Mississippi Valley Traveler
Driftless Area
Travel Guide

by Dean Klinkenberg

CONTENTS

Overview Map	4
Introduction	6
Regional History	13
Great River Road Route Overview	21
Hastings	24
William and Mary LeDuc	*26*
Prairie Island Indian Community	36
Eggleston	40
Red Wing	41
Red Wing's Difference Makers	*45*
Wacouta	59
Frontenac Station	61
Old Frontenac	63
Lake City	71
Lake Pepin	*76*
Camp Lacupolis	82
Reads Landing	83
Wabasha	86
Armistice Day Blizzard	*89*
Kellogg	99
Weaver	103
What is a Coulee?	*104*
Minneiska	106
Putnam Gray and His Castle	*108*
Minnesota City	110
Goodview	114
Winona	116
John Latsch	*119*
Homer	139
La Moille	142
Dakota	144
Life on the Frontier	*145*
Dresbach	148
La Crescent	150
Minnesota's Johnny Appleseed	*153*
Brownsville	156
Boathouses	*159*
Reno	162
Lansing	167

De Soto	174
Wisconsin's Amish Community	*178*
Victory	182
Genoa	185
Stoddard	190
La Crosse	194
Nathan Myrick	*197*
The Leona	*218*
Rivertown Brothels	*226*
French Island	232
Onalaska	235
Life in a Logging Camp	*241*
Holmen	245
God's Country	*248*
Brice Prairie	251
Midway	254
New Amsterdam	255
Trempealeau	259
Centerville	267
Marshland	269
Bluff Siding	271
Fountain City	272
Cochrane	280
Kenny Salwey	*283*
Buffalo City	284
Alma	291
The Gesell Family	*298*
Nelson	306
Pepin	310
Stockholm	319
Maiden Rock	328
Bay City	333
Hager City	337
Trenton	339
Diamond Bluff	341
The Sea Wing Tragedy	*343*
Prescott	345
Point Douglas	351
Regional Information	353
Index	362

INTRODUCTION

Welcome to the Driftless Area, 24,000 square miles of Wisconsin, Minnesota, Iowa, and Illinois bypassed by Pleistocene-era glacial ice and drift. The Driftless Area is a wonderland of coulees, valleys, and hollows amidst the Great Plains. The Mississippi River cut a deep valley through the heart of the region. The golden limestone bluffs stand as sentinels watching over the river; wide swaths of water stretch across the valley; raptors gently ride the thermals along the bluffs, rising to greater and greater heights. The Mississippi River from Hastings to Lansing is rich in natural wonders and spectacular scenery.

The Wisconsin side is populated mostly with small towns but also has the largest city, La Crosse, which, with its regional population of roughly 100,000, won't be confused with Chicago or Minneapolis. The Minnesota side has a four-lane highway and more development but also an abundance of public lands to explore. On both sides of the river, small villages snake along narrow plains, sandwiched between the river and tall bluffs.

The Mississippi River from Hastings to Lansing is a rewarding stretch to explore, but its pleasures are subtle and unassuming. Stop at a farmers market and relish the vivid colors and fresh flavors of seasonal tomatoes, squash, berries, and apples. Travel by houseboat and camp on an isolated island with fellow vacationers.

Share the river with young idealists on homemade boats and bond over the experience of dodging colossal barges. Or share the River Road with travelers on Harleys or in convertibles and bond over the experience of dodging an Amish buggy. Bike alongside a local farmer who is taking his John Deere to town for a little shopping. Devour a big burger or savor fine food while watching the river flow quietly by. Indulge in a slice of made-from-scratch pie and feel that stress melt away.

Don't Miss

On the West Bank

- LeDuc Historic Estate (page 29)
- Little Log House Power Show (page 31)
- Goodhue County History Center (page 47)
- Arrowhead Bluffs Museum (page 91
- Minnesota Marine Art Museum (page 121)
- Winona's summer cultural festivals (page 128)

On the East Bank

- Maria Angelorum Chapel (page 208)
- Trempealeau National Wildlife Refuge (page 267)
- Elmer's Auto and Toy Museum (page 274)
- Castlerock Museum (page 294)
- Eating local in Pepin (page 315)
- Stockholm Art Fair (page 322)
- Maiden Rock Bluff (page 323)

On Both Banks

- Lake Pepin (page 8)

Itineraries

The Lake Pepin Tour. Most people tour Lake Pepin as a day trip, but you will get more out of it by going at a slower pace and exploring it in two days (or more). On the Minnesota side, visit Christ Episcopal Church in Old Frontenac, Wiebusch's Windmill Haven, stroll the River Walk in Lake City, go to the National Eagle Center and Arrowhead Bluffs Museum around Wabasha. On the Wisconsin side, eat at least one meal in Pepin, tour the shops in Stockholm, hike at Maiden Bluff State Natural Area, and sip cider at the Maiden Rock Winery and Cidery.

The Pizza Trail. If you're in the mood for a pizza binge, there are several places on the Wisconsin River Road that make gourmet pizza with fresh, local ingredients. Most do it one night a week. Here's your agenda: On Tuesday, go to Suncrest Gardens near Cochrane; on Wednesday, eat at the Oasis Eatery at Nesbitt's Nursery south of Prescott; Thursday go to A to Z Produce near Stockholm; finish your binge at the Stone Barn outside of Nelson.

✔ TIP: Go to www.MississippiValleyTraveler.com for more itineraries..

About This Book

This is a travel guide, in case you haven't noticed. But, unlike many travel guides, this one includes more of the author, me, in the text. Yes, I want you to know about all the terrific attractions in the Upper Mississippi Valley, but I also want you to know some of the back story, like why certain places excite me.

I have a touch of attitude when it comes to travel. I am not a fan of chain stores, malls, mass consumption, or mass marketing. If all you want to do on vacation is lie on the beach, sip apple-tinis, and shop at Eddie

Introduction

Fishing in Lake Pepin

Bauer; if you buy all your art at the Pottery Barn; if your idea of a nice meal is the grilled chicken platter at TGI Fridays, then this book may not be for you. Sure, you can find national brands along the River Road—if that's what you need—but why not take a chance and try something that hasn't been focus-grouped and mass-marketed to the lowest common denominator? Why not sample some local flavor with a hand-crafted beer at the Pearl Street Brewery, or treat yourself to the homey atmosphere of a bed-and-breakfast? Relax, slow down, hang out, talk to people. That's my prescription for enjoying travel anywhere, and it will be very rewarding along the Mississippi Valley.

✔ **TIP: If you want to know more about my experiences writing this book, visit my website (www.MississippiValleyTraveler.com). I'll also be posting information that wouldn't fit in this volume.**

About My Picks

This book has no advertisements, paid or otherwise. No one paid to get a listing. No one gave me a free meal or free place to stay in exchange for a listing. The recommendations in this book, for better or for worse, are based upon my judgment of what is good, interesting, fascinating, or just worthy of your time. I have a strong preference for locally-run businesses, where you can get a feel for the community rather than fulfilling a corporate marketing department's idea of what puts you in the mood to spend more money.

Restaurants

Look, I can't possibly eat at every single restaurant that might be good. I don't have time for it, I can't afford it, and I don't want to look like the Stay Puft Marshmallow Man, again. That's just the way it goes. Restaurants get on my radar screen through recommendations from locals and visitors. I also pay attention to the places that are always busy. I try to find places that serve food that is a little bit different from the norm or that are very popular with the locals, even if the food isn't exactly cutting edge. If I don't eat at a particular restaurant, I stop by anyway to check out the visuals and to look over a menu. If a restaurant is busy and locals speak highly of it, I'll put it in the book, even if I don't get a chance to taste their food personally.

Note: Businesses change their hours often, and many have different hours at different times of year. Likewise, many businesses in smaller communities, especially restaurants and bars, don't keep exact hours. They may say they are open until 10pm, but, if they are really slow, will probably close earlier. Cut me some slack if I'm off by a bit.

Bars

My preferences tend toward dives and brewpubs. Along the River Road, you will find outstanding brewpubs and dozens if not hundreds of friendly neighborhood taverns and roadhouses. I can't stop at every single road house, regardless of how much fun that might be. The food at most of them is similar: burgers and fried stuff and beer. Let me know your favorites. Maybe we'll meet there for a drink, especially if you're buying.

Accommodations

I personally visited every accommodation listed in this book. If a place exists and it's not in this book, it either means I didn't care for it or my attempts to set up a visit were not successful, and believe me, I was very accommodating in my attempts to visit. I have listed a wide range of accommodation options, from campgrounds to bed-and-breakfasts to luxury hotels. My bias is to support independent motels, inns, and bed-and-breakfasts. I only provide detailed information for chain hotels that have a property on the river. Otherwise, I simply note where the chain hotels are located—after all, they tend to cluster like politicians around fundraisers. A note about the rates cited in the book: I asked for rates for two adults on a Saturday night during the summer, which is when most people travel to the region; peak season in some places is actually mid-September to mid-October, so you may pay a little more for a room at that time. So here's the disclaimer: room rates can vary tremendously depending upon a number of factors that are beyond my control. You may be able to do better than the rates quoted here, especially during the week, but many of the smaller places—bed-and-breakfast inns and mom-and-pop motels—have little room to bargain, unless you want to negotiate an extended stay. Also, I assume you know that budget motels (which I arbitrarily define as under $80/night for two people) are a mixed bag. Some are noisy, rooms are not always of consistent quality, and sometimes they get bad reputations, although often for reasons that are greatly exaggerated. But, they usually have the most affordable rates. If all you want is a cheap place to sleep, budget motels should suit you fine. If peeling paint and a few truck drivers scare you, however, you should probably stay somewhere else. So there, you've been warned.

✔ TIP: You can camp for up to 14 days on virtually any beach, sandbar, or island within the Upper Mississippi River Wildlife Refuge. You don't need any special permit, and it is free. You may have neighbors on summer weekends and there are no services, but it is a great way to experience the river. Head to their website for more details (www.fws.gov/midwest/UpperMississippiRiver/Documents/FSFRegs08.pdf).

For more information and updates, visit my web site at www.mississippivalleytraveler.com.

REGIONAL HISTORY

The First People

The Upper Mississippi Valley is the traditional home of the Dakota and Ho Chunk people. You may know the Dakota as the Sioux and the Ho Chunk as Winnebago, but these names were given to them by outsiders and are generally seen as derogatory. Within the Dakota nation, there were seven groups that lived in close proximity to each other in northern Minnesota before the year 1600. After 1600, the Dakota spread out, probably from increasing conflict with encroaching Cree and Ojibwe but also to be closer to trading posts along the Minnesota and Mississippi Rivers. The Ho Chunk lived throughout the Upper Midwest, with a large presence along the Mississippi River.

Growing European demands for resources would ultimately push the Dakota and Ho Chunk out of their homeland. Through a series of treaties (marred by broken promises, pressure tactics, and threats), lands were exchanged for cash. The Ho Chunk were moved many times; they spent several years in northern Minnesota where the US government wanted them to act as a buffer between the conflicting Dakota and Ojibwe before being moved further west. Over time, some Ho Chunk moved back to Wisconsin.

The Dakota ceded their lands with the 1851 Treaty of Mendota. Rumors about the new treaty opened the floodgates to settlers that the government could not stop. Some 20,000 illegal immigrants moved into Minnesota when the Dakota still held title to the land under US law. As part of the treaty, the Dakota moved to a new home along the Minnesota River, but the area had few remaining natural resources. To make matters worse, government annuities were not being delivered as promised, so the Dakota had to buy food on credit from traders. These creditors had first dibs on the money when annuities were finally paid; they could claim any amount and the government would pay it (like Haliburton), even if the Dakota kept their own records and disputed the amount. Faced with growing hunger and no money, some Dakota from the Upper Agency raided a government warehouse in 1862 and stole food. The government was convinced to withhold retaliation, but, when agents met with Chief Little Crow from the Lower Agency, they refused to make the same deal. At the meeting, trader Andrew Myrick said "So far as I am concerned, if they are hungry, let them eat grass or their own dung."

That's about all it took to ignite a major conflict. On August 18, a small band of Dakota from the Lower Agency went in search of food and ended up killing three men and two women. There was no turning back. The Dakota went on the offensive, raiding a warehouse and in the process killing 20 men, including Andrew Myrick who was found with grass stuffed in his mouth. The casualties could have been much higher but many Dakota helped settlers escape.

Little Crow knew that the Dakota had little chance of winning a war against the US, even when it was mired in civil war. They mounted attacks against forts and the city of New Ulm while undisciplined bands of Dakota rampaged through the country, killing settlers and their families. These efforts caused widespread damage and scores of casualties but ultimately failed to drive out the Americans. The Dakota surrendered in late September, although Little Crow escaped.

Minnesota officials quickly organized a kangaroo court and condemned 303 Dakota to death. Many of the accused denied killing anyone outside of battle; some denied killing anyone at all. Seventeen hundred Dakota, mostly women and children not accused of any crimes, were marched to Fort Snelling and imprisoned. The death sentences were appealed to President Lincoln, who overturned most of them. Still, on December 26, thirty-eight prisoners were hung en masse in Mankato, the largest mass execution in US history. After they were buried, some bodies were stolen from the graves, including one by Dr. William Mayo for "anatomical research."

Little Crow stayed on the move for a while but was killed in July 1863 by a farmer when he was back in Minnesota about to steal horses to provision for a long run on the lam. At that time, Minnesota had a bounty of $25 per head for any Dakota killed; the settlers who killed Little Crow got a $500 bonus. After the uprising of 1862, all Dakota were removed from Minnesota, first by steamer to St. Louis, then to a reservation in Crow Creek, South Dakota. About 1,300 arrived and less than 1,000 survived the first winter in the barren landscape. After three years, they were moved again, to Santee, Nebraska.

Black Hawk War

Further south, the Sauk and Mesquakie had troubles of their own. In the early 19th century, increasing numbers of settlers were moving into northwest Illinois. Treaties with Sauk and Mesquakie limited American settlements to specific areas, but, by the late 1820s encroachments on Indian lands grew more frequent. Two distinct philosophies about how to respond emerged in the Sauk and Mesquakie nations. One group believed they could not resist the Americans and should accept relocation to lands west of the Mississippi. This group was led by Keokuk. The other group believed that existing treaties were not valid because they had not been

Black Hawk (Davenport Public Library)

negotiated by Sauks with the proper authority. This group was led by Black Hawk, who was growing increasingly agitated at the treaty violations.

Under threat from federal forces, Keokuk and his followers agreed to permanently resettle west of the Mississippi. Black Hawk, however, continued to return to Saukenuk (their village on the east bank of the river) from winter grounds for the next two years. When he returned to Saukenuk in 1831, he found squatters living in the lodges. Black Hawk's return sparked several small skirmishes and renewed threats from the Illinois governor to exterminate the Indians if the federal government failed to remove them permanently. Weakened by the departure of many families, Black Hawk sought alliances with nearby Kickapoos, Potawatomis, and Ho Chunk. Among those who offered support was White Cloud, a prominent leader of Ho Chunk communities along the Rock River. By June of 1831, however, federal troops had moved into the area, prompting Black Hawk to return to the west bank of the Mississippi. Soon after that, the army moved into Saukenuk and torched it. Rebuked, Black Hawk signed a new treaty promising to stay on the western side of the Mississippi River.

Tensions between Indians and settlers never abated, however. White settlers regularly ambushed Indians and desecrated grave sites. Meanwhile, the federal government failed to supply the corn it promised under the terms of the treaty. Faced with starvation, some Indians returned to their ancestral lands in Illinois to harvest any remaining corn, but this move only exacerbated tensions with whites.

In the middle of this mess, Black Hawk accepted an offer from White Cloud to relocate to a Ho Chunk village along the Rock River in north-central Illinois, breaking his agreement with the US government. Encouraged by rumors that the British and other Indian nations would offer support, Black Hawk crossed the Mississippi in April 1832 with 2,000 men, women, and children. Black Hawk's actions did not go unnoticed; federal troops were dispatched from St. Louis, and Illinois rapidly organized several hundred volunteers to pursue him.

Very quickly Black Hawk realized that no help was coming from the British. Further, in spite of White Cloud's assurances, the Ho Chunk, fearing reprisals from state and federal officials, did not want the Sauks living in their village. Black Hawk moved northwest and, after the Potawatomis also refused to help him, was ready to give up and return to the west side of the Mississippi. Hopes for a peaceful settlement ended when a group of Illinois militia botched a surrender attempt by Black Hawk, triggering a brief fight known as the Battle of Stillman's Run. Although few people were killed in the battle, any hopes for a quick, peaceful settlement ended. Illinois mustered an additional 2,000 men, including a young Abraham Lincoln.

The ensuing war was more of a lengthy game of hide-and-seek, with Black Hawk and his followers on the run, trying to stay ahead of a motley group of undisciplined volunteers. Black Hawk made at least two additional attempts to surrender, both of which were misinterpreted by the militias. The Sauk moved through northwestern Illinois and into southern Wisconsin before making a break for the Mississippi River at Bad Axe Creek (north of Prairie du Chien).

On August 1, 1832, the steamboat Warrior, loaded with troops and armed with a cannon, encountered the Sauk; ignoring a white surrender flag, US troops opened fire, killing 23, before running out of fuel and returning to Prairie du Chien. Black Hawk and White Cloud tried to convince the group to continue north toward a possible safe haven, but most of those remaining wanted to cross the Mississippi as quickly as possible. Black Hawk, White Cloud, and a few others separated from the main group and went north.

On August 2, the pursuing armies converged on the main group. Initially, both sides fought in equal numbers, but federal troops and volunteers flooded into battle and turned it into a rout, killing at least 150 Sauk men and women. Meanwhile, another 150 Sauk had managed to cross the Mississippi safely into Iowa but were immediately detected by Wapasha, a Dakota chief who was aiding the Americans. Most of these Sauk were tracked and killed by the Dakota. Of the 1,000 who had followed Black Hawk across the Mississippi River back into Illinois, fewer than 200 survived. Black Hawk eventually surrendered to the Ho Chunk agent at Fort Crawford. In the aftermath of the war, many Indians—even those who had been friendly and cooperated with the United States—were forced by the American government to make additional land concessions. Europeans began arriving in large numbers. New Englanders accounted for many of the earliest settlers, but they were soon joined by immigrants from northern Europe.

Log raft on the Mississippi River

Logging

When Europeans first reached the area that is now Wisconsin, its 35 million acres were covered with 30 million acres of forest, or about twice what the state has today. The most common tree was white pine, which could grow to 250 feet tall and 8 ½ feet wide at the base. The seemingly endless forests were a big draw for Europeans.

The state's first sawmill was built near Green Bay in 1809, with the first along the Mississippi in 1819 at Prairie du Chien. Logging picked up in the 1850s, peaking between 1870 and 1900. From 1855 to 1899, six billion board feet floated down the Black River alone, which had 33 sawmills operating at various times.

The Black and Chippewa Rivers were two of the primary thoroughfares for transporting cut trees. Major sorting operations were located at the mouths of these two rivers and created prosperous villages at Reads Landing (Minnesota) and Alma and Onalaska (Wisconsin). Sawmills popped up in virtually every river town, but the industry was especially big at Winona, Onalaska, and La Crosse. Many logs were floated down the Mississippi River in huge log rafts to major processing centers in Clinton (Iowa), the Quad Cities, and St. Louis. As settlements grew in the North and West, sawmills along the Upper Mississippi increased production to meet demand for wood.

The industry was quite wasteful; only 40 percent of the trees harvested actually got to a mill. Trees that were considered blemished were often left to rot or burned. Some logs were lost in transit as they became waterlogged and sank (and are still being recovered today by entrepreneurs along the Mississippi River). Optimists in the 1850s believed that the pine forests of Wisconsin were inexhaustible. By the late 1890s, it was obvious that they were wrong. Processing was slowing down, and by 1905 most of the mills were closed and thousands of jobs were lost. There is still a logging industry in Wisconsin and Minnesota, but today it follows a more sustainable model.

GREAT RIVER ROAD ROUTE OVERVIEW

This book follows the Great River Road from the US Highway 61 bridge at Hastings, Minnesota to the Black Hawk Bridge that connects Lansing, Iowa to rural Wisconsin. The entire loop is 309 miles. This drive has spectacular views of the river, small towns, resort communities, and a couple of medium-sized cities. The route on the west bank covers roughly 152 miles in Minnesota and a small sliver of northeast Iowa. The route along the Great River Road follows:

On the West Bank (Minnesota/Iowa):

- US Highway 61 from Hastings;
- Minnesota Highway 316 is the official route, but I prefer going east on 10th Street in Hastings (it becomes Ravenna Trail/County Highway 54) and continuing on County Highway 68 (it becomes County Highway 18 past the Treasure Island Casino);
- Back to US Highway 61; and
- Minnesota Highway 26 from La Crescent to the Iowa border where the road becomes Iowa Highway 26 to Lansing.

The route on the east bank is about 157 miles long, mostly in Wisconsin but with a few miles of Minnesota pavement between Prescott and Hastings.

On the East Bank (Wisconsin/Minnesota):

- State Highway 35; and
- US Highway 10.

River Crossings

- The Hastings High Bridge is a steel truss structure with a suspended road deck; it was built in 1951 to replace the legendary Spiral Bridge (see page 25);

- St. Croix River Bridge (aka Point Douglas Drawbridge), a drawbridge built in 1990 for Minnesota Highway 10 that connects Point Douglas, Minnesota with Prescott, Wisconsin;

- The steel truss Eisenhower Bridge (aka Red Wing Bridge but called the Hiawatha Bridge when completed in 1960) that connects Red Wing, Minnesota with Hager City, Wisconsin via US Highway 63;

- The Wabasha-Nelson Bridge that connects Wabasha, Minnesota and Minnesota Highway 60 with Nelson, Wisconsin and Wisconsin Highway 25; the steel arch truss bridge was completed in 1988; its wide shoulders make it easy for bicycles to cross.

- The steel truss Main Channel Bridge connecting Winona, Minnesota and Minnesota Highway 43 with Bluff Siding and Wisconsin Highway 35/54; completed in 1942; it has a sidewalk for pedestrians and bicycles.

- The boring Interstate 90 Mississippi River Bridge, completed in 1967, that connects La Crescent, Minnesota with La Crosse, Wisconsin;

- The Mississippi River Bridge that connects La Crescent, Minnesota with La Crosse, Wisconsin via US Highways 14 & 61; this is actually two bridges: the north span with a steel girder and floorbeam construction, was built in 1939, while the south span uses tied-arch construction and was added in 2004. It has a sidewalk for pedestrians and bicycles; and

The Great River Road around 1900

- The Black Hawk Bridge, connecting 2nd Street in Lansing, Iowa with Wisconsin Highway 35 in rural Crawford County, Wisconsin via Iowa Highway 9/Wisconsin Highway 82. Completed in 1931, the Black Hawk Bridge is a visually striking configuration of two tall trusses linked by a low-arched truss that somehow looks a little bit off.

For more information and updates, visit my web site at www.mississippivalleytraveler.com.

HASTINGS

(18,204)

Hastings is a pleasant surprise. The previous sum total of my knowledge about Hastings was that it marked the gateway to (or exit from) the Twin Cities on my many road trips between La Crosse and Minneapolis. Now I know that Hastings has extensive green space along the river, a charming business district, and helpful locals.

Arriving in Town

US Highway 61 is Vermillion Street; it will get you through Hastings but not to many sites in town. The business district is mostly along 2nd Street.

History

In 1819, Lieutenant William Oliver led an expedition of keel boats from Fort Crawford upriver to Fort Snelling, but ice on the river forced them to stop for the winter. That's all it took for this spot to become known as Oliver's Grove for the next 30 years.

The village of Hastings was platted in 1853 by four men with deep ties to the fur trade: Alexander Faribault, Henry Sibley, Alexis Bailly and his son, Henry. This location had two important advantages as a town site: it was on a high plain and therefore didn't flood, and it had a good steamboat landing. These four men had trouble agreeing to a name, so they decided to settle the matter by drawing lots. Each put a name in a hat. The winning slip of paper had Hastings on it, which was the middle name of Henry Sibley. Sibley was later elected the first governor of Minnesota. In

Spiral bridge (Hastings Historical Society)

1856 the town claimed about 650 residents but one year later it had tripled to 2,000. Rampant land speculation drove prices to ridiculously high levels, though, so many settlers moved on in search of cheaper options. The financial panic of 1857 brought prices back to earth and Hastings settled into a typical growth pattern for that era: mills, a foundry, warehouses, wheat milling, shipping, railroad jobs, and breweries.

In 1895, Hastings got its first wagon/auto bridge. The initial design would have taken traffic over Second Street and away from the main commercial district, so town leaders insisted on an alternative that would ensure traffic would be routed directly to local businesses. The result was a unique spiral ramp that dumped traffic at the foot of Sibley Street. The road surface was constructed of three-inch oak planks, which didn't hold up well to increasingly heavy vehicle traffic. Approaching school busses had to stop and unload, then wait for the children to cross on foot before crossing and reloading on the other side. The current High Bridge was completed in 1951 and the spiral bridge demolished in the same year. Not only did the new bridge bypass the old commercial district, but two blocks of it were sacrificed for the construction.

William and Mary LeDuc

William LeDuc was a man who refused to give up. He tried his hand at many different occupations, and actually seemed pretty good at many of them, but he never made much money. LeDuc was born in Wilkesville, Ohio in 1823.

While living with an uncle, he became friends with William Tecumseh Sherman. Agriculture got his interest early, at least the science of it. He graduated from Kenyon College after paying his own way. In 1850 he moved to St. Paul; the city had 1000 residents and the Minnesota Territory was only one year old. He purchased land in Hastings in 1854 and sold his St. Paul interests just ahead of the crash of 1857. At the outbreak of the Civil War, he volunteered for the Army and got a position with the Quartermaster Corps, enlisting as a captain and leaving a brigadier-general.

His occupations included farming, copper mining, railroad promotion, and land speculation. Fellow Ohioan Rutherford B. Hayes appointed him Commissioner of Agriculture in 1877; while in this position he advocated programs that would turn the US from an importer of sugar and tea into a country that grew enough for itself—and it more or less worked, for tea, anyway.

Although he worked hard and struggled

financially most of his life, monetary success may not have been his highest priority. In a letter to his wife, he wrote "Money is nothing, enjoyment of life is everything. Money is only an accessory." It's not clear that his wife, Mary Elizabeth Bronson, felt the same way.

Mary was born in 1829 in central Ohio to a well-heeled family that could afford to send her to a private school, a rarity in that era. She was well-educated with wide-ranging interests and felt that life on the frontier was boring and isolating.

William had been part of a group that worked to expand the Hastings and Dakota railroad. When it was bought by the Milwaukee and St. Paul Railroad, several people got rich but LeDuc was not one of them. He felt cheated and betrayed by his partners. Decades later, in 1915, he received a gift of $100,000 from the estate of Mrs. Julia Butterfield; her first husband was one of LeDuc's partners in the railroad deal.

William was a widower and 93 years old at the time he received the gift. Mary had died in 1904 while William was in Tacoma, Washington scouting out a coal mine; he couldn't make it back in time for the funeral and spent the next year reading, fishing, and writing a book about spirituality. The gift allowed him to settle his debts and complete more work on the house before he died in 1917.

Hastings has had its share of industry over time, but one has had a lasting impact on the town. Charles Smead had a revolutionary idea for closing envelopes, specifically, manila ones (using durable metal clasps instead of the rubber band method that was common at that time). He searched for a manufacturer but found no takers, so he decided to make it himself. He secured money from three local investors in 1908 and launched Smead Manufacturing. Barely eighteen months after startup, however, he died in a freak accident, falling from the third floor of his hotel. P.A. Hoffman, one of the firm's original six employees, become the new owner in 1916; Smead Manufacturing has been managed by the Hoffman family ever since. In 1955, Ebba Hoffman became the company president after the unexpected death of her husband, Harold. It is now the largest US manufacturer of stationery, with more than 2,500 employees world-wide. The current leader is Ebba's daughter, Sharon Hoffman Avent.

Today, Hastings is growing again, this time as a suburban outpost of the Twin Cities, especially on the western part of town, where it looks like every other suburban community in America.

Tourist Information ⓘ

The **Hastings Visitors Center** is located downtown (111 E. 3rd St.; 651.437.6775; kiosk open daily but staffed M–F 8:30–5).

Attractions 💡

Lock and Dam 2 (651.437.3150) opened in 1930 but unexpected settling ruined the first structure, so it was rebuilt in 1948; it went through a major overhaul from 1987 to 1995. The dam is 822 feet long, and the lock has a maximum lift of twelve feet. The 4.4 megawatt power plant next door is operated by the City of Hastings.

Hey, what's that? In 2008, an experiment began below Lock and Dam 2 with the construction of the nation's first commercial hydrokinetic power generator. Hydrokinetic power takes advantage of existing river currents to generate electricity by placing turbines in the middle of the flow. At this site, a twelve-foot turbine hangs from a barge about three feet below the surface; it is expected to generate about one hundred kilowatts of electricity.

Hastings City Hall (101 E. 4th St.; 651.480.2350; M–F 8–4:30) was built as the Dakota County Courthouse in 1871 with a strong Second Empire vibe; the neo-Classical dome was added in 1912 when the building was expanded. It was purchased by the City of Hastings in 1991 after the new county courthouse opened. The interior is worth a walk-around to see the gorgeous art glass windows (hidden from World War II to 1992) and art enlivening the hallways. The **Pioneer Room** (651.480.2367; M,W 8–4:30, Th 8–Noon) has a number of local history artifacts, historical photos, and local records.

The landmark **LeDuc Historic Estate** (1629 Vermillion St.; 651.437.7055; guided tours W–Sa 10a, 11:30a, 1p, 2:30p, 4p; $6) is a grand Gothic Revival home built by big characters (see the LeDuc sidebar on page 26). William and Mary LeDuc spent two years planning the construction. Mary found the design for the house in an 1853 book called Cottage Residences by noted landscape architect Andrew Jackson Downing. The LeDucs wanted to build a prince's house on a poet's budget, so they were constantly juggling their dreams with their limited budget. Who hasn't been there. They moved into an unfinished house in August,

1865, after William was discharged from the service. The LeDucs had hoped to spend $2,000 on construction but estimated it would cost $5,000; in the end, they spent $30,000. The house had an unusual feature: an indoor outhouse. Your standard outhouse had to be relocated occasionally and the old hole filled. William, ever the innovator, put removable carts under the seats to collect the, um, material, so the carts could be rolled and dumped. The end result was a privy experience that was much more satisfactory than the standard one, especially during those long Minnesota winters.

Explore the ruins of an 1857-era mill next to the Vermillion River at **Old Mill Park** (800 18th St. West); originally built by Alexander Ramsey and Thomas Foster, the mill burned down in 1894 in a suspicious fire.

The Vermillion River carved a limestone ravine in what is now the middle of the city, creating a dramatic waterfall in the process. This is now part of **Vermillion Falls Park** (215 21st St. East), a pleasant place to picnic while accompanied by the sound of falling water.

Getting on the River

Through **Great River Boat Rentals** (1 King's Cove Dr.; 651.438.9999) you can rent a pontoon boat, a fishing boat, and a runabout ($200–$250/half-day, $295–$390/day on weekends); call ahead to reserve.

Culture & Arts

Great Rivers Art Gallery (301 E. 2nd St.; 651.437.2800; Tu–Sa 11–5, Su Noon–4) stocks mostly for-sale items from regional artists but also has a small gallery in the back.

Rivertown Days parade

Entertainment and Events ♪

Hastings has a twice weekly **Farmers Market** in the parking lot at Westview Shopping Center (8th St. W./Highway 55 at Pleasant Dr.; Tu,Sa 8a–2p). The **Saturday Night Cruise-In** features a mini-convention of classic cars in downtown Hastings on alternating Saturday evenings from late May until early October (5p–10p).

Festivals. At **Hastings Rivertown Days** (888.612.6122/651.437.6775) wander down to the riverfront and watch log burling and duck races, shop the arts and crafts booths, bird by canoe, fish in a tournament, and settle in for the grand parade where there is enough candy to send a diabetic into a coma. Most events are free but some require a festival button ($2). I love being surprised. I hadn't heard much about the **Little Log House Antique Power Show** (21889 Michael Ave.; 651.437.2693; $10/day, $20/weekend pass) and ended up wishing I had more time to experience it. The tractor parade is not something you'll see often. Sure, it has the usual food vendors, live music, flea markets, and artisanal crafts, but there are also buildings that represent a wide cross-section of rural life: a saloon that is a functioning saloon, a general store selling general merchandise, a village hall for the village, and a very unique two-story house built for bachelor Peder Egtvedt (July: last weekend; F–Su 8–5). If you miss the festival, you can see some of the buildings from 220th Street.

Bars/Clubs/Music. For something completely different, head down to the **Levee Café** (100 Sibley St.; 651.437.7577) on a Friday or Saturday night (8p–midnight) when a piano player sets up shop for a live sing-along, kinda like karaoke but with real music.

Sports and Recreation

Hastings has a dense network of paved trails around town, including many along the river; pick up the **Hastings Trail Map** brochure at the visitor center.

Hastings is the southern end of the **Mississippi National River and Recreation Area** (651.290.4160; www.nps.gov/miss/index.htm), 72 miles of parks, trails, and recreation areas managed by the National Park Service that go through the heart of the Twin Cities along the Mississippi River. Free guides are available throughout the region.

If you are disc golf enthusiast, you can indulge your passion at **C.P. Adams Park** (1301 18th St. East; 651.480.6175; free). The **Hastings Family Aquatic Center** (901 Maple St.; 651.480.2385) has several waterslides and a large pool (open swim times: M,F–Su Noon–8, Tu–Th Noon–5; $4.50–$6.50). In the winter, the **Hastings Civic Arena** (2801 Red Wing Blvd.; 651.480.6195) is the place to go for indoor ice skating arena; call for public skating times.

Shopping

The downtown commercial district has a mix of restaurants, antique stores, and boutique shops. **SECOND CHILDHOOD TOYS** (212 2nd St. E.; 651.438.7949; M–Sa 10–5:30) aims at a younger demographic (through an older one, of course) with puzzles, games, and toys meant to challenge or educate, including many classic toys that boomers will get nostalgic about. **THE EMPORIUM** (213 E. 2nd St.; 651.438.5444; M–Sa 10–5, Su Noon–5) has two floors of antiques, new and used books, and other collectibles. **MISSISSIPPI CLAYWORKS** (214 2nd St. E.; 651.437.5901; M,Tu,Th,F 10–5:30, W Noon–5, Sa 10–5, Su Noon–4) is the place to buy hand-thrown pottery by Ron Martino, as well as fine pottery from the southwestern US. If you need a snack, **CREATIVE CONFECTIONAIRE** (216 2nd St. E.; 651.437.7788; M–Sa 10–5:30, Su 12:30–5:30) sells delicious chocolates made in-house and ice cream ($2.50/one scoop). Just outside of downtown, the **UNDERGROUND ART GALLERY** (411 Vermillion St.; 651.438.9101; Tu–Sa 11–5) has a large stock of interesting work by local and regional artists working with a variety of media. The **ALEXIS BAILLEY VINEYARD** (18200 Kirby Ave.; 651.437.0413; F–Su 11–5:30) was one of the first vineyards along the Upper Mississippi River, and they have used their experience to produce better-than-average wines, especially for the Upper Midwest. The tasting room is in a scenic locale surrounded by grape vines (tastings fees: $2 to taste 3 wines, $3 for 5 tastings, $5 to sample all of their wines). You are welcome to sit outside and enjoy the atmosphere (wines $4–$6 by the glass), especially on the Sunday afternoons when they host live music.

Eating 🍴

The **RED ROCK CAFÉ** (119 2nd St. E.; 651.437.5002; M–F 6a–2p, Sa 7a–2p, Su 8a–1p) offers a full range of breakfast options from French toast to omelets ($5–$9), sandwiches for lunch ($6–$8.50), and, if you're still hungry, ice cream for dessert ($2.50/ single scoop).

THE LEVEE CAFÉ (100 Sibley St.; 651.437.7577; Su 8:30–2, M 11–2, Tu-Th 11–8, F,Sa 11–10) has a warm, modern ambiance with a well-executed menu of Midwestern standards (sandwiches and burgers $8–$10, entrées $9–$19).

The **AMERICAN LEGION POST 47** (50 Sibley St.; 651.437.2046; Su–W 7a–9p; Th–Sa 7a–10p) may not be the first place you would think of for food, but they have a decent menu of American standards and the only outside riverside dining in town, so you can enjoy great views of the river while eating a burger or a wrap (most items $6–$8; breakfast is generally a bit less); cash only.

LAS MARGARITAS MEXICAN RESTAURANT (2100 Vermillion St.; 651.480.0048; Su–Th 11a–9:30, F,Sa 11a–10p) serves up genuine Mexican dishes, with a number of seafood entrée options (entrées $8–$13).

Sleeping 🛏

Budget. The **HASTINGS INN** (1520 Vermillion St.; 651.437.3155; WiFi) has 31 clean budget rooms, each with microwave, fridge, and cable TV ($59+tax); they also have two kitchenettes ($80+tax).

Bed and Breakfast. THE CLASSIC ROSEWOOD INN (620 Ramsey St.; 651.437.3297; WiFi) is an 11,000 square foot Queen Anne behemoth built in 1880 for rags-to-riches Bavarian immigrants Rudolph and Marie Latto. They donated the house to the city for use as a hospital; in 1953 the building was converted into a nursing home. By the 1980s, the house was in such bad condition that it was condemned and nearly demolished. Pam and Dick Thorsen rescued the house at the last minute and spent years faithfully restoring the building; they opened it as a B&B in 1989. The house has enough space that, even in common areas, you are likely to enjoy privacy, if that's what you want. The eight guest rooms have a period feel and invite lounging around; most have whirlpool tubs ($97–$227+tax but most are $137–$157+tax). The rate includes a full breakfast that you are welcome to enjoy in your room, if you prefer.

✔ TIP: If you haven't stayed in a B&B in a while (or ever), you may not know how much they have adapted to changes in the hospitality market. Most now have a private bath for each room and many also offer the option of eating breakfast in your room, in case you are not a morning person, like me, and think it's best not to inflict yourself on other people before you've had that first cup of coffee.

Resources

- The local newspaper is the *Hastings Star Gazette* (651.437.6153).
- Post Office: 300 2nd St. East; 651.437.1663.
- Dakota County Pleasant Hill Library; 1490 S. Frontage Rd.; 651.438.0200; WiFi; M–Th 10–8:30, F,Sa 10–5:30, Su 1–5 (no Sunday hours in summer).

Getting Around 🚌

The **TRAC Bus** is one option for getting around town without a car (M–F 6a–6p); call to arrange service (651.437.8722; $2.25/ride).

PRAIRIE ISLAND INDIAN COMMUNITY
(199)

After generations of difficult times, the Dakota who live on Prairie Island are now finally enjoying some economic prosperity. Even if you're not a casino person, Treasure Island has so much going on that you can probably find something that will amuse you.

Arriving in Town

The only place you are likely to visit is the Treasure Island Casino and Resort, which is on Sturgeon Lake Road and stands out like bacon at a vegetarian buffet.

History

Following the Dakota Conflict of 1862, all Dakota were forced out of Minnesota and removed to reservations, first in South Dakota, then in Nebraska (see page 13). By 1880, squalid conditions prompted many Dakota to go back to their homeland, some walking the entire distance from Nebraska. These Dakota ended up at a place they called *Tinta Wita* but Europeans called Prairie Island. Europeans considered the land on the island unsuitable for farming, so it attracted few settlers. The Dakota, however, knew how to live off the land at Prairie Island and used many of the native plants in traditional medicine. The relative isolation of life on Prairie Island helped these Dakota maintain traditional aspects of life better than Dakota in other places.

The US government first recognized the Prairie

Island Indian Community in 1886, granting 120 acres reservation status. In 1936 the reservation was expanded to 534 acres, and a Community Council form of government was adopted, operating akin to a state government. The construction of Lock and Dam 3 in the late 1930s flooded low-lying sections of the island and reduced the number of habitable acres on the reservation to 300. Until the 1980s, Dakota living on the reservation had limited economic opportunities; poverty was the norm. Community members faced another insult in 1968 when a nuclear plant was built adjacent to the reservation.

In 1984, the Prairie Island Indian Community opened a bingo room with seating for 1400. After a 1989 agreement with the State of Minnesota, the community jumped into the gaming world with both feet by building their first casino. The casino now employs 1500 people. Gaming revenues have been used to build a community center, a health center, to improve sewer and water facilities, and to fund a wide range of charitable causes throughout the region.

Tourist Information ⓘ

Contact the **Treasure Island Casino and Resort** (800.222.7077).

Attractions

Lock and Dam 3 (651.388.5794) opened in 1938 and went through a major rehabilitation from 1988-1991. The dam is 365-feet long and the lock has an average lift of 10 feet.

Getting on the River

Spirit of the Water (Treasure Island Casino; 877.849.1640) is a 120-passenger luxury yacht that cruises on the Mississippi River (W–Sa Noon,6:30p, Su 11a,4p from early May–Aug., W–Sa Noon,5p, Su Noon,4p in Sept, Oct; $27–$33 for lunch/brunch cruises; $35 dinner cruises).

Entertainment and Events ♪

Festivals. The annual **Wacipi Celebration** (800.554.5483; July: 2nd weekend; free) offers a weekend full of traditional dancing, drumming, and singing that draws large numbers of Dakota participants; there are also a number of art and craft vendors.

The **Treasure Island Resort and Casino** (5734 Sturgeon Lake Rd.; 800.222.7077) is a huge place with 2500 slot machines, 40 blackjack tables, 10 poker tables, and a large bingo room. The resort also hosts nationally-known entertainers at the 3000-seat event center; the Parlay Lounge also hosts live music.

Eating ✕

TREASURE ISLAND RESORT AND CASINO has, as you would expect, several restaurants to choose from. The Thursday night seafood theme at the Tradewinds Buffet is a popular choice ($24).

Sleeping 🛏

Camping. TREASURE ISLAND RV PARK (651.267.3060) has nearly 100 sites with full hookups ($23/30-amp elec, $25/50-amp elec) plus room to pitch a tent ($15).

Moderate. TREASURE ISLAND RESORT AND CASINO (888.867.7829; WiFi) offers 480 stylish hotel rooms ($109–$269+tax); flat screen TVs are standard and many of the rooms have river views. The suites have larger flat-screen TVs and elegant walk-in showers with a luxury showerhead.

Getting To and Out of Dodge ✈

The casino operates free, roundtrip **mini-bus service** from places within a couple hours drive of the casino, including the Twin Cities, Rochester, La Crosse, and Eau Claire; call for details and to make a reservation (800.222.7077, x 2594)

✔ TIP: The casino has a complicated rate structure, partly because they offer a wide range of room types. If you are booking on-line (www.treasureislandcasino.com), look for package deals that combine a room with other options like a meal.

For more information and updates, visit my web site at www.mississippivalleytraveler.com.

EGGLESTON
(Uninc)

Named for the Eggleston brothers who were among the earliest settlers here: John and Joseph arrived in 1855 and were joined a short time later by Harlan and Ira. The village was home to a railroad station beginning in 1871 that served Prairie Island but was never more than a handful of businesses with a post office. Both the railroad and the post office are long gone and the town today is mostly a collection of mobile homes. And yet I write about it.

RED WING
(16,116)

A popular destination for daytrippers from the Twin Cities, Red Wing is a good place to use as a base to explore the surrounding area; stick around for a few days.

Arriving in Town

US Highway 61 enters town as Main Street, while US 63 connects to the Eisenhower Bridge via 3rd Street, if you wish to cross the river to Wisconsin. Red Wing's unique civic mall has a concentration of public and religious buildings; it is just west of downtown on a wedge of land between East and West Streets running from Main Street to 7th Street.

History

Let's start with the town's namesake: Red Wing. He was probably born about 1750 and was probably the nephew of Chief Wabasha I, though no one is sure. He was a shaman and a very successful military leader of the Mdewakanton Dakota in the latter part of the 18th century. In Dakota his name was *Tatankamani* (Walking Buffalo). French explorers, for reasons that are not well documented, called him *L'Aile Rouge* (Red Wing). He broke from Wabasha's band, leading a group of 100 who lived near the mouth of the Cannon River. He led an active life in the middle of changing times, chatting with the explorer Zebulon Pike in 1805 and fighting with the British against American interests before switching sides in the middle of the War of 1812. He traveled to Portage des Sioux (Missouri) in 1815 to sign a treaty of friendship with Americans. When he was older, he gave the name Red Wing to his oldest surviving son, Wakute, and called himself Shakea (The Man Who Paints Himself Red). He died March 4, 1829 while hunting.

The land around the Cannon River was not open to legal settlement until 1853, but a few Europeans still found a way to move in. The first to arrive were two families of Swiss missionaries: Samuel and Persis Denton in 1837 and Daniel and Lucy Gavin in 1838. They stayed until 1845, probably converting no one. Another group of Presbyterian missionaries and their families arrived in 1849 when Minnesota became a territory. At that time, Red Wing was home for about 300 Dakota. Among this group of missionaries were Joseph Hancock (b. 1816 in Orford, NH) and his wife Maria Houghton Hancock. Joseph built good relationships with the Dakota and learned their language. In 1850, Maria died during childbirth, and the next year his son died, too. Distraught, he left Red Wing for several years. John Day came from Wisconsin and moved—illegally—into the abandoned mission house, trying to establish a claim on land that still belonged to the Dakota. The Dakota were not amused, so they tore down the house. Day built a new house and the Dakota tore that one down, too. This process repeated itself about a dozen times before Day finally left.

The Dakota signed away the rights to their lands in the 1851 Treaty of Mendota and were removed from Minnesota by the 1860s. With the Dakota gone, Europeans flooded in and reshaped the area. Red Wing was platted in 1853 and became the county seat. Joseph Hancock eventually returned and played a central role in the city's development, serving as post master and writer of first county history, among other things.

Most early settlers were from the East, but there were also many Scandinavian and German immigrants. Hotels were built to house new arrivals, including an ill Henry David Thoreau who came for a four-day health respite in June 1861. He was trying to recover from tuberculosis but died the next year. While in Red Wing, he climbed Barn Bluff and was so moved he wrote about the river valley: "Too much could not be said for the grandeur and beauty."

Red Wing counted 1251 residents in 1860 and over 4000 just 10 years later. Much of Red Wing's early growth was fueled by wheat. In 1873, Red Wing had a warehouse that could store one million bushels of the grain; twice that amount shipped from town that year. The wheat trade declined in importance by 1880, but Red Wing had a strong, diversified economy with businesses like shoe manufacturing, sorghum processing, the Red Wing Iron Works (1866-1983), cigar factories (mostly 1870-1920), brewing, brick manufacturing, lumber, and quarrying.

Pottery makers have been mainstays in the local economy for generations. In the early years, local clay was plentiful and was an especially good raw material. The industry began with German immigrant Joseph Pohl in 1861; he later decided that farming was a better fit for him. William Philleo founded a terra cotta business in 1870 and had a nice run. He moved his company to St. Paul in 1880 and renamed it, but some of his former employees stayed in town and founded the Red Wing Stoneware Company. In 1906, the three existing pottery companies merged to form the Red Wing Union Stoneware Company, which produced pottery until 1967. In 1984, the Red Wing Pottery brand was brought back to life.

Red Wing's economy today is a mix of light manufacturing, healthcare, and tourism; the Red Wing Shoe Company is the largest employer.

Red Wing

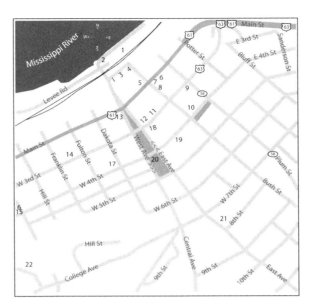

Map Key

Things to Do
10. Aliveo Military Museum
20. Band shell
19. Farmers Market
22. Goodhue County History Center
1. Levee Park
3. Red Wing Arts Association Art Gallery
6. Red Wing Shoe Museum
2. Rusty's River Rides
18. Sheldon Theater

Places to Sleep
14. Candlelight Inn
21. Golden Lantern Inn
15. The Guest House Next Door
16. Moondance Inn
17. Pratt-Taber Inn
5. St. James Hotel

Places to Eat
8. Bev's Café
11. Hanisch Bakery
9. Liberty's Restaurant and Lounge
7. The Nortons Restaurant
5. The Veranda/Jimmy's/The Port

Other
4. Amtrak Station
13. Post Office
12. Red Wing Public Library

Red Wing's Difference Makers

Red Wing has had more than its fair share of people who left a big mark. Frances Densmore (1867-1957) studied music at Oberlin Conservatory of Music. While studying in Boston with John Paine, she learned of the work of Alice Fletcher, one of the first people to record Native American music, and was inspired to follow her example. She spent much of her adult life documenting and recording the music of Native Americans, even as others were trying to erase their culture to force assimilation. In 50 years, she made some 3,000 recordings and published 20 books.

Francis Densmore recording Mountain Chief (Library of Congress)

Dr. Alexander P. Anderson (1862-1943) was a prominent scientist who invented Puffed Wheat and Puffed Rice. When they were first shown off to the public at the 1904 World's Fair in St. Louis, they were a treated like popcorn; Quaker Oats later used its marketing resources to convince the public to eat them for breakfast. His research had been conducted elsewhere, but he came back to Red Wing to live and work in 1915 and built a large complex called Tower View that now serves as a residential arts program.

Tourist Information ⓘ

The old rail depot, completed in 1905 and still used by Amtrak, houses the **Red Wing Convention and Visitors Bureau** (420 Levee St.; 800.498.3444/651.385.5934; M–F 8–5, and from Memorial Day thru Oct also open Sa 10–3, Su 11–3).

Attractions 💡

The standout geological feature in town is a chunk of land that rises 300 feet above the city. Known to the Dakota as *Khemnichan* (hill, wood, water), Europeans called it Barn Bluff because the general shape reminded them of a barn. You can explore **Barn Bluff Park** (500 East Fifth St.; 651.385.3674) via hiking trails that take you past abandoned quarries, next to limestone cliffs, and across goat prairies with great views of the area. You will also find remnants of Webster's Way, concrete steps to the top that were first built in 1899, rebuilt, then mostly destroyed by highway construction.

Memorial Park (542 E. 7th St.; 651.385.3674) sits atop Sorin's Bluff and is another place with great views of the area. A few thousand years ago, Barn Bluff and Sorin's Bluff were islands in a much wider and deeper Mississippi River.

From big views to big shoes. **The Red Wing Shoe Museum** (315 Main St., 3rd floor; 651.388.6233; M–F 9–8, Sa 9–6, Su 11–5) houses the World's Largest Boot, crafted for the company's 100th anniversary in 2005. The boot is 16 feet tall, 20 feet long, and 7 feet wide, measuring an impressive size 638 ½ D, perfect for that 120-foot tall person in your life.

The **Aliveo Military Museum** (321 Bush St.; 651.327.1569; F,Sa 10–4; free) showcases the collection of Bruce Sexton, a 30-year military veteran who served around the world and had a chance to collect some remarkable items: rare bayonets, a Philippine Moro Kris sword, a Zulu shield, and uniforms. The broadest collection of items is from WWII-era Germany and Japan but other places and wars are represented.

Red Wing has several riverside parks that would be fine spots to picnic. **Bay Point Park** (1392 Levee Rd.; 651.385.3674) is next to Boat House Village and the main channel. **Levee Park** (432 Levee Rd.; 651.385.3674) is a small, pleasant riverside park with a memorial to the *Sea Wing* disaster (see page 343). Further from downtown, **Colville Park** (510 Nymphara Lane; 651.385.3674) has plenty of places to spread out along the river.

The **Goodhue County History Center** (1166 Oak St.; 651.388.6024; Tu–F 10–5, Sa,Su 1–5; $5) has a wide-ranging collection that traces the history of the region from the earliest inhabitants to later arrivals. The collection includes displays on early agriculture and trades (don't miss the 18th century Lien family lathe), local characters like France Densmore and Eugenia Anderson, the lumber industry, and recent and distant history of the Native American population.

The **Red Wing Pottery Museum** (Pottery Place Mall, 2000 Old W. Main St.; 800.977.7927; M–Sa 10–6, Su 11–5; free) showcases the history of stoneware in Red Wing, with pieces that are functional and artistic. Did you know that mason jars were once made of stoneware, not glass? I didn't. Check out the impressive range of stoneware jars that range in size from minis barely large enough to hold a few tablespoons of salt to the 20 gallon monsters.

Eisenhower Bridge from Barn Bluff

Getting on the River

Rusty's River Rides (Levee Park; 612.859.6655) 90-minute narrated river cruises from mid-April through October (M–F 3:30p, Sa,Su 1p,3p; $12).

Ken of the **Lake Pepin Guide Service** (507.254.1174) is a fishing guide who also takes groups on tours of the Mississippi River in a pontoon boat ($250/half-day for 3 people, $400/day for 6 people).

If you prefer to take charge of your own transportation, **Ben and Joe's Fun Rentals** (1616 Old West Main; 651.388.4259) organizes kayak trips down the Cannon River to Bay Point Park in Red Wing; call for rates and times.

Culture & Arts

The **Red Wing Arts Association Art Gallery** (418 Levee St.; 651.388.7569; M–F 8–5, Sa 10–5, Su Noon –5 from May–Dec, Daily Noon–4 the rest of the year) maintains an impressive gallery in the old rail depot next to the visitors center.

If you want to sample performing arts, check out the schedule for the **Sheldon Theater** (433 W. 3rd St.; 800.899.5759/651.388.8700). The charming renaissance revival building opened in 1904 and still hosts live theater and movies.

Dr. Alexander P. Anderson, inventor of puffed rice and puffed wheat, built an estate and research center on the northern end of town that is now an artist-in-residence program called the Anderson Center at Tower View. Adjacent is the **Anderson Park Sculpture Garden** (163 Tower View Dr., 651.388.2009; daily dawn–dusk; free), a 15-acre space dotted with large-scale sculptures and a few interpretive signs explaining the different types of ecosystems native to Minnesota.

Tours

The **Red Wing Trolley Company** runs a 50-minute tour around town with stops at Pottery Place, the Sheldon Theatre, Barn Bluff, and Colvill Park (Red Wing Depot, 420 Levee St.; 651.380.3220; Th–M 11a–3p from Memorial Day weekend through October; $10/adult).

If you are a geek like me who enjoys seeing how things are made, you shouldn't miss the tour of **Red Wing Shoe Company** (314 Main St.; 651.385.5934; M–Th 1p, F 10a from mid-March–Oct.; free). The 90-minute tours give a nice overview of the shoe-making process; some of their sewing machines are 100 years old and still being used! You don't need a reservation; just show up at Plant #2 on the west end of town at US 61 and Cannon River Avenue at the designated time; park in the spots closest to Cannon River Avenue. You won't be allowed to tour if you are wearing open-toed shoes.

If you want a closer look at the process of manufacturing pottery, **Red Wing Stoneware** (4009 Moundview Dr.; 800.352.4877/651.388.4610) offers 20-minute factory tours (M–F 10:30a, 1p, 3:30p; $3).

Entertainment and Events ♪

Red Wing hosts a **daily Farmers Market** from mid-May to mid-October (Red Wing City Hall, 4th and Bush Streets), that occasionally includes live music on Saturday mornings. There is also a **weekly Farmers Market** on Saturdays (8a–2p) in Levee Park. If you are in town on a Wednesday evening between late June and early August, check out a concert at the **band shell** in Central Park (4th Street at East Street).

Festivals. Red Wing has festivals throughout the year, but two of the best ones are **River City Days** (800.498.3444) in early August that includes a Venetian boat parade and the **Fall Festival of the Arts** (800.498.3444), a juried art fair that celebrates local and regional art.

Music. One of the best venues for live music is just outside of town at the **Music Loft of Hobgoblin Music** (920 Highway 19; 877.866.3936/651.388.8400). They host events, often once a month, that bring in musicians that lean toward roots/Americana. Back in town, the British-pub inspired **Jimmys** at the St. James Hotel hosts live music on Friday evenings (8–10:30).

> ✔ TIP: If you want a nightcap but prefer a quality adult beverage, The Nortons Restaurant (307 Main St.; 651.388.2711) has a late night happy hour where you can get half-price rail drinks and a dollar off all draught beer (Tu–Sa 9p–10p).

Sports and Recreation ≋

The **Cannon Valley Trail** (507.263.0508) is a 20-mile former railroad line converted to a multi-use trail from Cannon Falls to Red Wing that is popular with bicyclists, in-line skaters, hikers, and cross-country skiers. The trail has an elevation change of 115 feet but it is so gradual, you probably won't notice. The trail is free for hikers but other users must purchase a pass ($3/day, $20/season wheel pass for bikers and skaters; $6/day, $20/season pass for skiers).

The **Hay Creek Trail**, a six-mile paved bike path connects to the Cannon Valley Trail and will eventually form part of the Goodhue Pioneer State Trail. The trail ends at **Dorer Memorial Hardwood Forest—Hay Creek Unit** (State Highway 58; trails open May 1–Nov. 1), a day-use recreation area with horse trails.

If you didn't bring your own horse, **Hay Creek Stables** (29491 Hay Creek Trail; 651.385.9395) offers guided horse rides through the Hay Creek Valley ($35/hr); call to schedule.

If you want to bike one of the trails but didn't bring a bicycle, no worries. Head to **Wheelhouse Cycles** (1932 Old West Main; 651.388.1082; M–F 10–7, Sa,Su 10–5), conveniently located a stone's throw from the trailhead of the Cannon Valley Trail ($20/day for a standard hybrid, $40/day for a Trek road bike). Get there early; they don't reserve bikes and on weekends, rentals are gone by 10am.

Ben and Joe's Fun Rentals (1616 Old West Main; 651.388.4259; Th–Sa) will also set you up with a bicycle ($5/hour, $20/day for a standard bike; $25/day for a tandem bike); if you were hoping for something with a motor to get you around town, they also rent scooters ($15/hour, $75/day).

For a swim, your best bet is the **Colvill Aquatic Center** (480 Nymphara Lane; 651.388.9234; daily Noon–7p from June to Labor Day; $6.50) and its large pool with waterslides.

You can go **mountain biking** or play **disc golf** at Memorial Bluff (542 E. 7th St.), or **rock climbing** at Barn Bluff.

For skiing or snowboarding, head to **Welch Village Ski and Snowboard Area** (26685 County Road 7 Blvd.; 651.258.4567); at press time,, fees were $47 for an all-day lift pass and $30 to rent a standard set of ski or snowboard equipment. Indoor ice skating is available at **Bergwall Arena** (215 Pioneer Rd.; 651.388.6088) and **Prairie Island Arena** (370 Guernsey Lane; 651.267.4346). Call for open skating times and fees. Outdoor skating rinks are abundant.

The giant boot

Shopping

FALCONER VINEYARDS WINERY produces wines from local grapes; I enjoyed the whites more than the reds, although I also liked their port (3572 Old Tyler Rd.; 651.388.8849; F,Su Noon–5, Sa 10–6 from late April–Thanksgiving, weekdays from Noon–5 added in the fall). **HOBGOBLIN MUSIC** (920 Highway 19; 877.866.3936/651.388.8400; M–F 8–5, Sa 10–5) is renowned for its hand-crafted Celtic harps; you can also get that accordion you've been pining for. The **POTTERY PLACE MALL** (2000 Old W. Main St.; M–Sa 10-6, Su 11–5) has a number of fun shops vending antiques, chocolate/candies, used books, kitchenware, etc. **RED WING POTTERY** (1920 Old W. Main St.; 800.228.0174/651.388.3562; M–Sa 9–6, Su 9–5) is a big store with plenty of pottery, some hand-thrown, plus home knick-knacks, candy, and t-shirts. You can watch a potter at work in the back of the store.

The downtown area has several boutique shops worth a visit. **BEST OF TIMES BOOKS** (425 W. 3rd St.; 651.388.1003; M–F 10–6, Sa 9–5, Su 11–3) has a good selection of new and used books. The **UFFDA SHOP** (202 Bush St.; 800.488.3332/651.388.8436; M–F 9–8, Sa 9–6, Su Noon–5 from May–Dec, otherwise open M–W,Sa 9–5, Th,F 9–8, Su Noon–5) sells Scandinavian-themed products like porcelain, glassware, candies, hand-knit sweaters, and books of Ole and Lena jokes. At the **RED WING SHOE STORE** (315 Main St.; 651.388.6233; M–F 9–8, Sa 9–6, Su 11–5), you can buy a pair of shoes or boots meant to take a beating. **THUNDER CLAN TRADING POST** (312 Bush St.; 651.385.0515; M–Sa 9–5) has Native American arts and crafts.

Eating

For a light breakfast, head to **HANISCH BAKERY** (410 W. 3rd St.; 651.388.1589; M–F 5:30a–5p, Sa 5:30a–3p; WiFi) and snack on fresh pastries and coffee.

BEV'S CAFÉ (221 Bush St.; 651.388.5227; M–F 5a–8p, Sa 6a–2p, Su 8a–1p) is a downtown diner that offers heartier, reasonably-priced breakfasts ($3–$8); check out the gritwurst, a house specialty.

For made-from-scratch goodness, head to **SMOKEY ROW CAFÉ/JENNY LIND BAKERY** (1926 Old West Main St.; 651.388.6025; M–Sa 7:30–6, Su 9–4; WiFi) and enjoy a wrap or sandwich on fresh bread ($6–$8); breakfast options include quiches, strata, and sandwiches ($5–$7).

LIBERTY'S RESTAURANT AND LOUNGE (303 W. 3rd St.; 651.388.8877; Su,M 8a–10:30p,

Tu–Th 8a–11p, F,Sa 8a–midnight) is a family-friendly restaurant with a wide-ranging menu of generally well-prepared foods from burgers to tacos to lasagna to walleye (sandwiches $6–$9, dinner entrées $10–$22); you can order breakfast all day (most items $4–$8).

Fresh and delicious Mexican standards are the norm at **FIESTA MEXICANA** (2918 N. Service Dr.; 651.385.8939; Su–Th 11–10, F,Sa 11–11); their menu includes a nice range of seafood options (entrées mostly $7–$11).

The St. James Hotel has three good choices for a meal. If you want casual dining, **THE VERANDA** (M–Sa 6:30a–8p, Su 7:30a–8p) is the only place in town that has outside seating with a river view. Breakfast items are mostly $7–$8; lunch and dinner menus lean toward salads, sandwiches, and light entrées ($8–$16). If you are more in the mood for gastropub fare at reasonable prices, head to the fifth floor and dine at **JIMMY'S** (daily 4p–10p) where you can eat heartier fare like fish and chips or Korean BBQ short ribs (entrées $9–$13) and pair it with a craft beer. Alas, if fine dining is what you crave, head downstairs to **THE PORT** (Tu–Sa 5–9). This inventive menu includes a vegetable strata called Beggar's Purse, plus bison ribeye, and other soul-satisfying concoctions (entrées from $16–$33). To make reservations at any of these restaurants, call 800.252.1875/651.388.2846.

THE NORTONS RESTAURANT (307 Main St.; 651.388.2711; M 11a–9p, Tu–Sa 11a–10p, Su 11a–8p) offers fine dining in a space with a sleek, modern décor. When I dined at Nortons, the menu had something of a Cajun theme, but that is not always the case; what is typical is finely crafted food that emphasizes seasonal ingredients. They offer half- and full-size portions for most of their dinner entrées, something I wish more restaurants would do (dinner entrée prices: half-portions from $12–$22, full portions from $20–$36).

Sleeping

Camping. About six miles from town, the **HAY CREEK VALLEY CAMPGROUND** (31655 Highway 58 Blvd.; 888.388.3998/651.388.3998) has plenty of overnight sights in a scenic valley adjacent to the Hay Creek Unit of Dorer State Forest; overnight sites are mostly in an open field with little shade but are large ($33). **HIDDEN VALLEY CAMPGROUND** (27173 144th Ave. Way; 651.258.4550; WiFi) is about 15 miles northwest of Red Wing, near the village of Welch and along the Cannon River Trail; it has several sites next to the Cannon River ($38/site); no reservations and no credit cards.

Budget. The only non-chain budget option in town is the **PARKWAY MOTEL** (3425 Highway 61 North; 651.388.8231; WiFi); rooms are in decent shape and clean and come standard with fridge, microwave, coffee, and cable TV ($49–$59+tax).

Bed and Breakfast. Red Wing has an impressive collection of bed and breakfast inns; you won't go wrong at any of these. Each includes a full breakfast.

THE CANDLELIGHT INN (818 W. 3rd St.; 800.254.9194/651.388.8034; WiFi) has five guest rooms in an Italianate home built in 1877 by Horace and Alice Rich; Horace was the President of Red Wing Stoneware, which later became Red Wing Pottery. Lynette writes about food and makes a mean breakfast. The house is decorated with a period feel and has rich, warm woodwork throughout ($159–$229+tax). **THE GOLDEN LANTERN INN** (721 East Ave.; 888.288.3315/651.388.3315; WiFi) has five rooms in the 1930s-era house built for J.R. Sweasy, the first president of the Red Wing Shoe Company. Check out the original art deco bathroom on the first floor. The rooms include two two-room suites and a third-floor suite with a more contemporary décor; all rooms have luxury options like gas fireplaces, king beds, and flat screen TVs. You can opt for breakfast in your room ($169–$209+tax). Don't be fooled by the imposing limestone Italianate house that is the **MOONDANCE INN** (1105 W. 4th St.; 866.388.8145/651.388.8145; WiFi in most rooms); the interior is welcoming and artful, decorated with French and Italian antiques. The house was essentially gutted after being rescued from neglect, so the rooms are in great shape and equipped with private baths including two-person whirlpool tubs ($169–$215+tax). **THE PRATT-TABER INN** (706 W. 4th St.; 651.388.7392; WiFi) is in an 1874-era house that went through a major overhaul; the four rooms, all with a private bath, have a seasonal theme and are decorated with a nod to the past but not handcuffed by it ($150+tax). **THE ROUND BARN FARM** Bed and Breakfast and Bread (28650 Wildwood Lane; 866.763.2276/651.385.9250; WiFi) is simply lovely. The house was built just a few years ago but it looks like a 19th century brick farmhouse thanks to generous use of reclaimed materials. The five guest rooms each have a private bath with whirlpool tub and individual climate controls, plus a fireplace, and feather beds with pillowtop mattresses ($159–$249+tax). Don't forget to check out the namesake round barn, built in 1914 and used primarily for special events.

Cabins/Houses. THE GUEST HOUSE NEXT DOOR (1117 W. 4th St.; 866.388.8145/651.388.8145) is a four-bedroom, two-bath house with a full kitchen and plenty of historic character, good for a family or group of friends traveling together ($325+tax; 2 night minimum).

Moderate. The **NICHOLS INN OF RED WING** (1750 US Highway 61; 651.388.6633; WiFi) is a newer hotel in a commercial district north of downtown with clean, contemporary rooms outfitted with fridge, coffee, and cable TV; some rooms have a microwave ($95–$154+tax, incl continental breakfast). The Grande Dame of local lodging is the **ST. JAMES HOTEL** (406 Main St.; 800.252.1875/651.388.2846; WiFi). This historic hotel was built in 1874-5 and has been a landmark in Red Wing for generations. In 1975, the Red Wing Shoe Company rescued the hotel from oblivion and completed a major overhaul that included building a new tower. No two guest rooms are identical. Each is named for a steamboat and has a handmade Amish quilt. The wide range of room types and sizes means rates can vary tremendously; most rooms run $175–$200 (+tax) on a weekend, but package deals help reduce costs.

Resources

- The local newspaper is the *Red Wing Republican Eagle* (651.388.2914).
- Post Office: 222 West Ave.; 651.388.8637.
- Red Wing Public Library: 225 East Ave.; 651.385.3673; WiFi; M–W 10–8, Th,F 10–6, Sa 9–3 from Memorial Day to Labor Day, M–W 10–8:30, Th,F 10–6, Sa 10–4 the rest of the year.

Getting To and Out of Dodge ✈

Red Wing is one of the stops on **Amtrak's Empire Builder** route; Amtrak uses the neoclassical Red Wing Depot (420 Levee St.) but does not maintain a service window. You can buy your tickets on-line (www.amtrak.com), by phone (800.872.7245), or on the train. Westbound trains depart Red Wing at 8:52p for destinations along the Mississippi River that include St.

Paul/Minneapolis (1 hour, 40 minutes), and St. Cloud (3 hours, 50 minutes) before continuing on through the western United States to Seattle. Eastbound trains depart Red Wing at 8:54a and pass through Winona (1 hour, 15 minutes) and La Crosse (1 hour, 45 minutes) before terminating at Chicago (7 hours). Fares can vary substantially; they are based on the number of available seats, so you will generally pay less the further in advance you book.

Getting Around

Limited bus service is available through **Hiawathaland Transit** (866.623.7505; M–F 6a–6:45p; $1.75). They operate two scheduled routes around the city; route 1 will be of most use to visitors.

For more information and updates, visit my web site at www.mississippivalleytraveler.com.

WACOUTA

(Uninc)

Wacouta is a small residential community with a number of lakefront homes and not much for a visitor to do, other than gawk at the big homes.

Arriving in Town

Follow Wacouta Road from US 61.

History

Wacouta was settled nearly as early as Red Wing. George Bullard arrived in 1850, He had been a trader and worked closely with the Dakota, so, when he platted the village in 1853 he chose a name to honor Chief Wakuta, one of the last Dakota chiefs in this area.

The founders of the village of Wacouta had high hopes for their town. In 1853, they went head-to-head with Red Wing for the county seat. Wacouta's proprietors pinned their hopes on getting votes from the lumbermen across the river who were regular customers at the village's hotels and businesses. Red Wing, still a small community at the time, imported 20 men to town, ostensibly to work for the village but, in reality, just to vote in the county seat election. Red Wing won. Wacouta didn't develop much after losing the election. It had a station on the Chicago, Milwaukee, and St. Paul railroad, but no major industry. Wacouta today is a small residential community with a number of lakefront homes, some new and very expensive.

Sports and Recreation 〰

The **Rattlesnake Bluff Trail** is a paved trail that passes through mostly flat terrain. You can ride/walk/run up to four miles; for route info, check out the sign by the township hall (go left at the Y in the road).

FRONTENAC STATION

(Uninc)

Frontenac Station is the place you pass through on the way to Frontenac State Park and Old Frontenac.

Arriving in Town

US Highway 61 forms the western boundary of town; whoever laid out the village chose street names to reflect the predominant ethnicities of area settlers: Germania, Hibernia, Scandinavia, Brittania.

History

Frontenac Station may lack the glamorous history of Old Frontenace, but it has nothing to hang its head about. The village came to life in the 1870s when the railroad built tracks along this alignment instead of through Old Frontenac. This decision was made at least partly because Israel Garrard didn't want trains rumbling through his bucolic resort community.

Frontenac Station developed into a solid, small community whose businesses served the local agricultural industry. By 1900, the village had a quarry, a grain elevator, a saloon, general stores, and blacksmiths. Stone from a nearby quarry was used in the construction of St. John the Divine in New York City.

Frontenac Station is also home to the oldest government building in continuous operation in Minnesota. The Florence Town Hall was completed in 1875 and is still serving the local community.

Tourist Information ⓘ

Your best bet to learn about the local scene is to stop in to the **Whistle Stop Restaurant** (33683 Highway 61 North; 651.345.5800; daily 6a–8p).

Attractions

Florence Town Hall (33923 Highway 61 Blvd), built on a lot donated by Israel Garrard, has been used as focal point for the town's business since it was completed in 1875; the interior has impressive details like maple floors, wainscoting, pieces of original furniture, and old voting booths.

Eating ✕

THE WHISTLE STOP RESTAURANT (33683 Highway 61 North; 651.345.5800; daily 6a–8p) is a standard small-town diner/dive, where you can get a big breakfast any time of day ($3–$7) or a burger ($5–$7).

OLD FRONTENAC
(Uninc)

Old Frontenac was home to a well-heeled resort—the "Newport of the North"—attracting folks from across the US. It is now a well-preserved Civil War-era community undisturbed by modern roads.

Arriving in Town

Old Frontenac is not directly on the Great River Road, but it is just a short detour away via County Highway 2, which loops around and through Old Frontenac and connects to the River Road north and south of Frontenac Station. At the point where County Highway 2 makes a sharp turn, take Lake Avenue Way to get to the heart of the old resort area.

History

The first European to live in the area was Rene Boucher, who set up a log stockade called Fort Beauharnois in 1726. He brought two Jesuit missionaries with them, Michel Guignas and Nicholas de Gonner, who established the Mission of St. Michaels the Archangel, possibly the first church in Minnesota. They abandoned the fort by 1763 when the French were forced to cede their North American lands to Great Britain. James "Bully" Wells was the next person to establish a significant presence. He ran a trading post that was established by 1840. After the Treaty of Mendota opened the Minnesota Territory, more settlers moved in. Everet Westervelt bought Wells' claim around 1854 and built the first store in the area; at that time it was known as Western Landing.

One of the former resort homes

Brigadier General Israel Garrard and his brother, Lewis, visited the area on a hunting trip in 1854 and were so enchanted they vowed to return. In 1857, Israel bought 4,000 acres from Jean Baptiste Faribault and divided it into quarter shares: one for each of three Garrard brothers and one for Westervelt, reserving 320 acres for a town site they called Westervelt. Israel Garrard bought out Westervelt in 1859 and renamed the village Frontenac in honor of Louis de Buade de Frontenac, a governor general of New France who commissioned several explorations of the Mississippi Valley.

Garrard built a home he called St. Hubert's lodge (in honor of the patron saint of hunters) and the village attracted a few settlers, many of whom were from Cincinnati where they had previously worked for Garrard. While the village of Frontenac attracted some industry, its main claim to fame was the resort on a point of land at the northeast end of town. Garrard converted a warehouse into the Lakeside Hotel; turned a general store into a hall with a theater, billiards, and tavern; and built nine cottages for summer resort guests. For seventy years, Frontenac was a favored summer vacation spot for the genteel on holiday.

After the resort waned in popularity, Methodists

View from Latsch State Park, Minn.

Marina on Lake Pepin

Boathouses at Latsch Island, Winona, Minn.

Can't have a parade without a clown, Lake City, Minn.

Little Log House, near Hastings, Minn.

Mississippi River near Wabasha, Minn.

LARK Toys snowman, Kellogg, Minn.

Hot dish at Grumpy Old Men Days, Wabasha, Minn.

bought the former Lakseside Hotel and ran it as a retreat center for decades. Many of the buildings later fell into decline until a gradual effort to restore them began in 1987, largely through the efforts of Bill and Linda Flies. What makes Frontenac unique today is not so much the number of Civil War-era buildings but that an entire community from that period is essentially intact and undisturbed by modern development. The former resort buildings are being restored but are now private residences.

Tourist Information

Your best bet to learn about the local scene is to stop in to the **Whistle Stop Restaurant** (33683 Highway 61 North; 651.345.5800; daily 6a–8p).

Attractions

Frontenac State Park (County Road 2; 651.345.3401; $5/day vehicle permit) has plentiful hiking and picnicking, much of it with great blufftop views of Lake Pepin. The park has sections of bottomland hardwood forest that are popular with birders.

Christ Episcopal Church (County 2 Blvd.; 612.345.3531) was completed in 1869 as the resort area was coming into prominence; the logs used to build it were floated down the St. Croix and Mississippi Rivers. Other than the addition of a few electric lights and forced air heat, the church is just as it appeared when built.

Sports and Recreation

The **Florence Township Beach** is by the boat ramp at the end of Garrard Street.

Sleeping

Camping. The main campground at **FRONTENAC STATE PARK** (County Road 2; 651.345.3401; $5 daily vehicle permit + camping fee) is in a heavily wooded area and the sites are nicely spaced apart ($18/ without elec, $22/ with elec). There are also six primitive, cart-in sites that are a quarter-mile walk from the parking lot ($12).

Budget. Villa Maria opened in 1880 by Ursuline nuns as a boarding school for girls; the school was a big success, which required new buildings. Israel Garrard donated a large tract and the new school and dormitory buildings opened in 1890. The school did well for decades but came to an abrupt end when the school was struck by lightning in March 1969 and burned to the ground. The sisters decided not to rebuild and closed the school, but they found another use for the former dormitory, creating the interdenominational **VILLA MARIA RETREAT AND CONFERENCE CENTER** (29847 County 2 Blvd.; 866.244.4582/651.345.4582; WiFi) on its expansive 70 acres. The rooms were once dorms for a private, parochial school, so they are small, don't have a TV or phone, and share common bathrooms and showers. They are perfect for that quiet retreat you have been craving (Weekends: one night costs $73.50/person and includes three meals; two nights will run you $110/person with meals included from Sa breakfast through Su brunch).

LAKE CITY

(4,950)

Lake City, more so than any other community in the region, feels like a resort town, with busy streets, boutique shops, a large marina crowded with sailboats, and unattractive waterfront condominiums. The lake (see the Lake Pepin sidebar on page 76) abounds with natural beauty and recreational options, which explains why the city's summer population swells to 12,000.

Arriving in Town

US Highway 61 enters town as Lakeshore Drive; US Highway 63 heads west near the center of town and is Lyon Avenue from that point on. The small commercial district is located northeast of US 61 from Lakeshore Drive to Lake Pepin and along Washington and Franklin Streets.

History

Jacob Brody arrived in 1853 and gets the credit as Lake City's first settler; he was joined by his brother Philip and other settlers the next year, most of whom came from New England. Before Lake City amounted to much, the towns of Florence and Central Point were attracting settlers, but those communities faded away as it became clear that Lake City had the superior steamboat landing; in 1858, alone, Lake City counted 1,500 steamboat dockings.

As the population exploded from 300 in 1856 to over 2500 in 1870, business boomed. For a brief time, Lake City was busy with clamming, button manufacturing, and grain shipping. The railroad arrived in

1872 and the grain elevators were moved from the lakefront to the railroad tracks. With the decline in steamboat traffic, Lake City grew into a commercial center for local farmers. During the Depression, all three banks in town closed; only one eventually reopened.

Wiebusch Windmill Haven

Lake City residents have been witness to two major disasters on Lake Pepin. The *Sea Wing* was an excursion boat that sank near Lake City on July 13, 1890, killing 98 of 215 passengers (see the sidebar on page 343). A half century later, a B-24 Liberator crashed in Lake Pepin on December 15, 1944 during a snow storm. The four-engine prop plane was a long-range bomber being moved from St. Paul to Kansas City. The plane exploded on impact and sank; the bodies of the three crew members could not be recovered until six months later because of ice on the lake.

Tourist Information ⓘ

You can stock up on brochures at the **Lake City Tourism Bureau** (101 West Center St.; 877.525.3248; M–F 9–5, from April–Oct. also open Sa 10–3).

Attractions

Lake City has a number of parks along the waterfront that would be a fine place for picnicking or quiet contemplation, including **Gold Star Mother's Park** and **Ohuta Park** along Park Street, **McCahill Park** near the marina, and **Roschen Park** on South Lakeshore Drive. There is also a small park at the end of **the point** in the middle of town that juts out into Lake Pepin. Follow Chestnut Street past the beach and mobile homes for a great panoramic view.

Hey, what's that? Scotland may have the Loch Ness Monster, but Lake Pepin has Pepie, a mysterious, very large fish, or monster, or very large tree stump. Stories about a monster in the lake go back to Native American oral traditions. Pepie even got a mention in the 1871 edition of the Minnesota Historical Society's Book of Days Almanac. Maybe you'll be one of the folks who claims to have seen this mysterious creature, but you are more likely to see a Pepie t-shirt than the actual monster. If you are the lucky one to get the first video of Pepie, you could be the next YouTube star.

The **Lake City Historical Society** set up a few displays about Lake City's past in the second floor ballroom of the 1899-era **City Hall** (205 W. Center St.; 651.345.5383; M–F 8–4:30; free); the ballroom is at least as interesting as the display cabinets.

It's a bit of a detour from the river, but **Ralph Wiebusch's Windmill Haven** (36225 County Road 72) is worth a 15-minute drive. Ralph is one of those folks who walks a fine line between serious collector and obsessive. His interest in windmills dates back to the 1970s when he moved them from farms in the Midwest to ranches in the West. Over the years, he has purchased and restored about three dozen of them; two dozen currently adorn his yard. The windmills were used primarily between the 1880s and 1930s to pump water from wells. To get there from Lake City, travel south on US 63 toward Zumbro Falls; just be-

The Point

fore reaching town, turn left on County Road 72. The windmills are 0.7 miles on the right.

Getting on the River

You can't rent a boat around here, but you can pay someone else for a ride. The **Pearl of the Lake** (100 Central Point Rd.; 651.345.5188) is a paddlewheel replica that offers 90-minute cruises on Lake Pepin from April through October (W–Su 1p; $15).

Culture & Arts

Lake City has two places where can view (and buy) the work of local artists: **Serendipity Coop Art Gallery** (110 S. Washington; 651.345.5734; W–Sa 10–4) and **Local Elements Art Gallery** (210 S. Lakeshore Dr.; 651.345.4278; F,Su 10–2, Sa 10–5).

Entertainment and Events

The local **Farmers Market** is on Thursday evenings from 6p–8p at the Chestnut Street beach.

Festivals. Enjoy the scenery of Lake Pepin with an extended bike ride around the lake as part of **Tour de Pepin** (early June). Options include a 12-mile ride to

Wabasha with return by bus; a 32-mile ride to Stockholm (Wisconsin) with return on the *Pearl of the Lake* paddlewheeler; or biking the entire 72-mile route. You must register for the event ($50). Ralph Samuelson invented water skiing in 1922 on Lake Pepin, which naturally the town must celebrate with a festival; it has been doing just that since 1972 with **Waterski Days** (last weekend in June). The 18-year old Samuelson strapped two pine boards to his feet, each board eight feet long by nine inches wide, and got behind a motorboat operated by his brother; when his brother hit the throttle young Ralph was lifted out of the water. No doubt inspired by Samuelson, in 1973 Lake City resident Dennis Francis, then 27-years old, waterskied the Mississippi from Coon Rapids (Minnesota) to the Gulf of Mexico. The festival includes a parade on Sunday afternoon and a waterskiing demonstration. Celebrate the apple harvest with **Johnny Appleseed Days** (1st weekend of October); expect plenty of art and craft vendors, an apple pie competition, and a children's peddle tractor pull. Contact the tourism office for details on these events (877.525.3248).

Sports and Recreation

Take a pleasant stroll along the waterfront on the 2 ½ mile paved path called the **River Walk**.

Lake City has **two swimming beaches**, one at the foot of Chestnut Street (651.345.3905) and another in Hok-Si-La Park (2500 N. Highway 61; 651.345.3855).

Shopping

HUETTL'S LOCKER (1903 N. Lakeshore Dr.; 651.345.3424; M–F 8:30–5:30, Sa 8a–Noon) is an old-fashioned butcher and meat shop, making a variety of specialty sausages and cured meats that you should

Lake Pepin

Sailing on Lake Pepin

Lake Pepin is a 25,000 acre natural lake formed by the Chippewa River delta. The Chippewa deposits more silt and sand than the Mississippi can carry away, so a natural dam has formed. The lake (so-called because there is essentially no current) is 22 miles long and has a maximum width of 2 ½ miles, with a depth that is usually 20–32 feet. It is a popular place for sailing in summer and ice boating in winter.

Father Louis Hennepin wanted to name it *Lake of Tears*, maybe because he was captured by Dakota in 1680 near its southern end, but French explorers who did not have the kidnapping experience called it *Lac Bon Secours* or Lake of Good Hope. Ultimately, the name that stuck is probably derived from Pepin the Short, ruler of France from 740 to 768, who was Charlemagne's father.

The Lake is facing serious environmental threats, most notably from runoff (primarily from farming) carried down the Minnesota River. The latest studies found that 10 times the normal amount of silt is being dumped into the lake, a pace that would fill the 10,000-year-old lake completely in about 300 years but that is already filling in shallow side channels.

buy in large quantities. **MISSISSIPPI MERCANTILE** (106 E. Center St.; 651.345.4800; W–Sa 10–5, Su 11–4) has some interesting antiques and collectibles, many with a nautical theme. **TREATS AND TREASURES** (108 E. Lyon Ave.; 651.345.2882; M–F 10–5:30, Sa 9–5, Su 11–4) has an eclectic mix of books, Pepie t-shirts and sweatshirts, and gourmet chocolates. **GREAT RIVER VINEYARD & NURSERY** (35680 Highway 61 N.; 651.345.5331) sells locally-grown grapes in season, plus fresh grape juice, jelly, and jam. **BUSHEL & PECK** (35878 Highway 61 N.; 651.345.4516; M–Sa 9–6, Su Noon–6 from May–Nov.) sells morel mushrooms in May, fruit in summer, and apples in fall. **PEPIN HEIGHTS ORCHARD** (1775 S. Highway 61 S.; 651.345.2305; daily 9a–6p from mid-Aug–Dec) is another option for apples in the fall.

Eating and Drinking

SKYLINE ON PEPIN (1702 N. Lakeshore Dr.; 651.345.5353; M–Th 11–9, F,Sa 11–11, Su 9:30–9) has a large outdoor patio that is a fine place to enjoy a drink.

RABBIT'S BAKERY (304 S. Washington; 651.345.3199; W–Su 6a–3p in summer, W–Su 7a–3p the rest of the year; WiFi) bakes pastries, bread, and other yummy food from scratch. Settle in with a pastry and a cup of coffee to read the newspaper or search YouTube for Mississippi Valley Traveler videos. Lunch options include soups and sandwiches on fresh bread ($7.50 with a side). The first Sunday of the month, they fire up the brick oven for pizza night (5p–8p).

RHYTHM AND BREWS COFFEE HOUSE (220 E. Chestnut St.; 651.345.5335; Tu–W 7a–1:30p, Th–F 7a–1:30p, 5–8, Sa 8a–1:30p, 5–10, Su 8–3) is another option for coffee.

MARIEN'S DELI (716 W. Lyon Ave.; 651.345.2526; M–F 7–7, Sa 8–5, Su 10–2) prepares fresh salads and sandwiches at very reasonable prices ($5 for a 10" sub).

CHICKADEE COTTAGE CAFÉ (317 N. Lakeshore Dr.; 651.345.5155; open mid-April–October M–Sa 8–2:30, Su 9–2; open F,Sa 5–8 in summer) is popular with the ladies-who-lunch set, plus just about everyone else. The café is retrofitted into an early 20th century cottage-style home; you are eating where someone previously read a book or played with the kids. The creative menu of freshly prepared food includes dishes like the uff da omelet, which is filled with smoked salmon (breakfast entrées mostly $5–$7). Lunch options include salads, wraps, sandwiches, and mains like three cheese lasagna and quiche ($7–$10). For dinner, they offer a number of pasta dishes, walleye, steaks, and seafood ($10–$18), plus sandwiches and salads.

HOPE'S HARVEST (130 S. Washington St.; 651.345.3690; daily 8a–6p, reduced hours in winter) offers freshly-prepared sandwiches, soups, and salads with organic and local ingredients; you can eat for about $5 here.

BRONK'S BAR & GRILL (101 E. Center St.; 651.345.2123; kitchen open Su–Th 11a–9p, F,Sa 11a–10p) has an art deco feel outside that carries inside to the bar. The menu is essentially bar food with a few twists like an Asian Chicken Salad, vegetable quesadilla, and entrées like fried walleye ($15), but the big burgers are probably the most popular items (sandwiches, salads, and burgers mostly $6–$8).

NOSH RESTAURANT AND BAR (310 ½ S. Washington St.; 651.345.2425; M,W–Sa 4–9, Su 3–8 in summer, reduced hours in winter) offers the best fine dining option in town with an emphasis on seasonal ingredients from local sources. The changing menu has Mediterranean influences; the summer night I visited, entrées included seafood paella and grilled lamb chops (entrées from $17–$27). If you just want a snack with a drink to enjoy on the patio, they have several smaller plates and salads ($5–$12).

Sleeping

Camping. HOK-SI-LA PARK (2500 N. Highway 61; 651.345.3855) is the site of a former Boy Scout camp. The tent-only sites are rather close together but some have lake views; weekdays are a better value ($30/night on weekends from Memorial Day to Labor Day, $15/night weekdays or before Memorial Day/after Labor Day). **LAKE PEPIN CAMPGROUNDS AND TRAILER COURT** (1010 Locust St.; 651.345.2909) has a decent amount of shade in a compact site south of the highway ($15/tent site; $20/elec, $23/water & elec, $26/full hookup; all + tax).

✔ TIP: If you've been roughing it for a few days, the Marina has public showers where you can make yourself presentable again.

Budget. SUNSET MOTEL (1515 N. Lakeshore Dr.; 800.945.0192/651.345.5331; WiFi) offers simple, clean, well-maintained rooms, many of which have a microwave and fridge ($80+tax), small cabins that are a bit roomier ($89+tax), and one-and two-bedroom kitchenettes ($119–$225); the motel has a heated swimming pool.

Bed and Breakfast. B&Bs often try to carve out an identity but few do it as well as **THE FROG & BEAR BED AND BREAKFAST** (411 West Center St.; 800.753.9431/651.345.2122; WiFi), as Dale and Betty have decorated their inn with the objects they collect obsessively. (I think you can guess what they are.) No two guest rooms have identical features, but each of the the four rooms is cozy and has a private bath ($129+tax).

House Rental. DRAGONFLY DREAMS RETREAT CENTER (120 W. Lyon Ave.; 651.345.2764; WiFi) targets crafters (quilters and those of a similar ilk) who want to spread out and work, but it would also work for a family or group traveling together. The house has a full kitchen, four bedrooms, satellite TV, and three bathrooms (one with a Jacuzzi tub); one of the bathrooms is reputed to be the oldest functional indoor bathroom in town ($600+tax/8 people; 2 night minimum).

Moderate and up. JOHN HALL'S ALASKAN LODGE (1127 N. Lakeshore Dr.; 800.325.2270/651.345.1212; WiFi) has nine spacious suites with lake views equipped with a fireplace, microwave, and coffee (most also have a fridge), and decorated generously with natural materials ($129–$149+tax). If you like the timeshare lifestyle, there are two options in Lake City. **VILLAS ON PEPIN** (1215 N. Lakeshore Dr.; 651.345.5188; WiFi) has several one-and two-bedroom units overlooking Lake Pepin that come with full kitchens, balconies, and a homey feel; check out the roof-top patio. Another option is **WILLOWS ON THE RIVER CONDOMINIUM RESORT** (100 Central Point Rd.; 651.345.9900; WiFi), with one-and two-bedroom units with similar amenities but a minimalist décor, good views of the lake, and an indoor swimming pool ($185+tax /one-bedroom, $260+tax /two bedroom; two-night minimum in summer).

For more information and updates, visit my web site at www.MississippiValleyTraveler.com.

Resources

- The local newspaper: is the *Lake City Graphic* (651.345.3316).
- Post Office: 111 S. High St.; 651.345.3760.
- Lake City Public Library: 201 S. High St.; 651.345.4013; WiFi; M,Th 10–8, Tu,W Noon–8, F 10–6, Sa 9–1.

Getting Around 🚌

Limited bus service is available through **Hiawathaland Transit** (866.623.7505; M–F 7:30a–4:30p; $1.75); call to schedule a ride.

CAMP LACUPOLIS

(Uninc)

Located at the southern tip of Lake Pepin, Camp Lacupolis was once a quiet stagecoach stop; it is now a quiet fishing camp.

History

Founded in 1861 with the catchy name Lake-Opilis; the name is derived from Greek and means something like "Camp Lake City." It never got big enough to justify a post office. It once had a stagecoach stop. Overland visitors from the west would stop for the night, then continue on to Lake City by boat in the morning. It is now a village of log cabins and campers.

Sleeping

Camping. CAMP LACUPOLIS (71000 US Highway 61; 651.565.4318) has a few sites with water and electric that are close to the water ($25; May–Oct).

Cabins. CAMP LACUPOLIS (71000 US Highway 61; 651.565.4318) has 19 cabins in a range of sizes, all with air conditioning and supplied with linens, but you'll need to bring towels, soap, shampoo, toilet paper, garbage bags, and paper towels; most cabins have a small kitchen ($75–$160 + tax, but $10/night discount if staying two or more nights; March–early Dec).

READS LANDING
(Uninc)

When you pass through Reads Landing today, it's hard to believe that this community was once in the running to be the state capital and had a population of nearly 2000. Life is much more laid back in Reads Landing today than it was in its heyday as the scene of sin and vice for vacationing lumberjacks.

Arriving in Town

US Highway 61 bisects this small community; the riverfront is along 2nd Street, just one block east of the highway.

History

The village of Reads Landing is on the site of a former trading post (known as *Waumadee* to the Dakota) that was operated by successive generations of Rocques beginning around 1810. They sold the land to Edward Hudson, so naturally this spot became known as Hudson's Landing. After he died, Englishman Charles Read purchased Hudson's claim. Read emigrated to the US at age 10 with his brother's family. He served in the American army that invaded Canada in 1837; the 17-year-old Read was captured by the British and sentenced to hang. Luckily for Mr. Read, Queen Victoria pardoned him and let him return to the US. In 1844 he settled in Nelson's Landing (Wisconsin), before moving across the river a few years later to establish a trading post, which angered Alexis Bailly, who already had a trading post in the area near Hastings. Read platted the village in 1856 and incorporated it in 1868 with a great deal of optimism. Reads Landing was a thriving community with a bustling steamboat port that served the logging trade. Logs coming down the nearby Chippewa River were assembled into large rafts, then floated downriver for processing. Several hundred raftsmen would stay in town awaiting their turn to assemble and go. Reads Landing was one of the lumbermen's favorite places for R&R—with nearly two dozen hotels and saloons to pick from!—which led to the inevitable "scenes of violence and lawlessness staged on its streets", as described in a county history book. As the lumber trade declined, Reads Landing descended rapidly into irrelevance, and the village disincorporated in 1896.

From 1882 until the 1950s, trains crossed the river via a 2900-foot pontoon bridge. A 400-foot pontoon section would swing open to let boats pass through; the pontoon sank 14 inches when a train crossed. The bridge was a maintenance headache because of frequent damage from ice and flooding. In 1951, ice and high water caused severe damage to the bridge, and the railroad chose to abandon it rather than fix it again; the bridge was disassembled the next year.

Attractions

Housed in a the standout Italianate former schoolhouse, the **Wabasha County Historical Society Museum** (70537 206th Ave.; 651.565.4158; Sa,Su 1–4 from May–Oct.; $5) has a nicely maintained period classroom and a fun collection of exhibits that includes displays about clamming, 19th century clothing, and farm tools. Don't miss the wonderfully disorganized basement and the large shed in back that has a 1916 Model T and horse-powered farm implements like a cabbage planter.

Eating and Drinking 🍸 🍴

There is an informal **TIKI BAR** along the riverfront that serves as a community gathering place; you are welcome to BYOB and hang out there with your friends.

Sleeping 🛏

Bed and Breakfast. The **RIVER NEST BED & BREAKFAST** (20073 County Road 77; 651.560.4077; WiFi) has two suites overlooking the river, each with a private entrance. Each suite is outfitted with a Jacuzzi tub, cable TV, fridge, walk-in shower, fireplace, and deck; one suite is wheelchair friendly ($149 incl tax and full breakfast).

Moderate. The **ANCHOR INN** (112 W. 2nd St.; 800.482.8188/651.565.3509; WiFi) has a four-bedroom second floor apartment available for overnight rental in a historic riverfront building that began life as a tavern; the apartment is equipped with a full kitchen and living room and would be a fine place to stay for a family or group of friends traveling together ($289 + tax).

★ **Author's Pick:** The **AMERICAN EAGLE BLUFF BED & BREAKFAST** (651.564.0372) is housed in an 1870s-era farmhouse on 40 spectacular blufftop acres overlooking the confluence of the Chippewa and Mississippi Rivers; views of both rivers abound. Relax in an Adirondack chair in the yard or inside the screened porch, enjoying the views and verdant (and expansive) gardens. The two guest rooms have a number of luxury touches like showers with glass block walls and the absence of a television ($175+tax incl full breakfast).

WABASHA

(2,599)

Known for bald eagles and the *Grumpy Old Men* movies, Wabasha is a pleasant river town and an enjoyable place to kick back and watch the world float by. Wabasha is also among the few towns where the riverfront is undisturbed by railroad tracks, so you can enjoy the scenery in relative peace.

Arriving in Town

To get to town from US 61, follow Minnesota Highway 60; it enters town as Pembroke Avenue and will get you to Main Street and the riverfront. If you keep following the signs for Minnesota 60, you will eventually end up in Wisconsin.

History

Wabasha claims to be Minnesota's oldest city, and it's certainly hard to argue the point. Europeans first arrived in 1826. Duncan Campbell and a few other settlers trickled into the area in the 1840s as a small community developed, many of them of mixed Native American/European ancestry. The city was named Wabashaw in 1843 for the Dakota chief who lived in the area; the last "w" was dropped in 1858 when the city incorporated. The village was formally platted in 1854; the early population included a mix of French Canadians, Native Americans, English, and Americans who were later joined by German, Irish, and Scandinavian immigrants.

Wabasha had a few lumber mills and companies producing finished lumber pieces, but many people

Early Wabasha (Wabasha County Historical Society)

also made a living directly from the river through fishing, clamming, ice harvesting, and boat building. Between 1860 and 1870, the city's population nearly doubled from 894 to 1739. Wabasha was among the many communities that served as a transit spot for local wheat, at least until wheat farming ended in the 1880s. The St. Paul and Chicago railroad reached Wabasha from St. Paul in 1871; this ensured Wabasha's future and ended Reads Landing's.

Wabasha's first highway bridge opened in 1931, ending nearly 70 years of ferry service. The ramp into town had an s-curve that bent to Pembroke Avenue so traffic would flow through the commercial district. It was replaced in 1989 with one that has a ramp that goes right over the top of the commercial district, so traffic now bypasses it. (You now know better and should detour down to the commercial district.)

Wabasha served the retail needs of the local farming community until the availability of automobiles made it easier for folks to drive to bigger cities to shop. Wabasha also suffered from the general decline in the farm economy. In recent years, the city has had modest growth in light industry and has retained grain mills.

Wabasha

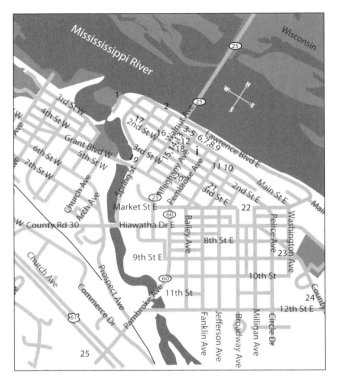

Map Key

Things to Do
22. Broadway Theater
6. Down by the River Gallery
21. Grace Memorial Episcopal Church
13. Heritage Square Park
11. Kautz Saddle Company
8. National Eagle Center
15. River Rider
20. St. Felix Catholic Church
1. Swimming beach
19. Troy's Bait Bucket
23. Wabasha Community Pool

Places to Sleep
4. America's Lofts
25. Coffee Mill Motel & Suites
2. Eagles on the River Vacation Rentals
5. Lofts on the Mississippi
24. Wabasha Motel & RV Park
17. Wabasha Municipal Campground

Places to Eat
7. Chocolate Escape/Big Jo Espresso/Flour Mill Pizzeria
16. Eagles Nest Coffee House
12. Olde Triangle Pub
14. The Scoop
10. Stacy's Kitchen
3. Vinifera

Other
9. Post Office
18. Wabasha Public Library

Armistice Day Blizzard

The morning of November 11, 1940 was unusually warm. Temperatures reached 60° along the Upper Mississippi River. A perfect day for duck hunting, even if the forecast called for colder temperatures and snow flurries. Or so it seemed.

In late morning, light rain began to fall, which turned to sleet, then, as temperatures plummeted, the snow began. Winds blew up to 70 miles per hour, creating five-foot waves on the river. Because of the warm morning, most of the hunters were not prepared for the rapidly falling temperatures, and their shallow skiffs were no match for the wind and waves. Many were stranded on islands and forced to survive the blizzard on their own; a few drowned trying to get back to shore.

Temperatures fell into the single digits overnight and the storm roared on into the next day, wreaking havoc through a thousand mile path of the Midwest. The blizzard dumped 16 inches of snow on Minneapolis and left behind 20-foot high snow drifts in places. The storm claimed over 150 lives throughout the Midwest. In Minnesota, about half of the 49 dead were duck hunters; most froze to death. The Alma Historical Society Museum (page 294) has a moving display about the blizzard with an audio recording of hunters telling about their experiences on that day.

Tourist Information ⓘ

The **Wabasha-Kellogg Convention and Visitors Bureau** (137 Main St. West; 651.565.4158; M–F 8–5, Sa 9–3) has all the brochures you could possibly want, and more.

Attractions 💡

One of the best regional attractions, the **National Eagle Center** (50 Pembroke Ave.; 877.332.4537/651.565.4989; daily 10–5; $8) has exhibits on the special talents of a bald eagle and the symbolic role eagles have played in many cultures. You can also get close to live eagles at the center; these birds were rescued from life-threatening injuries but are not good candidates for release.

The riverfront **waterfall** was designed by local residents John and Marcia Bouquet and built in 2009. It pumps water from the Mississippi River into the fountain, then sends it cascading back into the river. A **statue of Chief Wapashaw** was installed in 2010.

The **Kautz Saddle Company** (113 Pembroke Ave.; 507.951.0985; Th–Sa) has a nice collection of items from the Old West in a 2nd floor exhibit space; most of the collection, as you would expect, focuses on horse-riding gear like saddles, bridles, and spurs, but there are also some unique pieces of longhorn art and Native American cultural artifacts. If you're in the mood, you can buy a custom saddle from the downstairs shop.

Grace Memorial Episcopal Church (205 3rd St. E.; 651.565.4827) is a gem of a church. The parish dates to 1857, but the current English Gothic edifice was completed in 1901 from local limestone with a roof of Vermont blue slate. The *Resurrection Window* over the altar was made by the Tiffany Company; it was shipped by rail to Wabasha, escorted by four armed guards.

National Eagle Center

The congregation of **St. Felix Catholic Church** (117 3rd St. W.; 651.565.3931) dates to 1858; the current church was completed in 1893. The Gothic Revival church still has its original high altar and, just above the sanctuary, an unusual stained glass window in the ceiling.

The **Arrowhead Bluffs Museum** (17505 667th St.; 651.565.3829; daily 10–5 from May–Oct.; $4) is a tribute to the sportsman's world, with more than a passing nod to man's dominance of the natural world. It's a fascinating place. Cabinet after cabinet of guns (old and new), ammunition, shells, scopes, and stuffed animals galore, all personally shot by proprietors Les or John Behrens. If that's not enough, check out the legion of fishing lures, frenzy of fossils, assembly of antiques, array of arrowheads, bevy of belt buckles, even a box of bowling trophies. About those animals—they are the centerpiece of the collection and grab your eye as soon as you walk in the door. Deer, moose, polar bear, small mammals like skunks and fox, and more birds than you may see in your lifetime fill the spacious interior. Don't miss it. To get there from Wabasha, go west on Minnesota Highway 60 to the top of the bluff, then turn left on 667th Street (a gravel road).

Getting on the River

Troy's Bait Bucket (406 W. Grant Blvd.; 651.565.4895; daily 6a–6p) rents paddleboats ($10/1 hour, $15/2 hours), kayaks ($5/1 hour, $10/3 hours,

Looking down to Wabasha.

$25/day), canoes ($25/half day, $50/day), and pontoon boats ($175/day).

If you want someone else to drive, **Big River Adventures** (651.565.9932) will take up to four people on a 90-minute guided tour of the backwaters in a jon boat ($32). Call to arrange a tour.

Culture & Arts

Down by the River Gallery (152 Main St.; 651.565.5414; Sa,Su Noon–4) has rotating exhibits of work by local artists.

Entertainment and Events

Wabasha has a twice weekly **Farmers Market**: Mondays in the parking lot at St. Elizabeth Medical Center (1200 Grant Blvd. W., 3p–5:30p) and Thursdays under the bridge downtown in Heritage Square Park (4:30–6:30 from mid-May–mid-Oct.). On Friday nights in summer, the city hosts **live concerts** in Heritage Square Park. Check the schedule for the **Broadway Theater** (611 Broadway Ave.) to catch a movie or a live show.

Festivals. Wabasha has festivals throughout the year, so you'll just have to come back. If you only go to one it should be **Grumpy Old Men Days** (late February; 651.565.4158). Inspired by the movies penned by Minnesota native Mark Steven Johnson, the festival has a host of fun events that will keep you smiling: a hot dish luncheon, minnow races, and the requisite ice fishing contest. Stick around into March, for an **eagle watch weekend** at the National Eagle Center. The Wabasha Public Library hosts **worm races** in mid-June (651.565.3927), which is a nice bookend to the minnow races in February. The big city party is called **Riverboat Days** (651.565.4158), which has a fishing contest, pancake-eating, and a parade in late July. If you have one more festival in you, check out the **Wabasha County Fair** (651.565.4158) in mid-July.

Sports and Recreation

Just west of the river, **Kruger Recreation Area** (651.345.3401), part of the Richard Dorer Memorial Forest, has a good network of trails for hiking and mountain biking. Follow Minnesota Highway 60 west for five miles, then take County 81 for half a mile.

River Rider (257 Main St. W.; 651.565.4834; Tu–Sa 10–5) is a good source of expert advice about where to ride, as well as for bicycle sales and repairs.

Head to **Coffee Mill Ski & Snowboard Resort** (99 Coulee Way; 651.565.2777; W,Th 4–9:30, F 1–9:30, Sa 10–9:30, Su 11–7) to ski or snowboard. At the time of this writing, a weekend lift ticket was $30, ski rental was $22, and snowboard rental was $28, but check their website for specials and current rates (www.coffeemillski.com).

There is a public **swimming beach** near the Gazebo at the west end of Main Street. The **Wabasha Community Pool** (888 Hiawatha Dr. East; 651.565.2375; daily 1p–5:30p, 6:30p–8:30p; $3) is another option; it has a big waterslide that I'm sure you'll love.

Another good outdoor option is a **hike along the dike** to Lock and Dam 4 for great views of the river and Alma, Wisconsin. During my 45-minute hike, I saw Canadian geese, a snake, turtles, ducks, and a bald eagle. To reach the dike from Wabasha, take County Highway 30 south to the second turn for County Highway 24, then 652nd Street to 140th Avenue; park in the small lot with the sign that reads "Public access" (and has the address 64938 140th Ave.).

Shopping

Don't be fooled by the name; the decoys made at the **LOON LAKE DECOY COMPANY** (170 Industrial Court; 651.565.2696; M–F 8–4; weekend hours from Sept.–Dec.) are not meant to float in the water but are compelling and beautiful works of art with a wildlife theme that are meant to sit on a shelf in your home. **THE CHOCOLATE ESCAPE** (152 W. Main St.; 651.565.0035; Th–M 10a–8p) lives up to its name, with gourmet chocolates, some made in-house like the turtles (nuts bathed in caramel and covered with dark or milk chocolate plus something extra like sea salt); check out the wall-sized mural depicting the journey of a cocoa bean from forest to store shelf. **WIND WHISPER WEST** (128 Main St. West; 651.565.2002; Tu–Su Noon–4) is an unlikely shop for a small town like Wabasha, carrying some 2000 ceremonial kimono, a dying art form, while a typical department store in Japan is likely to carry fewer than ten. Think of this like visiting an art gallery. **THE BOOK CLIFFS** (161 Pembroke Ave.; 651.565.5312; Tu,W,F,Sa 10–Noon & 1–5, Th 10–Noon & 2–6) is a small independent bookstore with a good collection of items of local and regional interest.

Eating and Drinking 🍸 🍴

SLIPPERY'S BAR & GRILL (10 Church St.; 866.504.4036/651.565.4748; M–Th 11a–1a, F 11a–2a, Sa 8a–2a, Su 8a–1a), the bar made famous by the *Grumpy Old Men* movies, can be a fun place to get a drink, although the mood is occasionally soured by large tour buses that dump scores of drinkers on the scene. If you don't like crowds, avoid coming here on a summer weekend.

STACY'S KITCHEN (116 Main St.; 651.565.4408; W–M 7a–2p) is a small-town diner offering hearty breakfast options of skillets, sandwiches, quesadillas, and omelets ($5–$8).

At **FLOUR MILL PIZZERIA** (146 W. Main St.; 651.560.4170; Th–M 10a–8p) you can buy pizza by the slice (about $4) or whole pies with some creative specials like a pesto pizza with chicken or the southwest chipotle (7"–18"/$9–$32 for specialty pizzas; 2 topping pizzas from $7–$24 for 7"–18"); enjoy your pizza on the deck where you can stare at the river.

The **OLDE TRIANGLE PUB** (219 Main St. W.; 651.565.0256; kitchen open daily 11a–9p, bar open later) serves up burgers, sandwiches, and salads (most around $6) plus a few Irish specialties like shepherd's pie and Irish stew (mains generally $6–$8), all of which you can enjoy with a pint of Guinness.

VINIFERA (260 W. Main St.; 651.565.4171; Th 4–8, F 4–9, Sa 2–9, Su 2–8 in summer; reduced hours in winter) is the place for casual fine dining. The seasonal menu pairs foods from predominantly local sources with wines from the world's great vineyards. When I visited, the menu included cedar plank salmon and pan roasted pork tenderloin ($7–$18); portion sizes tend to be small by American standards. Reservations are advised.

Ice cream addicts have three options: the previously mentioned **CHOCOLATE ESCAPE** (152 W. Main St.; 651.565.0035; Th–M 10a–8p), where you can wash it down with a cappuccino at the adjacent **BIG JO ESPRESSO**; **THE SCOOP** (Heritage Park, F 11–9, Sa 11–7, Su 1–5 from Memorial Day–Labor Day), which is under the bridge; and **EAGLES NEST COFFEE HOUSE** (330 2nd St. West; 651.565.2077; M–W 7a–2p, Th–Sa 7a–4p, Su 8a–2p), which also includes the option of an espresso.

Sleeping

Camping. KRUGER RECREATION AREA (County Road 81; 651.345.3401) has 19 large but primitive sites in a heavily-wooded area with a common water source ($12). The **WABASHA MOTEL & RV PARK** (1110 Hiawatha Dr. E.; 866.565.9932/651.565.9932; WiFi) has 14 large sites, all with water, electric, and sewer hookups ($32.50 + tax). The **WABASHA MUNICIPAL CAMPGROUND** (Main & Church; 651.565.4568) has a few sites available for overnight rental on a first-come, first-served basis in a crowded but shady area ($35/water, elec, sewer). **PIONEER CAMPSITES RESORT** (64739 140th Ave.; 651.565.2242; WiFi) is a large campground near the backwaters with cramped sites set in deep shade amidst tall pine trees ($25/primitive, $28/water & elec, $30/water, elec, sewer).

Budget. The **WABASHA MOTEL & RV PARK** (1110 Hiawatha Dr. E.; 866.565.9932/651.565.9932; WiFi) has 10 clean, bright rooms with cable TV ($64–$69 + tax).

Cabins. The folks at the **WABASHA MOTEL & RV PARK** (1110 Hiawatha Dr. E.; 866.565.9932/651.565.9932) built a cabin in 2010 so you know it's in great shape. The Park Model home has a full kitchen with grown-up size appliances, a flat screen TV, and a bedroom with a queen bed ($129 + tax, 2 night minimum).

Moderate. The **COFFEE MILL MOTEL & SUITES** (50 Coulee Way; 877.775.1366/651.565.4561; WiFi is $5 extra) has 21 rooms in a variety of styles and sizes, all with cedar walls and ceilings, cable TV, coffee pot, microwave, and fridge. Standard rooms are downstairs and have lower ceilings ($79+tax); the chalet rooms are upstairs and have high ceilings ($89+tax); suites have king beds (and two have hot tubs) but aren't much larger than standard rooms and are decorated in themes that barely register ($99–$139+tax). Unless you really plan on using a hot tub, the best deal is to stick with the standard or chalet rooms; they also rent an apartment that has a fireplace and full kitchen that could comfortably sleep six ($196 incl tax). Check their website for special package deals, especially in winter (www.coffeemillmotelandsuites.com). **LOFTS ON THE MISSISSIPPI** (212 Main St. W.; 507.261.1450; WiFi) are two units that would serve anyone well as a home: a one-bedroom unit on the second floor with a deck that has river views ($129+tax); and a two-bedroom unit on the third floor with features like French doors and a Jacuzzi tub ($159+tax). Each unit has nice touches like wood floors and exposed brick, walk-in showers, fireplaces, full modern kitchens, and cable TV. **AMERICA'S LOFTS** (800.482.8188/651.565.3509; WiFi in most) consists of eight units in recently rehabbed historic buildings in downtown Wabasha; while the amenities vary from unit to unit, most have full kitchens, balconies or patios, a fireplace, and a Jacuzzi tub ($149+tax). **EAGLES ON THE RIVER VACATION RENTALS** (800.482.8188/651.565.3509; WiFi in most) has six fabulous rental units on the riverfront;

most have cable TV, fireplace, full kitchens, grills, washer and dryer, and boat docks ($189 + tax/one-bedroom unit, $289 + tax/two-bedroom unit).

Resources

- The local newspaper is the *Wabasha County Herald* (651.565.3368).
- Post Office: 109 Main St. E.; 651.565.3909.
- Wabasha Public Library: 168 Alleghany Avenue; 651.565.3927; WiFi; M 10–7, Tu,Th,F 10–5, W 10–6, Sa 9–Noon.

Getting Around

Limited bus service is available through **Hiawathaland Transit** (866.623.7505; M–F 7:30a–4:30p; $1.75); call to schedule a ride.

For more information and updates, visit my web site at www.MississippiValleyTraveler.com.

KELLOGG
(439)

Located in the Zumbro River delta with the Mississippi River, the village of Kellogg is within close proximity to a number of wildlife areas.

Arriving in Town

Belvidere Street is the town's main drag. It intersects the Great River Road. The town's eastern boundary is Dodge Street, aka State Highway 18.

History

In 1854, Isaac Cole settled on section 22 of Greenfield Township on the south bank of the Zumbro River. He established ferry service and built a hotel; a post office opened in 1862 for a place called Pauselim. In 1863, residents built a Methodist church and platted the village. A few other buildings went up but when the railroad built a depot a bit further east, Pauselim faded away and Kellogg sprang to life. The Methodist Church was moved to Kellogg in 1882.

John Huddleson was among the first arrivals in the Kellogg; he built a home around 1870. The village was was named by railroad officials to honor a Milwaukee man who supplied signs for the depot. How I long for the days when all you had to do get a town named after you was to donate a couple of signs! Kellogg had 200 residents by 1880, thanks to its role as a shipping point for area farmers' products, and enough economic stability to survive a major fire in 1880. Kellogg has been a small town heavily dependent on agriculture since it was founded.

Tourist Information ⓘ

Direct your questions to the **Wabasha-Kellogg Convention and Visitors Bureau** (137 Main Street West; 651.565.4158; M–F 8–5, Sa 9–3).

Attractions

LARK Toys (171 Lark Lane; (507.767.3387; M–F 9–5, Sa,Su 10–5) is a joyous place to pass some time. It is unusual to find an independent toy store anymore, and certainly very rare to find one in the middle of a rural area. The store has a wide range of items spread through several rooms: books (*Doctor Seuss* to *Harry Potter*), silly masks, buildings blocks, aerobies, plastic spiders and snakes, kits for science experiments, a photo booth, matruyskas, puzzles, games, and wood toys they craft by hand. Don't miss the carousel with beautiful pieces handcarved by local artist Todd Pasche; the carousel runs every 30 minutes ($1). They also have a nostalgic display of toys from the past called Memory Lane (free) and an 18-hole mini-golf ($6).

Getting on the River

If you brought your own canoe or kayak, check out the **Halfmoon Canoe Trail** (507.454.7351), five miles of easy paddling through the backwaters. From US 61, take County Highway 18 through Kellogg and turn right on S. Dodge Street, then turn left on County 84; after 4 miles, turn left on 622nd Street and follow it to Halfmoon Landing.

Culture & Arts

The **Jon Hassler Theater** (412 W. Broadway; 507.534.2900) is a performing arts center in the nearby village of Plainview; their season generally runs from June through December.

Entertainment and Events ♪

The sand prairies around town are ideal for growing watermelon, so it shouldn't be a surprise that the village has been throwing a festival for decades to celebrate the fruit. The **Kellogg Watermelon Fest** (507.767.4953) is held in September, the first weekend after Labor Day.

Sports and Recreation ≋

The **Snake Creek Management Unit** of Richard Dorer Forest (651.345.3216) is a popular spot for hikers and off-road vehicle drivers. The north section has a five-mile trail for hiking and cross-country skiing, while the south area's 13.5 mile loop is popular with ATV drivers and mountain bikers.

Take a short detour down Highway 84 from Kellogg through a tranquil rural setting to reach two unique nature preserves. At the **Kellogg-Weaver Dunes Scientific and Natural Area** (612.331.0750) explore a sand prairie remnant, with rolling dunes, some 30 feet high, covered in light vegetation in most places but occasionally just open sand. The dunes were created by deposits from the Zumbro, Chippewa, and Mississippi Rivers. The area is home to a number of threatened species of plants (like purple sand grass, beachheather) and rare brids, plus the threatened Blanding's turtle; you may see these turtles crossing the road, especially in June when they are laying eggs or in late August when the youngsters hatch. Try not to run them over. Access to the north tract is about four miles from Kellogg; park on the east side of the road at the sign. The South tract is about six miles from Kellogg at Township Road 141. Adjacent to the dunes is **McCarthy Lake Wildlife Management Area** (651.296.6157), an area rich in wetlands created by an old channel of the Zumbro River. If you visit at the right time of year, you are likely to see sandhill cranes, bald eagles, or tundra swans. Access is four miles south of Kellogg.

Eating

TOWN AND COUNTRY CAFÉ (320 E. Belvidere Ave.; 507.767.4593; M–Th 6a–3p, F 6a–9p, Sa 6a–8p, Su 6:30a–1p) is a cozy small town eatery where you can get breakfast all day (most items $5–$7) but they are especially popular for their pies. When I visited, they had 12 types of pie to choose from. Twelve! I had a slice of butterscotch walnut with a scoop of ice cream for $3.21.

Please don't squish the turtles

Sleeping

Camping. You can pitch a tent by the parking lot at the south end of the **SNAKE CREEK MANAGEMENT UNIT** (651.345.3216); there are no services.

Resources

- Post Office: 345 E. Belvidere St.; 507.767.4993.

WEAVER

(Uninc)

On the verge of being a ghost town after losing many buildings to highway construction, Weaver today is just a few houses surrounded by great scenery.

Arriving in Town

Minnesota Highway 74 goes through what is left of town.

History

Andrew Olson and his family, who arrived in the 1850s, were probably the first to settle in what became Weaver, but they didn't stay. The village was platted in 1871 and named for William Weaver, one of the original town proprietors who arrived in 1857 from New York and settled on the Olson farm. It never attracted much industry—a couple of sawmills and an ice house—settling for a minor role as regional commercial and transportation center thanks to a railroad station. As the village declined in the 1930s and trains stopped less and less often, a creative system was rigged to continue mail delivery. The mailbag destined for Weaver was thrown from a moving train as it passed the town; simple enough. Getting mail out of town required greater ingenuity, however. Mailbags going south were clipped vertically between two pipes dangling from a pole; a crewman on the approaching train would extend a mechanical arm that was supposed to hit the bag and flip it into the baggage car where it could be sorted. It worked most of the time, but occasionally the mailbag would get sucked under

What is a Coulee?

You may have heard folks in this area talking about coulees. What the heck is a coulee? Geologists use the term to refer either to a stream-like lava flow or abandoned sluiceways which once carried glacial meltwaters. I'm sure that's just as clear to you as it is to me. Another source said that it is a widely used term in western Wisconsin that refers to stream beds that are usually dry.

The word is derived from the Scotch word *combe* (koom), which means a dale, ravine, valley, or dingle. Or, it might be derived from the French word *couler*, which means "to flow." Whatever. In everyday use, it just refers to the scenic narrow valleys of the driftless area; these coulees can be great fun to explore. Pick a small country road or state highway and wander through the coulees.

If you want a specific route to follow, I really love the scenery along Minnesota Highway 74 as it follows the Whitewater River to Whitewater State Park (507.932.3007). The drive from Weaver to the park office is 15 miles, some of it on a gravel road; most of this stretch is part of the Whitewater Wildlife Management Area (see page 105).

Whitewater State Park is one of the most popular in Minnesota. Highlights include Chimney Rock, the Elba Fire Tower, several miles of hiking trails, and a swimming beach. The campground has generously sized sites with shade; some are along the Whitewater River, but they fill up quickly, so call ahead if you want to camp here. When you are done, head back via County Highway 26 and State Highway 248 to Rollingstone, then back to US Highway 61.

the train and letters would be tossed about and shredded, sending Weaver residents scurrying to collect the scattered, ripped letters and put them into a new bag to try again. Some of the town's buildings were razed when US Highway 61 was rerouted and expanded to four lanes.

Sports and Recreation ≋

Whitewater Wildlife Management Area
(507.932.4133) is 37,000 acres of sublime beauty of Whitewater River marshland. The area is rich in wildlife, especially birds. There are many places to pull over and get out of your car to hike or fish (or cross-country ski in winter).

MINNEISKA
(116)

Minneiska has been called "The town that refused to die" because it has survived several major fires (the latest in 1947), a tornado, and highway construction.

Arriving in Town

Bennett Avenue is pretty much the only street in town; it is elevated a few feet above the highway.

History

Michael Agnes arrived in 1851 from St. Louis; he and two other early settlers tried to make a living by selling cordwood to steamboats but had a tough go of it. Their community was initially known as Whitewater but was given the name Minneiska when the village was platted in 1854. *Minneiska* is the Dakota name for the nearby Whitewater River.

In 1884 (and still today), the town stretched for a mile along the Mississippi but had only one street. A major fire devastated the town in January 6, 1884; firefighting efforts were hampered by temperatures of -30° F. Another fire in 1900 destroyed half the town, but the 400 residents dutifully rebuilt again. Minneiska was never a boom town, but had a small, stable population, at least until 23 homes and eight businesses, most of them in the oldest section of town, were sacrificed for the widening of Highway 61 in 1959.

Most of the village today runs along a side road that is elevated a few feet above the highway, with the remaining older buildings in Wabasha County and many of the newly rebuilt businesses in Winona County.

Minneiska around 1900 (Wabasha County Historical Society)

Culture & Arts

Minneiska might not have a lot going on, but somehow it became home for two exceptional woodcarvers, who also happen to have their studios right next to each other: **Carven Critters** (207 Riverview Dr.; 507.689.2070) is the studio for Todd Pasche, who specializes in carousel characters (see LARK Toys on page 100), and **Langseth Norsk Woodcarving** (514 Bennett Ave.; 507.689.4208; open mid-April–Dec.) where Hans Langseth makes many traditional Norwegian designs; if they're there, they're open. Hans, by the way, is a descendent of another Hans Langseth who holds the record for the longest beard on record; ask him about it.

Sports and Recreation

The primary activity at **John Latsch State Park** (US Highway 61; 507.932.3007) is a hike to the top of the bluff—450 feet above the parking lot—up a long series of wooden steps; at the top, you are rewarded with magnificent views of the valley. This is not an easy hike because of the incline, but the steps make it more tolerable.

Putnam Gray and His Castle

Gray's Castle (Wabasha County Historical Society)

In the late 1800s, an eccentric inventor/riverman named Putnam Gray built a home next to the river in a style that one could call Victorian packrat and that ultimately looked more like a grounded steamboat than a house. The house was such a landmark that it appeared on postcards. Gray's sisters would wrap themselves in sheets when they heard a boat coming at night, then dance on the balcony so they would look like ghosts when the boat's light shone on them. This helped the house develop a reputation for being haunted. The house eventually collapsed, or burned, or flooded; no one seems too certain about the details, other than that it had disappeared by the early 1900s.

Putnam Gray left his mark in other ways, too. Some believe he invented what was later called the Ferris wheel. His sons, Lafayette and Verenzo, exhibited a wheel like the first Ferris wheel at a Winona fair where George Ferris saw it. Ferris followed the brothers to Fountain City and convinced them to let him exhibit it, which he did at the Chicago World's Fair in 1893, although his design was much larger than Gray's.

Hey, what's that? If you look up in the hills above town, you may find Minneiska's famous fish. (Trees make it hard to find in summer.) Putnam Gray (see sidebar on page 108) erected the first fish above town—a 16-foot wooden weathervane on a 20-foot pole that grew into a local landmark; it was replaced with a tin version in 1901 and has been repaired many times because some folks can't resist shooting it.

Eating and Drinking

The **EAGLE VIEW BAR AND GRILL** (208 Bennett; 507.689.4578; Tu–F 11–10, Sa 9a–10p, Su 9–9) is a casual small town eatery with very good, affordable food, including dozens of varieties of sandwiches and burgers (most <$6); folks love the fries but get a half-order unless you brought a small army to share them with ($2.75). Check out the weekend specials like the Saturday prime rib, which, if you miss it on Saturday, you can enjoy on Sunday as a delicious sandwich. If you are in the mood for a drink after eating, walk next door to **BUCK'S BAR** (206 Bennett Ave.; 507.689.4183; daily 9a–close) and enjoy a view with your preferred beverage.

MINNESOTA CITY
(1,449)

Founded by people with big ideas and high hopes, Minnesota City never lived up to the hopes of its founders. Today, it is a quiet village near the Mississippi River backwaters and not the state capital some had hoped for.

Arriving in Town

From US Highway 61, you enter town on Bridge Street, which connects to the highway north and south of town; the highway used to run along Mill Street, which was once the village's commercial strip.

History

When New Yorker William Haddock started the Western Farm and Village Association in 1851, he wanted to help interested city folks leave the urban environment and resettle in the country. Members paid $5 to join; most were mechanics from New York City and were foreign-born; they hoped that by banding together, they could buy supplies in bulk and thus more cheaply than as individuals. Scouts for the company traveled on ice skates upriver from La Crosse on the frozen Mississippi to search for land. They purchased 160 acres from Israel Noracong and founded a village they initially called Rolling Stone Colony; the name was translated from the Dakota word *Eyan-omen-man-met-pah* (the stream where the stone falls) after a rock in a nearby river that, according to legend, would rock mystically during periods of high water. The village was platted in March 1852 and renamed Minnesota City by a unanimous vote of association members;

the name reflected optimism that their new city was destined to be the new state capital. It attracted settlers very quickly—500 in the first year. Few stuck around, however, once they realized that the land was not ideal for farming and that the village was not directly on the Mississippi River. The initial scouting party had mistakenly believed their site was on the main channel because the water had been unusually high during their scouting trip. Only 20 families stuck out the first winter.

With most of the original colonists gone, others settlers began moving in. In 1880, the village had about 200 residents. The town developed primarily around agriculture with feed and flour mills and other businesses serving area farmers; cabbage was an important crop for decades. Many early farmers came ready to experiment, including some who made the first attempts to grow apples in the region. Minnesota City also had a strong railroad presence with connections not only north and south along the Mississippi River but also westward to Rochester.

Over time, though, Minnesota City suffered a number of setbacks. The widening of US Highway 61 rerouted traffic from Mill Street and the heart of town to its fringe; portions of town were annexed by neighboring Goodview. The local school was absorbed by Winona and eventually closed. Severe flash flooding in 2007 damaged many older buildings. Minnesota City is a bedroom community today.

Tourist Information ⓘ

You best bet is to contact the **Winona Visitors Center** (924 Huff St.; 507.452.2278; M–Sa 9–5, Su 11–4 from April–Oct, the rest of the year open F,Sa 9–5 but closed last two weeks in Dec.).

Attractions

Lock and Dam 5 (507.689.2101) is a few miles north of town; it opened in 1935 at the height of the Depression and went through major rehabilitation from 1987 to 1998. The dam is 1619 feet long, and the lock has an average lift of six feet.

The **Minnesota City Historical Association** (140 Mill St.; 507.689.4103; archives open 9:30a–11:30a 2nd & 4th Sa from June–Aug) is based in an 1870s frame First Baptist Church that still has the original hand-carved chairs—100 of them—and many other original touches like the organ, stove, and the galvanized tin baptismal bath. While the original church was built for a Baptist congregation, the church had a long history of hosting interdenominational services. The historical society has a small collection of historic photographs, plus a number of records from the village's past.

Getting on the River

Canoeists and kayakers might want to check out the **Verchota Landing Canoe Trail** (507.454.7351), a challenging 11.2 mile route that involves paddling upstream on the Mississippi River at times. The Verchota landing is just east of the boat club on Prairie Island Road.

Entertainment and Events ♪

Minnesota City Day (3rd Saturday in May) is a community-wide festival to mark the day the first settlers arrived with music and historical reenactments.

For more information and updates, visit my web site at www.mississippivalleytraveler.com.

Sleeping 🛏

Camping. The **BASS CAMP RESORT** (23651 Rolbiecki Lane.; 507.689.9257) is a few miles north of town between the highway and the river but shielded from highway noises. The sites are nicely shaded and not so close that you feel like you're having dinner with your neighbors every evening; most have views of the river ($15/tent sites, $30/RV sites w/elec).

GOODVIEW

(3,373)

The newest community in the area, Goodview has grown quickly from a subdivision to a fully functioning village.

Arriving in Town

US Highway 61 skirts along the western edge of the village; 6th Street is more or less the main drag through town.

History

The village of Goodview is a just a kid, albeit a quickly growing one (like many of our children in the US). Built as a housing subdivision called Goodview by Clarence Witt, residents organized in 1946 and voted to incorporate as a village when there were 336 residents spread over 789 acres. Goodview has been primarily a residential community for most of its existence, with the biggest growth happening after World War II. The village created the fire department in 1953 (Leo Borkowski was the first chief) but didn't hire its first full-time police officer until 1974.

Tourist Information ⓘ

Get your questions answered at the **Winona Visitors Center** (924 Huff St.; 507.452.2278; M–Sa 9–5, Su 11–4 from April–Oct, the rest of the year open F,Sa 9–5 but closed last two weeks in Dec.).

Sports and Recreation 〰

Goodview manages **LaCanne Park** (6280 US Highway 61), a lovely space on a small lake with a playground, picnicking, basketball courts, paved multi-use path, and a swimming beach.

Shopping

CATHEDRAL CRAFTS (730 54th Ave.; 507.454.4079; M–F 9–2) is one of the region's renowned art glass studios, restoring older windows and creating new ones. They operate a small retail store where you can buy samples of their work or place an order for that custom art glass window you've always wanted in your great room.

Sleeping 🛏

Budget. THE MIDWESTERN MOTEL (7115 Martina Rd.; 800.213.9136/507.452.9136; WiFi) has 19 spacious rooms in good shape. Most rooms have a microwave and fridge, and the fresh scent is free ($49 + tax/one bed, $59 + tax/two beds).

WINONA

(27,069)

Winona is knee-deep in river history but, sadly, has one of the most neglected riverfronts in the region. On the plus side, this blue-collar town has a surprisingly rich cultural scene.

Arriving in Town

The Mississippi River runs nearly west-to-east at Winona, so if you're heading toward the river from Winona, you are going north (or northeast). US Highway 61 skirts the edge of town and is home to the soul-killing chain stores. To get into town, go north on Mankato Street or Huff Street; the business district is mostly from 4th Street north to the riverfront. You can park for free on the downtown streets for up to two hours; if you think you're going to be around for a while, try to find a spot at the lot between 1st and 2nd Streets at Lafayette Street.

Winona's street planners have gone out of their way to confuse visitors. Some numbered streets also have names, so 8th Street is also Sanborn, 6th Street is also Broadway, etc. If that doesn't confuse you, then the way buildings are numbered just might. Rather than increasing by 100 for each block (so the buildings between 7th and 8th Street would all be numbered in the 700s, for example), building numbers only advance by half that for each block, so the buildings between 7th and 8th Streets are actually numbered 350-399. This numbering system applies to all streets, so if you are looking for an address in the 400-449 range and you see an address for 220, you have four blocks to go, not two. That's probably way more than you need to know, but, hey, that's why I'm here.

History

Around 1800, a band of Mdewakanton Dakota built a summer village they called *Keoxah*. They were led by a series of chiefs named Wapasha, so the prairie became known as Wapasha's Prairie. The village spread out over a large area, with four long houses located next to the river elevated to avoid getting wet during spring floods, a dozen round huts known as wigwams, and a small patch of cultivated land for growing maize.

Europeans knew at least three Chief Wapashas. The first moved his group to a location along the Upper Iowa River around 1780. His son (who lost an eye as a child during a game of La Crosse and styled his hair to resemble an eye patch) moved the group to this prairie around 1807. Wapasha III took over in 1837 and is the one who signed the Treaty of Mendota. Around this same time, other bands in the same Dakota family branch were led by Red Wing and Little Crow. After signing the treaties of Mendota and Traverse des Sioux, the Dakota moved to reservation land along the Minnesota River.

Steamboat captain Orrin Smith made the first land claims. He arranged transportation for three men to the town site on the steamboat *Nominee*. Just two years later, the new settlement had grown to 300 residents. By the time Winona incorporated as a city in 1857, it had 3000 residents and more than 1000 annual steamboat landings. The city is named for *Wenonah*, who, according to legend, jumped to her death from Maiden Rock because she was not allowed to marry the man she loved (see page 328).

From 1870 to 1900, Winona prospered because of transportation (steamboats and railroads), lumber (sawmills), and wheat. In 1875, A.G. Mowbray and L.C. Porter opened a large mill at the foot of Franklin Street that later became Bay State Milling; it is still in business. Winona was also a major supply point for settlers continuing west, so it is not surprising that the city's first millionaire, John A. Latsch, was a wholesale grocer (see sidebar on page 119).

Peak immigration to Winona was from 1860 to 1900. The first wave of settlers was mostly riverboat captains and educated folks from the East. Germans were 29% of the population in 1880; they formed self-sustaining neighborhoods where they spoke German, printed German-language newspapers, and generally kept to themselves. The first Poles arrived in 1855 and were 11% of the population by 1880. Most of the Poles came from Kashubia (a small region near Gdansk and Bytow), speaking a language that may be older than standard Polish but that has essentially disappeared from Poland today. A handful of Winona residents still speak it. In 1880, the Irish were 9% of the population, Norwegians 4%, and Bohemians 4%.

Winona went into a recession after the northern forests were depleted and the lumber mills closed. (The last mill closed in 1909.) One of the new businesses that thrived was the Watkins Medical Company. J.R. Watkins founded the company in nearby Plainview but demand for his new product, *Dr. Wards Liniment*, outstripped his ability to produce it in his kitchen, so he moved his operation to Winona in 1885. The Watkins Company grew into one of the nation's largest suppliers of health products, supplements, and flavor additives; you may have used their vanilla. Education has also provided a stable base for the region's economy. The State Normal School (now Winona State University) began in 1858. The College of St. Teresa was founded in 1907 and began admitting men in 1912.

John Latsch

John Latsch

John Latsch loved paddling around the backwaters of the Mississippi River, and, being a bachelor, he had plenty of time to take his canoe for a spin. On one of his trips, he got caught in a storm and landed on an island to seek shelter. Unfortunately for Latsch, the island was owned by a gentleman named Scrooge who used his shotgun to motivate Latsch to get off the island.

This also motivated Latsch to use his considerable resources—he became fabulously wealthy as a grocer—to buy property along the Mississippi River and donate it to the public so everyone would have access to its shores. By the time he died in 1934, he had spent more than two million dollars to acquire 18,000 acres for the public. His largess led to the creation of John A. Latsch State Park and Whitewater State Park in Minnesota, Perrot State Park and Merrick State Park in Wisconsin, plus city parks in Winona.

Like folks in many river towns, Winonans had a live-and-let-live attitude about certain behaviors. The city had an active red light district for generations that was concentrated along 2nd Street between the depot and downtown. It flourished until a raid in December 1942 shut it down, at least for a while; Winona seems to have had active brothels into the 1990s (see sidebar on page 226). During Prohibition, local police were not enthusiastic enforcers of the ban on alcohol; the city had at least 200 speakeasies and "blind pigs" (home taverns) and over 500 places to buy liquor. The local liquor trade flourished until federal agents got involved in the late 1920s and began regular raids.

Winona, like many established communities in the US, faced perplexing problems in its older core as new homes and businesses pushed the boundaries further away the center of town. The city fell victim to some of the same misguided urban renewal plans of the early 1970s, razing entire blocks from the historic downtown core. The loss of a chunk of the city's architectural heritage and the failure of these efforts to deliver the promised growth led to stronger preservation efforts.

Winona today is a regional commercial and cultural hub, surprising for its range and depth and cultural opportunities, as well as for the depressing monotony in the restaurant scene. Perhaps the most recent arrivals, Hmong and Hispanic immigrants who began to move into the area in the 1980s, can help with the latter.

Tourist Information ⓘ

The **Winona Visitors Center** is a great place to stock up on brochures and answers (924 Huff St.; 800.657.4972/507.452.2278; M–Sa 9–5, Su 11–4 from April–Oct, the rest of the year open F,Sa 9–5 but closed last two weeks in Dec.)

Attractions

For a bit of perspective on the city of Winona, head up to **Garvin Heights Park** (Garvin Heights Road) and take in the panoramic views 530 feet above the city. If you'd like to stretch your legs, you can hike to the top instead of driving,

The **Minnesota Marine Art Museum** (800 Riverview Dr.; 507.474.6626; Tu–Sa 10–5, Su 11–5; $6) is part of the surprisingly rich cultural scene in Winona. The nautically-themed collection of fine art includes a permanent gallery with paintings from the Hudson River School (like Winslow Homer), Impressionists, and the recently acquired *The Beach of Scheveningen* by Vincent van Gogh. There are also three galleries that host rotating exhibits; I saw an exhibit on fishing lures. The museum also has several remarkable photographs of the Mississippi River Valley by Henry Bosse, a 19th century mapmaker and photographer who worked for the Army Corps of Engineers.

The **Winona National Bank** (204 Main St.; 507.454.4320; lobby open M–F 8:30–5) is two parts fine architecture and one part silliness. The bank, designed by George Maher and completed in 1916, has an Egyptian Revival exterior but a Prairie School feel inside. The interior has impressive bronze work and an art glass window made by the Tiffany Studio. For the silliness, check out the **African Safari Museum** on the second floor.

Merchant's Bank (102 E. 3rd St.; 507.457.1100; M–F 9–4; free) was completed in 1912, designed by William Purcell and George Elmslie, former associates of Louis Sullivan. Mostly Prairie School in design, the bank has an outstanding collection of art glass windows. Albert Fleury painted the mural on the north wall; it depicts the valley behind Sugar Loaf Bluff.

Winona (Region)

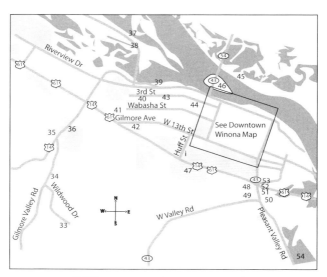

Winona (Central)

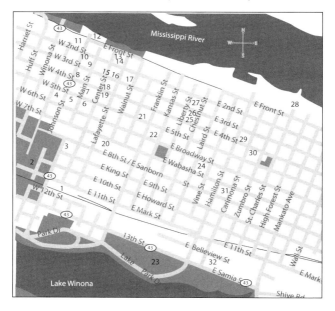

Winona, Minnesota

Map Key

Things to Do
18. Adventure Cycle and Ski
45. Aghaming Park
43. Bob Welch Aquatic Center
28. Bud King Ice Arena
9. Farmers Market
47. Garvin Heights Park
2. Krueger Library
23. Lake Park
17. Merchant's Bank
39. Minnesota Marine Art Museum
27. Polish Cultural Institute
38. Prairie Island Park
36. St. Mary's University
30. St. Stanislaus Kostka
48. Sugar Loaf Bluff.
46. Swimming beach
5. Theatre du Mississippi
25. Watkins Administration Building
26. Watkins Heritage Museum
20. Watkins Manor
21. Winona Arts Center
8. Winona County History Center
7. Winona National Bank

Sleeping
22. Alexander Mansion B&B
40. Alverna Center
3. Carriage House B&B
34. Dory's Place
53. Express Suites Riverport Inn
33. Heaven's Valley Lodge
49. Nichols Inn & Suites
50. Plaza Hotel and Suites
37. Prairie Island Campground
41. Sterling Motel
51. Sugar Loaf Motel
35. Village House Inn
44. Windom Park B&B

Places to Eat
14. Acoustic Café
13. Betty Jo Byoloski's
24. Bloedow Bakery
15. Blooming Grounds Coffee House
11. Blue Heron Coffee House
10. Bluff Country Coop
19. Bub's Brewing Company
12. Cane Pole Café
29. Chong's Noodle House
32. Lakeview Drive Inn
31. Poot's Tavern
42. Rubio's
54. Signatures
16. Winona Garden

Other
1. Amtrak Station
52. Jefferson Lines bus stop
6. Post Office
4. Winona Public Library

The **Polish Cultural Institute of Winona** (102 Liberty St.; 507.454.3431; M–Sa 10–3 from May–Oct.; $2) is housed in the former headquarters building for the Laird Norton Lumber Company, which employed many Poles. The collection focuses on the daily life of Winona's Polish community, with displays about work and church. The collection also includes a few Polish costume dolls.

The dome of the **Church of St. Stanislaus Kostka** (625 E. 4th St.; 507.452.5430) rises stately above the floodplain, visible for miles up and down river. This Baroque/Romanesque gem was completed in 1894. The vast, ornate interior uses a Greek cross design and can seat 1800.

If you want to learn more of the story about the Watkins Corporation, check out the **Watkins Heritage Museum** (E. 3rd St. between Liberty and Chestnut Sts.; 507.457.6095; M–F 10–4, Sa 10–2; free), which has several detailed displays documenting the corporation's history, with many fun examples of products the company has made and sold over the years. Don't miss the **Watkins Administrative Building** (150 Liberty St.; M–F 10–4), another local landmark designed by Chicago architect George Maher. Built for a staggering $1.2 million from 1911–1913, the exterior is blue Bedford stone, and the entrance vestibules are covered with Italian marble. The interior makes good use of rich mahogany and mosaics, and has an ornate dome and art glass windows depicting local scenes.

For a free look inside one of Winona's famous houses, head to **Watkins Manor** (175 E. 7th/Wabasha; 507.494.7496; M–F 8:30–4:30; free). Built in 1927 for Paul Watkins, the nephew of the company founder, and his wife, Florence, the house is now part of an assisted living facility. You are welcome to walk

St Stanislaus Kostka

around the first floor of the house where you will see an interior that is mostly English Tudor, with elaborate wood work in the parlor and an impressive Great Hall—adorned with tapestries—that will make you feel like you are in a medieval castle.

Hey, what's that? The stub of rock that rises above the south end of town is a landmark known as Sugar Loaf Bluff (the Dakota called it Wapasha's Cap). Most of the bluff was quarried in the 19th century, leaving just the portion you see today.

The **Winona County History Center** (160 Johnson St.; 507.454.2723; M–F 9–5, Sa,Su Noon–4; $5) has a fun and varied collection of items that illuminate Winona's past: replicas of 19th century storefronts, sleighs, carriages, and big stuff like a 19th century water pumper from the fire department, a sulky reaper with sail, a delivery wagon, and a hearse. One of the highlights is a replica of the La Moille cave art, which was flooded when the lock and dam system was completed. Upstairs, a timeline wraps around the track outlining the area's history from Native American through the frontier era to the present.

The centerpiece of Winona parks, **Lake Park** (Lake Park Drive) is a grassy expanse surrounding Lake Winona, a body of water formed when the main channel of the Mississippi River changed course and left behind this remnant. The park has a band shell for outdoor concerts, a 5.5 mile paved multi-use trail, and many options for a scenic spot to picnic.

The **Arches Museum of Pioneer History** (507.454.2723; W–Su 1–5; $4) is a pleasant 15-minute drive from Winona on US 14. The museum offers a peek at pioneer life, with a one-room schoolhouse (with original furnishings) and a furnished log cabin. The museum also emphasizes the ingenuity of the pioneers through its collection of 19th century farm equipment and tools (much of it for planting potatoes) and implements of daily life.

Getting on the River

It's not the Mississippi, but you can paddle around **Lake Park** in a canoe or kayak from early June to late August; get them at the Lake Lodge (M–F 4:30–8, Sa 7a–11a; free).

The **Prairie Island Campground** (1120 Prairie Island Rd.; 507.452.4501) rents a 12-foot aluminum fishing boat with oars and trolling motor ($50/day) and canoes ($5/hour, $10/half day, $15/ day).

Culture & Arts

The **Krueger Library** at Winona State University (175 W. 11th/Mark St., 507.457.5140, hours vary with the academic year) has a nice collection of art scattered throughout its three floors, including a display of freshwater pearls harvested from the Mississippi River and Native American pottery from the Southwest.

The **Winona Arts Center** (228 E. Fifth St.;

507.453.9959; gallery open W 3p–6p, F 4p–7p; free) has a small gallery featuring rotating exhibits from local artists and shows independent films on some weekend nights (F,Sa 8p; $5).

The **Theatre du Mississippi** (Masonic Temple, 255 Main St.; 507.459.9080) is a performing arts center that is active throughout the year.

St. Mary's University has an active performing arts program presented through the **Page Series** (www.pagetheatre.org); the programs include dance, theater, and music and typically runs from October through April. **Winona State University** also has an active set of cultural programs; check their calendar for events.

Tours

The Trester Trolley (507.429.9101) takes passengers on a guided tour around Winona (45 minutes–one hour; $10/adult for groups of 10 or more). You can call to schedule a tour or go with one of the regularly scheduled tours on Saturdays.

> ✓ TIP: Winona has been called the stained glass capital of the Midwest because of the presence of two-nationally known studios (Cathedral Crafts and Willet Hauser Architectural Glass) and an impressive collection of windows around town. While you can only tour the shops as part of a large group, there's nothing stopping you from checking out the windows. Pick up a brochure to Winona's stained glass treasures at the visitors center and take a self-guided tour of the windows in the Watkins Administrative Building, Merchant's Bank, Winona National Bank, the County Courthouse, and the Winona County History Center.

A most unusual sight at the Steamboat Days parade

Entertainment and Events ♪

Winona hosts a twice-weekly **Farmers Market** from May to October in the parking lot at Second & Main Streets (W 2p–5p, Sa 7:30a–Noon). **Fringe Friday** is an art celebration on the last Friday of the month downtown. If you don't want to get on a horse but like looking at them, the **Minnesota Equestrian Center** (24621 Gilmore Valley Rd.; 507.452.5600) hosts a number of shows throughout the year; check their website for a list of events (www.minnesotaequestrian.com).

Festivals. Winona has an abundance of fun festivals throughout the year. Begin with the **Frozen River Film Festival** (507.459.8090), an event of growing stature that features provocative films from around the world with an emphasis on cultural and environmental themes (late Jan.; $7/individual tickets but passes also available). In early June, the **Great Dakota Gathering and Homecoming** (507.452.2278) reunites Dakota from around the region; programming for the public has an educational focus. The learning tent is a unique opportunity to experience Dakota culture.

Steamboat Days (800.657.4972) is a celebration of Winona today with a big parade, midway, concerts, and fireworks, but no steamboats and not much about the river; the parade on Sunday draws most of the town (mid-June; free). **The Minnesota Beethoven Festival** (507.457.1715) from late June to mid-July is one of the events that makes Winona a special place in the summer. In 2010, the festival included a performance by Yo-Yo Ma; most shows are $25 but the Minnesota Orchestra performs a free show in Lake Park on one evening. The other major cultural event in the summer is the **Great River Shakespeare Festival** (507.474.7900). There are several shows each week at the Performing Arts Center on the campus of Winona State University ($27–$37 on weekends, $20–$32 during the week, $10 on Tuesdays). Concurrent with the Shakespeare Festival, the Theatre du Mississippi performs **Drops and Drama**, an event that shows off some of the 98 historic drops—vibrant pieces of art painted on cotton muslin and linen—that were originally used by the Masons as part of their secret rituals; the annual show is staged with a theme (Norse mythology when I attended) and selected drops are used to illustrate it ($5).

Music. ED'S (NO NAME) BAR (252 E. 3rd St.; Tu–Su 4p–1a) is the place for live music, good beer, and friendly folks.

Sports and Recreation

Aghaming Park (Latsch Island) has nearly 2000 acres of floodplain forest; it is a popular place for bird watching. There aren't a lot of developed trails, so it is a good idea to wear long pants if you hike here.

Prairie Island Park (Prairie Island Rd.) is located near a backwater channel and has some hiking trails.

Bob Welch Aquatic Center (780 W. 4th St.;

507.453.1646/507.457.8210; daily Noon–7p) is a swimming pool with a lot of bells and whistles; it is open from early June to late August ($4 adults). There is also a **swimming beach** at Latsch Island Park. The adjacent boathouse community is one of the last on the Mississippi River (see the sidebar on boathouses on page 159).

Big Valley Ranch (22076 E. Burns Valley Rd.; 507.454.3305) offers guided trail rides on horseback from May to October ($20/30 min, $35/1 hour, $60/2 hours).

In winter, there are a number of outdoor skating rinks. The place for indoor skating is **Bud King Ice Arena** (670 E. Front St.; 507.454.7775); call for open skate times and prices.

If you want to rent a bicycle, **Adventure Cycle and Ski** can take care of your needs (178 Center St.; 507.452.4228; M–F 10–7, Sa 10–5, Su 10–2; $5/hour, $20/day).

Shopping

THE BOOK SHELF (162 W. 2nd St.; 507.474.1880; M–W, F 8–6, Th 8–8, Sa 8–5, Su 10–2) is the source for new and used books. **BLUE HERON GALLERY AND STUDIO** (168 E. 3rd St.; 507.474.6879; M–Sa 10–5) is a small gallery displaying works of visual art, primarily the paintings of Julia Crozier but sometimes including works by other artists, as well. **MAGNOLIA'S** (177 Lafayette; 507.452.5077; M,W–F 10–4, Sa 10–3) stocks items crafted by local and regional artisans, plus imported Polish pottery which is very beautiful and affordable and you should buy some. **PIECES OF THE PAST** (79 E. 2nd St.; 507.452.3722; M Noon–5:30, Tu–F 9:30–5:30, Sa 10–5, Su 11:30–4) has some interesting knickknacks, home décor items, rustic furniture, and accents. **SUGAR LOAF ANTIQUES** (1023 Sugar Loaf Rd.; 507.452.9593; M,Tu,Th,F 10–5, Sa 10–4, Su 11–4), located in the former Bub's Brewery, is a sprawling complex of rooms packed with treasures and junk, but the real treasure is the building itself. At the **GARVIN HEIGHTS VINEYARD** (2255 Garvin Heights Rd.; 507.313.1917; Tu–Su 10–6 from May–Oct.) you will be charmed by the enthusiasm of owners Marv and Linda and the beautiful ridge-top location, even if the wines themselves are a work in progress ($3/4 samples).

Eating and Drinking ȳ ✕

BUB'S BREWING COMPANY (65 E. 4th St.; 507.457.3121; daily 11:30–close) is another friendly place that is a favorite among locals.

Coffee. This being a college town, there are plenty of options for good coffee. I wish the same could be said of the restaurant scene. **THE ACOUSTIC CAFÉ** (77 Lafayette St.; 507.453.0394; M–Th 7:30a–10p, F 7:30a–11p, Sa 9:30a–11p, Su 9:30a–9p; WiFi) has an eclectic, creative clientele; you can get a pita or half-sandwich for about $5 or a bowl of freshly-made soup for $4. The **BLUE HERON COFFEE HOUSE** (162 W. 2nd St.; 507.452.7020; M–W, F 7–6, Th 7–8, Sa,Su 8–5;WiFi) has a local food/organic food aesthetic; sandwiches run about $7, but they also serve fresh salads and soups ($3–$5.50). They also host the occasional theme-night dinner where you can sample world cuisine. **BLOOMING GROUNDS COFFEE HOUSE** (50 E. 3rd St.; 507.474.6551; M–F 7–7, Sa 7–5, Su 9–4) makes a very satisfying cup of coffee, which you can sip with a wrap, Panini, or salad (food items $7 or less).

If you prefer something baked for breakfast (or a snack), head to **BLOEDOW BAKERY** (451 E. 6th/

Broadway; 507.452.3682; M–F 6a–5:30p, Sa 7:30a–3p) where you can get a big cinnamon roll ($1) or a handful of donuts.

POOT'S TAVERN (579 E. 7th/Wabasha St.; 507.452.9952; M–F 11a–1p,3p–5p, 6p–1a, Sa,Su 6p–1a) is a quintessential neighborhood tavern. Owner Matt Pellowski, who has been running the bar since 1976, puts together a different lunch special each weekday (M–F 11a–1p) and also makes a popular pizza that is a discounted early in the week (Su–Tu get a 9" pizza with 3 toppings for $5 that you can wash down with $2 bottles of beer); stop in, chat, and learn a few things about the neighborhood.

THE BLUFF COUNTRY COOP (121 W. 2nd St.; 507.452.1815; M–F 8–8, Sa 8–6, Su 11–6) has a small selection of prepared foods like sandwiches and salads, plus plenty of fresh produce.

CANE POLE CAFÉ (2 Johnson St.; 507.474.2520; TuW,Su 11–4 Th–Sa 11–8 from May–Sept.) is nearly the only riverfront dining option; you can get a freshly prepared sandwich or salad for under $6, and follow it with ice cream ($2/single scoop in a cone).

THE LAKEVIEW DRIVE INN (610 E. Sarnia; 507.454.3723; daily 10:30a–10p from mid-March–mid-Sept.) is the oldest restaurant in Winona; they have been making Winonians happy since 1938. They have a standard menu of diner foods that are freshly prepared and can be rolled out to your vehicle by a carhop; they also make their own delicious root beer. Wednesday is classic car night (6:30p–9p), so roll up in your '57 Chevy.

Housed in an attractive historic building, **BUB'S BREWING COMPANY** (65 E. 4th St.; 507.457.3121; M–Sa 11:30–10, Su 11:30–8; bar open later) offers more sandwich options that you can shake

Mississippi River bridge at Winona

a pickle at, mostly varieties of burgers and chicken sandwiches ($7–$8); the Cajun chicken sandwich actually has some kick to it.

BETTY JO BYOLOSKI'S (66 Center St.; 507.454.2687; kitchen open daily 11a–10p, bar open later) is another local favorite where the atmosphere is more interesting than the food but at least they have a good beer selection. The interior of the former riverfront warehouse is brick-intensive, accented with neon beer signs and large transportation-themed mobiles hanging from the ceiling. Choose from the standard meat and grill-centric entrées like a ribeye or fish and chips ($10–$15), sandwiches and wraps ($7–$8), or pizza. Burgers are two-for-one on Sundays (4p–10p).

The **WINONA GARDEN CHINESE RESTAURANT** (62 E. 3rd St.; 507.454.1950; M–Sa 11–9) may have Chinese in their name, but they also have an extensive menu of competently-executed Thai dishes ($6–$9).

CHONG'S NOODLE HOUSE (578 4th St.; 507.961.0203; M–Sa 11–8:30) is a hole-in-the-wall family-run restaurant with a modest menu of Vietnamese/Lao/Hmong items. You could probably make a meal just from the large spring rolls. I am a big fan of the fish salad larb ($7).

RUBIO'S (1213 Gilmore Ave.; 507.474.4971; M–Sa 11a–9p) occupies space in the nearly empty Winona Mall, dishing out tasty Mexican cuisine (dinner entrées $8–$13); the lunch buffet is a good deal (M–Sa 11a–3p; $7). If I find out you went to Taco Bell instead of Rubio's, I'm coming after you.

SIGNATURES RESTAURANT (22852 County Highway 17; 507.454.3767; M–Sa 11–2, 5–9, Su 10–2, 4–8) is the choice for fine dining. The exterior screams clubhouse chic, but the inside has a modern, miminalist decor accented by signed photos of celebrities. The menu changes with the seasons, but you can generally expect dinner entrées to average $20–$25. The lunch menu has a number of affordable items in the sandwich and salad genre (most under $10).

Sleeping

Camping. PRAIRIE ISLAND CAMPGROUND (1120 Prairie Island Rd.; 507.452.4501) has a quiet spot on a backwater channel with large sites, mature trees that provide copious amounts of shade, and a small swimming beach. There are two clusters of sites: one with 111 sites with electricity ($21) and a separate area of 90 primitive sites ($17).

Budget. The **STERLING MOTEL** (1450 Gilmore Ave.; 800.452.1235/507.454.1120; WiFi) is a 1960s-era motel with 32 moderately-sized rooms with enough space for a couple of beds and chairs; the rooms are well-maintained and a good bargain ($42+tax/room with a standard and a double bed, $65+tax/room with two queen beds and a double bed). The **SUGAR LOAF MOTEL** (1066 Homer Rd.; 507.452.1491; WiFi) has 20 small-ish rooms that are clean and in good shape with adorable period bathrooms decorated with bright pastel colors ($60+tax/1 bed, $65+tax/2 beds).

Bed and Breakfasts. THE CARRIAGE HOUSE B&B (420 Main St.; 507.452.8256; WiFi) is literally an old carriage house converted to four comfortable guest rooms. Many features of the carriage house were retained, like the original hay door. Rooms are decorated with a nod to period style but are not stuffy or uncomfortable; two rooms have a Jacuzzi tub ($99–$159 + tax incl expanded continental breakfast). If you're nice, the owners might take you for a ride in their 1929 Ford Model A. At the **WINDOM PARK B &B** (369 W. 6th/Broadway St.; 507.457.9515; WiFi), you will feel like you are staying in a home rather than an inn, especially when you are enjoying the shaded front porch. The early 20th century Colonial Revival house is furnished with family heirlooms; each room of the six rooms has a private bath and places to sit and read. The two carriage house rooms have a modern touch ($120–$195 + tax incl full breakfast). **THE ALEXANDER MANSION B&B** (274 East 6th/Broadway St.; 507.474.4224; WiFi) is a spectacular example of 19th century Victorian style (and persistence in rehabbing an old house). The house has gorgeous woodwork throughout, plenty of places to sit and relax, and is a short walk from downtown. The four guest rooms have been restored to their 1880s appearance complete with period furniture ($149–$229 + tax incl full breakfast).

Cabins/Houses. DORY'S PLACE (990 Gilmore Valley Rd.; 507.454.4020; WiFi) is a bedroom, two-and-a-half bath house, furnished like you would furnish your own home. The whole-house rental can sleep 12 comfortably and is popular with families ($500/night + tax); it also popular with the crafting crowd, as it has a space separate from the living areas to set up your crafting tables and leave your work out all weekend without being nagged by your family ($50/night extra for workshop). **HEAVEN'S VALLEY**

LODGE (300 Wildwood Dr.; 507.454.4020) is in a peaceful setting at the end of a gravel road tucked into a coulee. Perfect. The converted barn has two bedrooms, a bathroom down a short flight of stairs, and a few dead animals on the walls to keep you company. Outside, enjoy the bonfire pit and harvest fresh eggs for breakfast from the chicken coop behind the house ($165+tax).

Moderate. The **VILLAGE HOUSE INN** (72 College Rd.; 888.507.6655/507.454.4322) is an 1870s farmhouse located near St. Mary's University. It was gutted and rehabbed into a modern guesthouse with a nod to the past. The four rooms are spacious, comfortable, and each has a private bath; the first floor room is wheelchair accessible ($110–$130 + tax incl continental breakfast). Although they rent individual rooms, whole house rentals are increasingly common ($390/weekend night). The **NICHOLS INN & SUITES** (1025 Sugarloaf Rd.; 507.454.6066; WiFi) has 60 impeccable, moderately large rooms decorated with a modern feel ($82 + tax). The **ALVERNA CENTER** (1175 W. 7th/Wabasha; 507.457.6921; WiFi), a former monastery, has 30 comfortable no-frills rooms with private baths, a double bed, a desk, and a small TV with cable ($75 incl tax). The building has plenty of room to spread out. While mostly geared toward conferences, individual travelers are welcome to stay but call during the day to make a reservation. The **PLAZA HOTEL AND SUITES** (1025 US Highway 61 East; 507.453.0303; WiFi) has 135 large rooms equipped with microwave, fridge, coffee pots, and TVs in the bathrooms; some rooms are accessible for folks with a hearing impairment or in a wheelchair ($125–$185 + tax incl continental breakfast). The first floor rooms have direct access from the parking lot via patio doors. You can upgrade to a family suite for just

$10 more and get an extra sitting area and real dishes to eat from. The **EXPRESS SUITES RIVERPORT INN** (900 Bruski Dr.; 800.595.0606/507.452.0606; WiFi) has 106 generously-sized rooms in great shape ($110–$130 + tax incl expanded continental breakfast); they also have four fantasy suites that include two rooms with a bed in an old Chevy (the bed is small and probably better for kids than adults), a bridal suite, and a room with a Roman bath theme ($160 + tax incl expanded continental breakfast).

Resources

- The local newspapers are the *Winona Daily News* (507.453.3500) and the free twice weekly *Winona Post* (W,Su; 507.452.1262).
- Post Office: 67 W. 5th St.; 507.454.5268.
- The Winona Public Library (151 W. 5th St.; 507.452.4582; M,W 10–6, Tu,Th 10–7, F 10–5, Sa 9–2; WiFi) is a Beaux Arts building that opened in 1897, designed by Warren Powers Laird. The exterior is built of Bedford stone and accented with columns of Georgia marble, with steps of Winona limestone; inside there is a marble replica of Canova's *Hebe* and murals by Kenyon Cox.

Getting To and Out of Dodge ✈

Winona is one of the stops along **Amtrak's Empire Builder** route. The train station is near the Winona State University Campus (65 E. 11th/Mark St.; 800.872.7245/507.452.8612; office open daily 8a–11a, 6:30p–9p); westbound trains depart Winona at 7:50p for destinations along the Mississippi River that include Red Wing (1 hour), St. Paul/Minneapolis (2 hours 40 minutes), and St. Cloud (4 hours, 50 minutes) before continuing through the western United States to Seattle. Eastbound trains depart Winona at 10:11a and pass through La Crosse (36 minutes) before terminating at Chicago (5 hours, 40 minutes). I'd like to quote some fares for you, but Amtrak bases ticket prices on the number of seats available, so prices can vary quite a bit. In general, you should expect to pay less the further in advance you book, but, if there is only one seat left, you will pay a premium for it, even if it is a month in advance.

Jefferson Lines (800.451.5333) operates regional bus service with once daily eastbound connections to La Crosse, Madison, and Milwaukee (M–Th, Sa 11:05a, F,Su 4:20p; 5 hours to Milwaukee) and once daily westbound connections to Rochester and Minneapolis (M–Th, Sa 3:55p, F,Su 5:55p; 2 hrs 40 min to Minneapolis). Schedules and fares are so damn confusing and change so often, you are better off just calling them directly for the most current info. What I can tell you is that the cheapest rates are for a 21-day advance purchase, especially for travel Sunday through Thursday. The bus stop is at the Quality Inn at the intersection of US Highway 14/61 and State Highway 43 (956 Mankato Ave.; 507.452.3718); buy your bus tickets at the front desk.

✔ **TIP: If you are buying tickets at the last minute, check fares for Amtrak, too. You might get a better deal.**

Getting Around

The **Winona Transit Service** (260 W. 3rd St.; 507.454.6666) operates the local bus system (M–F 6a–6p; $1). They also operate a free late-night service on weekends when the universities are in session called Safe Route, so you don't have to drive after a night out at the bars (F,Sa 7p–1:55a).

HOMER
(Uninc)

Homer is one of a string of old rivertowns between Winona and La Crescent that sacrificed much of their historic core for the widening of US Highway 61.

Arriving in Town

Old Homer Road is about the only street in town; it is elevated about the highway.

History

Around 1831, Francois du Chouquette, a blacksmith, set up shop at the future village site but didn't stick around long. Next on the scene was Willard Bunnell, who arrived in 1849 and didn't leave. Bunnell and family had initially settled on the Wisconsin side of the river at Trempealeau and Holmes' Landing (now Fountain City). In 1849, the US government granted Bunnell a trading license, which allowed him to negotiate a deal with Chief Wapasha. Just north of Bunnell's Landing, as the new settlement was known, the village of Minneowah attracted a few settlers and a couple of sawmills. Unfortunately, Minneowah's original platters, the Minneowah Stock Company, forgot to file their claim, so the first settlers had no legal title to their land. Minneowah was abandoned when Homer was platted in 1855 and settlers moved in like sharks to make new claims and divide up the former Minneowah. One of them, Daniel Dougherty, had exceptionally good luck and drew lots that included the hotel and many other parcels. Mr. Bunnell was exceptionally pissed off about this, so the two men duked

Bunnell House

it out. Dougherty nearly bit off Bunnell's thumb before the fight ended. Life settled down in Homer (named for Bunnell's birthplace in New York) and the village attracted a number of New Englanders among the early settlers. Never a boom town, Homer had 125 residents in 1910; much of the town's older building stock was razed for the widening of the highway.

Attractions

Built in the 1850s for Willard and Matilda Bunnell, the three-story "Steamboat" Gothic **Bunnell House** (36106 Old Homer Rd.; 507.454.2723; W–Sa 10–5 Su 1–5 from June–Aug; $5) is the oldest home in Winona County. The house has many period furnishings plus a few items owned by the Bunnell's like the piano in the parlor.

> **RANDOM FACT:** *Willard's brother, Lafayette Bunnell, named Yosemite Valley in California.*

Sleeping

Camping. PLA-MOR CAMPGROUND (22718 Little Smokies Lane; 877.454.2267/507.454.2851) has two groups of campsites flanking the highway; the sites are rather close together but most are shaded. The sites east of the highway are close to the river and have a view of Trempealeau Mountain ($27/tent sites, $35/water & elec, $40/water, elec, sewer, all + tax).

Cabins. PLA-MOR CAMPGROUND also has four simple cabins that are like camping but with walls, two with bathrooms ($50 + tax) and two without ($65 + tax); bring your own bedding; no heat or AC.

Budget. If you want one more option, **PLA-MOR CAMPGROUND** also has a one-bedroom suite ($77+tax; WiFi) above the campground office; it has a full kitchen, full bath, and air conditioning.

LA MOILLE

(Uninc)

There isn't much left of the village, but a mill and a state park give visitors good reason to stop in the area.

Arriving in Town

What's left of La Moille is concentrated along La Moille Road, of course.

History

The village was initially known as McGilvery's Landing because a guy named McGilvery ran a ferry from here. The village was named after a town in Vermont, presumably because one of the founders was from there, but no one really knows. La Moille was a bustling place for a time: it had a railroad station, a steamboat landing, and ferry service. Much of the shipping business came from the products of nearby Pickwick Mill. Most of the town's buildings were sacrificed to progress when the highway was widened.

La Moille was the longtime home of Dan Hafner, a renowned rattlesnake hunter, who was so adept at hunting and handling them, he didn't bother to wear gloves, boots, a hat, or a shirt when searching for them. He could reach into a lair and pull them out before they struck and was apparently never bitten. Don't try that at home, kids.

Near La Moille, there was a cave with centuries-old pictographs, representations of animals carved in the sandstone that included a bird with its wings spread 3½ feet by 3 feet. The cave was flooded when the lock and dam system went operational, but it had already been vandalized by that time. There is a replica of the cave at the Winona County History Center (page 125).

Attractions

Wilson and Timothy Davis and George Grant opened the **Pickwick Mill** (26421 County Highway 7; 507.457.0499; Tu–Sa 10–5, Su 11–5 from June–Aug, Sa 10–5, Su 11–5 in May, Sept., Oct.; $3) in 1858 and did their job so well that it was a working mill until 1978. Mary Davis chose the name after reading Charles Dickens' novel *Pickwick Papers*. The mill is an impressive six stories tall, built from limestone quarried at nearby La Moille. The 20-foot overshot waterwheel produced the power to turn the millstones, helping the mill produce over 100 barrels of flour every day at its peak. A flood in 1980 caused extensive damage; local folks rallied to save it from demolition. There is a 20-minute video describing how the mill worked that is worth watching..

Entertainment and Events

Pickwick Mill Day (2nd Saturday in Sept.; 507.457.3296) celebrates the mill's history with craft demonstrations, but the highlight is watching the mill's original grinding operation put back in action (10:30a & 2p).

Shopping

LAVENDER LANE GIFTS (23337 Lamoille Rd.; 507.452.2048; Tu–Sa 10–5, Su Noon–4) is housed in the former Precious Blood Church, and it smells heavenly. They sell a mix of handcrafted soaps, candles, cute home furnishings, and gourmet food products.

DAKOTA

(329)

The village of Dakota forms one end of the Apple Blossom Scenic Drive.

Arriving in Town

River Street is the primary road through town. Center Street connects to the Apple Blossom Scenic Drive and the southbound Great River Road; continue north on River Street to connect to the northbound Great River Road.

History

John Reed was a premature arrival in this area; he tried to open a trading post in the 1840s but the Dakota, who still had legal claim to the land, evicted him. Jeremiah Tibbetts arrived in 1847 with a group of Dakota and built a small trading post; he gets the credit for coming up with town's name. Nathan Brown, a native New Yorker, showed up in 1849 and organized the village. Brown could not get a trading license from the US government, either, but he successfully negotiated a deal directly with Chief Wabasha for trading rights. The early settlers lived in an area known as Old Dakota that was platted in 1855. In 1873, the town was re-surveyed on higher ground. All development from that time forward took place in the new plat; nothing remains of Old Dakota. Dakota was devastated by a severe measles epidemic in 1882 that killed many residents and brought the town's economy to a halt. When folks recovered, Dakota did a nice business shipping grain downriver. The town also got a boost from the arrival of the railroad in 1872, which, besides

Life on the Frontier

Kartingi Tuininga, the wife of one Mr. Johannes Tuininga was bitten by a rattlesnake. They had no money for a doctor, so he began to slaughter their chickens and used the bloody corpses as a salve. He went through all two dozen of the flock, yet Mrs. Tuininga did not appear to be improving.

As he was losing hope, a stranger rode by their farm and Johannes told him the story. The man was moved by their dire predicament and gave Johannes $10 to take his wife to the doctor. She recovered.

The man who gave them the money was supposedly Henry M. Rice, who was Minnesota's first US Senator. Tuininga was part of the group of Friesians who left the Netherlands in 1853 and founded New Amsterdam, Wisconsin (see page 255). The Tuiningas traveled with their five children, but Anna and Garret died during a yellow fever epidemic on the ship and were buried at sea.

Not the Tuininga homestead but still an awesome picture

shipping people all over the Midwest, also shipped a lot of cattle before the Depression. In the 1910s, the good folks of Dakota fought a battle with the War Department (the bureaucratic home of the Army Corps of Engineers, which has jurisdiction over shipping along the Mississippi River) over a proposal to shift the main channel of the river from the Minnesota side (in front of Dakota) to the Wisconsin side. Many residents made their living from working on the river and feared that changing the channel would hurt their business. They lost, and they were right. In 1951, the rail depot closed, but for a few years afterwards, locals could still board a passenger train by flagging down one of the trains as it passed through town. Like many of its neighbors, Dakota lost most of its older buildings to highway construction in the 1960s. Dakota today is a quiet bedroom community.

Attractions

Steve Morse Park (Center and River Sts.) is a small corner park with a gazebo and a river view and a pleasant place for a picnic lunch.

Sports and Recreation

The 3000 acre **Great River Bluffs State Park** (County Road 3; 507.643.6849; $5/daily vehicle permit) has seven miles of hiking trails, many of which end at dramatic overlooks of the river valley. In winter, enjoy nine miles of trails for cross-country skiing or snowshoeing. To reach the park, go west on Interstate 90 from the River Road for four miles to exit 267 and follow the signs.

For more information and updates, visit my web site at www.mississippivalleytraveler.com.

Shopping

SOUTHWIND ORCHARDS (45440 County Highway 12; 507.643.6255; daily Aug.–mid-Nov.) has a big retail store where you can buy apples in season, plus a number of other fall crops and some crafts.

Sleeping

Camping. GREAT RIVER BLUFFS STATE PARK (County Road 3; 507.643.6849) has a 31-site campground atop the bluff, with plentiful shade and space but no electric hook-ups ($16 + $5 daily vehicle fee). Along US 61, there is also a five-site bicycle campground with a water source but no other services ($12).

Resources

- Post Office: 745 Frontage Rd.; 507.643.6555.

DRESBACH

(Uninc)

Dresbach is part old river town and part new suburban community with few attractions for visitors.

Arriving in Town

The main drag is Riverview Drive.

History

Ashel Pearse built a log cabin in 1833, one of many French settlers who worked out a deal with Native Americans to live here for a while. The town got its name from one George B. Dresbach, Sr., an Ohio native who, in 1857, bought the earlier claims and invested $50,000 of his own cash to start a village. Mr. Dresbach was a busy man; he started a quarry and a brickyard and served in the Minnesota House of Representatives. The village platting kick-started some interest in development: in 1857 eleven houses were built and the town got its first general store and post office. Dresbach's effort to develop a bustling town, however, was never the success he hoped; he lost most of his money in the process and died with little material wealth. Dresbach the village puttered on, boasting 175 residents in 1910, getting an economic boost from the construction of Lock and Dam 7 in the 1930s. Dresbach took a big hit from the construction of Interstate 90 a few decades later. The village lost many of its buildings and a big chunk of its (small) population; even the graves of George Dresbach and family had to be moved to a new cemetery. Dresbach today is a bedroom community with a few impressive houses along the river and a few modest homes in the older part of town.

RANDOM FACT: *George Dresbach's brother was one of the first lion tamers for the P.T. Barnum circus.*

Tourist Information ⓘ

The **Interstate 90 rest area** near Dresbach has a stock of brochures for the local area, as well as the entire state of Minnesota.

Attractions

Lock and Dam 7 (507.895.2170) was completed in 1935 and underwent a major overhaul from 1989 to 2002. The lock has a maximum lift of nine feet; the dam is 940 feet long. There is a small visitor center that presents the Corps' history of managing the river for navigation, and a viewing platform to watch boats locking through.

✔ TIP: Many of the locks offer public tours (M–F 9–3 from March–Oct; free), but you must call in advance to schedule it, and they generally limit tours to groups of six or more people.

Hidden below Riverview Drive, **Dresbach Park** (Old Mill Rd. @ Mulder Rd.) is a small riverfront park with a couple of picnic tables, a playground, and a nice view of the river.

Getting on the River

The **Best Dam Fishing Float** (608.484.1656; daily 7a–5p; $15/day) is one way to get on the river without a boat. Raise the red flag at the boat ramp below Lock and Dam 7, and they'll send a small boat to pick you up, so you can spend the day fishing from their platform in the river; bring a fishing license.

LA CRESCENT

(4,923)

When John S. Harris planted apple trees in southeast Minnesota in 1857, skeptics heckled. Through persistence and selective breeding, he eventually proved them wrong and created apples that could thrive in the often harsh Minnesota climate. Fast forward 150 years and the apple orchards are well established and LaCrescent is the *Apple Capital of Minnesota*, producing multiple mouth watering varieties like Honeycrisp and Keepsake every year.

Arriving in Town

The highways (State Highway 16, US Highways 14 & 61) skirt the eastern edge of town. A few orchards have storefronts along this road. The small business district is concentrated along Main Street and Walnut Street. Elm Street gets you started on the Apple Blossom Scenic Drive.

History

When Peter Cameron, a native of New York, built a log house in 1851 and Thor Halverson, a native of Norway, did the same the following year, they joined a long line of people who were attracted to this small, elevated prairie near the Mississippi River. The future village site was marked by dozens of burial mounds and evidence abounded of ancient peoples who lived here.

Cameron had been trading along the Upper Mississippi since the early 1840s and had business interests in La Crosse. He and his wife Emma were married in

La Crescent, Minnesota

1845 in La Crosse, the first couple to be married in the city. Emma was quite familiar with the marriage ritual; she went through it 11 times; Peter was her fourth husband. Peter had big plans for La Crescent that were hampered by poor access to the Mississippi River; the village was separated from the river by a mile of sloughs and marshes. Cameron figured the best solution was to build a canal that would connect the town to the river (and in the process might have diverted the main channel from La Crosse to La Crescent), but he died in 1855 while building a sawmill in La Crosse, and the canal plan also came to a permanent end.

The village was platted in 1855 by Harvey and William Gillett on part of Cameron's old claim and renamed from Camerons to Manton. They sold all their lots in a year, most of them to the Kentucky Land Company, then left town, probably for a beach in Mexico. The land company wanted a more appealing name, something with a loftier sound, so they chose La Crescent, which they felt evoked the shape of the bluffs. That's the story that has survived, anyway.

The Kentucky Land Company got busy building a village. In short order, they built a dozen homes, all very similar two-story houses decorated with elaborate trim, then built a road across the marsh to connect the town to the ferry landing. For 20 years, the only way for La Crescent residents to cross the Mississippi River was down the muddy road to the ferry. This did not encourage rapid growth.

John Harris arrived in 1854 determined to grow apples (see the sidebar on page 153). When he planted his first crop, skeptics were plentiful, because they assumed the Minnesota climate was too harsh. The critics were wrong, however, and his apples eventually grew very well. Other growers followed suit and orchards became one of the largest industries in the area.

Although the number of orchards has declined from forty in the 1960s to a handful today, the number of acres dedicated to growing apples is about the same.

Like other small towns in the area, La Crescent experienced a housing boom after World War II as it grew into a suburb of La Crosse. In 1940, the village had just 815 residents or about one-fifth of what was counted in the 2000 census.

Tourist Information ⓘ

The **La Crescent Chamber of Commerce** maintains a visitor's information center inside the State Bank of La Crescent (109 S. Walnut; 800.926.9480/507.895.2800; M–F 9–4); go to the entrance on the right-hand side, not the main entrance for the bank.

Attractions

The **Apple Blossom Scenic Drive** (800.926.9480/507.895.2800) is a lovely route that loops 10 miles from La Cresent to Dakota atop a ridge and down a coulee. Along the way, you pass by orchards, nice views (stop at the Apple Blossom Scenic Overlook), and retail stores selling produce in season.

Eagles Bluff Park (McIntosh Rd. E.; 507.895.2595) is a protected natural area in the midst of the city with nice views of the river valley. From the starting point described below, the first two-thirds of the hike follows a gentle uphill slope, but it gets steeper for the last leg. When you reach the top, go left and follow the ridge trail to get to a small goat prairie with a view. Allow at least an hour for the round trip. To reach the park, take Elm Street to McIntosh Road and turn east. After the stop sign you will see a sign for the West Bank Addition; park on the street and walk up the hill.

Minnesota's Johnny Appleseed

John Harris proved his skeptical neighbors wrong when he figured out a way to grow apples in the harsh Minnesota climate.

Born in Seville, Ohio in 1826, the industrious Harris opened his first nursery at age 11. He moved to La Crosse in 1851 to recover his health after serving in the Mexican War. Determined to grow apples, he moved across the river to La Crescent in 1854.

In 1856 he founded Sunny Side Garden and began experimenting the following year. Every season he selected the best specimens by taking seeds from the plants that had survived the winter. Severe winters in 1872-73 and 1884-85 nearly put him out of business, but he held on and continued to tinker throughout his life, even planting other types of fruit trees (pear, plum, cherry).

He began exhibiting his fruit at fairs in 1864 and did so every year until his death in 1901, winning many awards and the informal title of Godfather of the Minnesota State Horticultural Society. Sunny Side Garden no longer exists, and, remarkably, there is no apple named in his honor. The John S. Harris Memorial Park (North Elm Street and McIntosh Road) has a marker with his picture and a brief biography; the park is in a subdivision that was once the location of Sunny Side Garden.

La Crescent's history is on display at **Heritage House** (328 S. 3rd St.; 507.895.1857; by appt.), which has fun items like 19th century ice skates, photos from the city's history, and a shed full of items that tell the history of the local apple industry.

Entertainment and Events ♪

Applefest (800.926.9480/507.895.2800; mid-September) is La Crescent's celebration of itself, but it has moved away from its roots celebrating the apple industry into a generic town festival; at least you can tour an orchard and get a slice of apple pie.

Sports and Recreation ≋

For frozen fun, the **La Crescent Community Arena** (520 S. 14th St.; 507.895.4160) offers indoor ice skating; check their website for ice times (lacrescent.govoffice.com).

Shopping

APPLE VALLEY GIFTS (329 Main St.; 507.895.4268; M–F 11–5:30, Sa 10–5) sells cute home furnishings, fragrant soaps, and other stuff to scent your body and house; the second floor has a few shelves of local and regional-interest books.

There are two apple stands south of the stoplight on State Highway 16: **HEIN APPLE STAND** (507.895.4495) and **LEIDEL'S ORCHARD** (507.895.2404); both are open daily during the harvest season, which is usually August through early December. **BAUER'S MARKET** (221 N. 2nd St.; 507.895.4583; M–F 8–8, Sa,Su 8–6) sells seasonal produce, including apples from a variety of orchards.

Eating and Drinking 🍸 🍴

THE SPORTS HUB (25 N. Walnut St.; 507.895.2715; kitchen open daily 11a–10p, bar open later) is a neighborhood sports bar with a recently renovated interior and friendly people. The grill menu is a notch above most bars. I enjoyed the southwest chicken wrap ($6), but they also have several burger options ($4.75–$7.25); even better, they have Guinness on tap.

Resources

- Post Office: 230 Main St.; 507.895.2233.
- La Crescent Public Library: 321 Main St.; 507.895.4047; WiFi; M,Tu,F 10–6, W,Th 10–8, Sa 10–2.

Getting To/Around La Crescent

Bus service is available through the **La Crosse MTU** Route 10, aka The Apple Express, (608.789.7350), which operates Monday-Friday with hourly departures from 6:42a to 5:12p at 5th & State Streets in La Crosse; buses depart from downtown La Crescent hourly from 6:24a to 5:53p.

For more information and updates, visit my web site at www.mississippivalleytraveler.com.

BROWNSVILLE

(517)

A classic river town that experienced a boom period fueled by great expectations, followed by the bubble bursting. Brownsville today is a pleasant small town that is still strongly connected to the river, albeit more for recreation than for economic reasons.

Arriving in Town

State Highway 26 skirts the eastern edge of town; Main Street (State Highway 3) runs west from there.

History

Job Brown went west from his birthplace in Yates County, New York in 1823. He worked the lead mines in Galena and served in the Mexican War before heading upriver and staking a claim at the base of Wildcat Bluff in 1848. According to an old history book, Job "…attained quite a notoriety as a reckless and desperate man, especially when under the influence of liquor, to the use of which he was moderately addicted."

The area by Wildcat Bluff had a favorable location for a boat landing; slowly a small settlement grew among the scree. In 1854, Job, his brother Charles, and James Hiner platted a village they called Brownsville; I guess Hinerville didn't have the same cachet.

From 1855 to 1856, the village's population jumped from 50 to 228 and reached 806 by 1875. Early businesses included a grist mill, a sawmill, and a brewery. The basics. On July 4, 1855 the town celebrated Independence Day in a big way. Fred Gluck traveled to Iowa and bought an ox (which had been gener-

Church of the Holy Comforter

ously paid for by Mr. L.A. Smith). The ox was butterflied and cooked slowly over hot coals (along with a pig and other goodies). Charles Brown gave a speech, and a local citizen read the Declaration of Independence. The festival drew hundreds of people and a story in the local newspaper, but no one tweeted about the event or posted any pictures on their Facebook page.

Brownsville had a reasonably busy steamboat landing for a number of years and was connected by stagecoach to several area towns. A small pox epidemic in 1857 killed 16 people but folks forged ahead. Brownsville was another regional transit point for a while, especially for grain shipping. Given its location next to the Mississippi River, fishing, trapping, clamming, and ice harvesting supported many people.

In spite of its early promise, Brownsville never hit it big. Job Brown moved away by 1860, although he stayed close to the Mississippi River for much of the rest of his life. In 1868 he cleaned up his act, found Jesus, and became a preacher. His brother, Charles, who was generally regarded as a kind and generous man, especially to struggling travelers, had a mental breakdown and died in 1873 at the St. Peter Insane Asylum.

The town named after them never sustained much economic success. Fires took a toll on the old business district, which disappeared almost completely in 1950 when Minnesota Highway 26 was built; the business district now runs west from the river along a higher plateau. Brownsville settled into the role of a small river town. Today, most residents commute to work elsewhere.

Tourist Information

Direct your questions to the **Brownsville village office** (104 N. 6th St.; 507.482.6732; M–F 8a–Noon, Sa 9a–Noon).

Attractions

The **Church of the Holy Comforter** (Main St.; 507.725.3884 or 507.482.6724) is a fine example of period design. The Gothic Revival church was inspired by Richard Upjohn's 1852 book *Rural Architecture*. The building was completed in 1870 for an Episcopal congregation; the side room was used as sleeping quarters for visiting pastors. The small building served their needs until the fortunes of Brownsville declined; it was closed in 1924. From the 1930s to the 1950s, the building was home to the Emanuel Evangelical Lutheran Church, then closed again. In 1973 the Houston County Historical Society purchased the building and has been maintaining it since. The church is typically open to the public during Brownsville Days, but otherwise there are no regular hours; call to set up a visit.

Entertainment and Events

Brownsville Days (June; 507.482.6732) is a small town festival with a parade and good-sized crowd that is sponsored by the local Lions Club.

Boathouses

If you're paying attention as you drive around, you may notice some curious structures in places along the shores of the Mississippi. The small floating buildings, topped with a tin roof look big enough for just a room or two are usually found in clusters. Are they shacks? Fish houses?

Actually, they are boathouses. In most cases, they have just enough space to store a boat and for weekend living quarters. Here's some background.

In the early 1900s, folks living off the river (clammers, fishermen, trappers) built floating houses that they could maneuver through the backwaters. During the Depression, many more families tried to make a living (or simply get food) from the river; some had nowhere else to live. When the lock and dam system was built in the 1930s, the water level stabilized and suddenly boathouses were more practical.

Thousands were built; there was essentially no regulation until the 1970s. In 1986, legislation passed that granted the Corps responsibility for regulating boathouses; the act protected the right of existing boathouses to continue to exist but prohibited the construction of new ones. Naturally, the states also have some say with boathouses, so you won't see any in Iowa, because their Department of Natural Resources won't allow them.

The boat houses float atop plastic barrels, pontoons, or wooden logs. They are held in place with spud poles and are connected to shore via a walkway; they are stationary, although they rise and fall as river levels change. They usually have electricity but are not allowed to have a bathroom; the community has to maintain outhouses on land. Many no longer have a boat well, as they have evolved into weekend living spaces where groups of friends and families get together to experience the Mississippi River as their backyard.

The only place where boathouses can be used as a year-round residence is at Winona's Latsch Island community. Other places you where you can see communities of boathouses are around Fountain City, La Crosse, Brownsville, and Red Wing.

If you want to read more about boathouses and to look at lots of pretty pictures, check out book *The Floating Boathouses on the Upper Mississippi River: their history, their stories* by Martha Greene Phillips.

Eating

THE COPPER PENNY (201 Main St.; 507.482.7019; Sa,M–Th 6:30a–1:30p, F 6:30a–8p, Su 6:30a–1p) is a small diner that is worth a stop for a piece of pie ($2), like the strawberry rhubarb I ate.

SACHSEN HALLE (702 Main St.; 507.482.4255; M,W,Th 5–9, F,Sa 4–10, Su 4–9) feels like a traditional German rathskeller but began life as a blacksmith shop; they make a good thin crust pizza (12" cheese/$7, 16" cheese/$12).

Sleeping

Camping. WILDCAT LANDING AND CAMPGROUND (Minnesota Highway 26; 507.482.6250; May–Sept) is a cramped campground with little shade, but, hey, it's right next to the river ($20/primitive sites, $32/elec or river sites).

Resources

- Post Office: 508 Main St.; 507.482.6652.

✔ TIP: Life in the country progresses at a different pace than life in the city. This is also true of country drivers. Yes, some drive very fast, but, for the most part, country drivers are not in as much of a hurry as you are, so slow down and take your time.

RENO

(Uninc)

Barely more than a few houses, the small village is surrounded by a large state forest.

Arriving in Town

The main road—actually, the only road—is Hillside Road.

History

This area was notorious during the Civil War as a hideout for a gang of pirates, but Reno was built by the railroad, not gangsters. The mouth of Crooked Creek was the transfer point for trains on the westbound narrow gauge with the north-south tracks along the river. In 1882, Reno had a railroad station, a roundhouse, a residence for the agent, a coal shed, a water tank, a few houses, and a post office, which is more than it has today. This was never going to be a big community because of geography: between the slough and the bluffs, there just isn't much room to build a town. Eleven inches of rain on June 16, 1946 led to flash flooding down the Crooked Creek valley, washing out roads, the railroad, and some pigs. Today, the unincorporated village has a few houses and a lot of scenery.

Sports and Recreation

Reno Recreation Area (Hillside Rd.; 507.724.2107), part of the Dorer Memorial Hardwood Forest, has thousands of acres of wilderness for camping, hiking, and horseback riding. There is an overlook on Reno Bluff that is an easy 10-15 minute hike uphill on an old quarry road. To reach the overlook, drive one mile past the camping area to another small parking lot on the right. On the trail, go right at the T intersection and stay to the right when you reach the quarry; the overlook is just above the quarry. In an hour, you can explore both the high overlook and walk along the ridge. But don't limit yourself to these areas. The Reno Recreation Area has a 17-mile network of trails that are popular with hikers, horseback riders, and cross-country skiers.

Getting on the River

Take your canoe or kayak to **Reno Bottoms** (563.873.3423), a 10-mile one-way trail that begins at the spillway for Lock and Dam 8 and goes downstream to New Albin, Iowa, passing through backwaters that will give you a feel for what the Upper Mississippi River was like before the lock and dam system was built in the 1930s.

Sleeping

Camping. The **RENO RECREATION AREA** (507.724.2107) has several different areas for primitive camping, many of which are popular with groups traveling around by horse ($16/horse sites; $12/others).

NEW ALBIN
(527)

New Albin is located a bit off the river in a broad, flat plain called Ross's Bench. There are many recreation opportunities nearby.

Arriving in Town

The river road enters town as Railroad Avenue; Main Street is one block east (on the other side of the railroad tracks).

History

Before there was New Albin, there was a place called Ross's Landing just north of Winnebago Creek. This small community later become known as Jefferson and might have had a bright future, except for the fact that village officials sued the expanding railroad for additional compensation for land the railroad was taking to build tracks. The railroad responded by refusing to build a station at Jefferson, then founded the nearby town of New Albin, Iowa, which sucked away what little commerce had been conducted at Jefferson. The station at New Albin was completed in 1872. On July 4 of that year, 11-year-old Albin, the son of Joseph Rhomberg, one of the proprietors of the town, was playing near a bonfire with pockets full of gunpowder. This was not a good idea, and, sure enough, the gunpowder ignited and exploded, mortally wounding young Albin. The town was named in his honor, but they had to use New Albin to avoid confusion with the Iowa towns of Albia and Albion. The little village grew into a shipping point for grain and produce and had a number of commercial fishing operations. The population has been relatively steady since the 19th century: 423 residents in 1880, 588 in 1910, compared with 527 in 2000.

Tourist Information

Tourism information is available through the **Allamakee County Economic Development** (800.824.1424/563.568.2624; M–F 8:30–4:30).

Attractions

If you are into unusual buildings, check out the **Reburn Barn** (1641 Pool Hill Dr.), a 12-sided structure that was built in 1914; it is a quarter-mile off the River Road on the south end of town. The **New Albin Town Hall** (Main Street) is much the same as it was when completed in 1895.

Fish Farm Mounds State Preserve (2692 State Highway 26) is a three-acre site with about a dozen Woodland-era Native American burial mounds. The mound group—primarily conical in shape—is a short uphill climb from the parking lot. The Fish family donated the property to the State of Iowa, hence the somewhat confusing name.

Getting on the River

The **Mississippi River Canoe Trail** (800.824.1424/319.568.2624) follows a path through the backwaters from New Albin to Lansing. There are several options for putting in, but one of the more interesting is to start at Black Hawk Bluff on the Upper Iowa River (just off Highway 26) and paddle to Lansing through Big Slough (13 miles).

Entertainment and Events ♪

New Albin Town Days (mid-July; 563.544.8062) is the town's day to celebrate its identity, with the usual events: sports, music, food, and a parade.

Sports and Recreation ≋

Many of the backwater areas around New Albin are public lands; one of the most accessible areas if you don't have a boat is **Pool Slough Wildlife Management Area**, which is great for birding, general wildlife watching, and fishing. Pool Slough is along Army Road, which you can reach by following Ross Avenue, then, after crossing Main Street, Elm Street.

Shopping

CITY MEAT MARKET AND GROCERY (199 Railroad Ave.; 563.544.4236; M–Th,Sa 8–6, F 8–7) is a local staple run by five generations of the Meyer family, a grocer with an important difference: they make awesome jerky. Check out the savory beef jerky (go for the hot one!) or the surprisingly sweet and tender pork jerky. This is not your standard convenience store jerky, as you will notice by the price ($12.99/pound). They also have a variety of other fresh meat products and groceries.

Resources

- Post Office: 190 Main St.NE; 563.544.4248.
- New Albin Public Library: 176 Elm St.; 563.544.4747; M,W,F 4p–7p, Tu,Th 9a–11a & 4p–7p, Sa 9a–11a.

LANSING

(1,012)

Lansing is a consummate river town, with an economy that has historically, for better or worse, been dependent upon the Mississippi River. Even if the Lansing of today has fewer people making a living from river-related jobs, the Mississippi remains central to the town's identity.

Arriving in Town

Main Street is the primary east-west road, beginning at the Mississippi River and exiting town as State Highway 9 toward Waukon. Front Street parallels the Mississippi River and becomes County Highway X52 as it exits town to the south as the River Road.

History

Europeans moved into the area in 1848, just as the Ho Chunk were leaving. Among the first settlers was William Garrison of Lansing, Michigan. He did not stick around, but his name for the town did. The following year, Galena transplants John Haney and his son, James, arrived, followed in short order by H.H. Houghton. They built a few mills in Lansing and prospered. Houghton used part of his fortune to build a stone mansion on the side of Mt. Hosmer in 1863 (it is still there).

Lansing was a remote outpost in those early years. Boats passed town just a few times a month. Communication with the outside world was sporadic in the winter with mail arriving only once a week. Residents had to travel across the frozen Mississippi to Prairie du

Chien, which had the nearest railroad. When the ice was not thick enough to walk across, Lansing residents were on their own. The town had a good steamboat landing and eventually became a key supply point for the region; Lansing grew five-fold in 20 years—from 440 residents in 1854 to 2280 in 1875.

Just south of nascent Lansing, the town of Columbus also had a bustling boat landing. Columbus was chosen as the first county seat in 1851. When the town was platted in 1852, two acres were set aside for county buildings, but nothing was ever built and when the county seat was moved, Columbus essentially disappeared. A name change in 1857—to Capoli, in honor of the bluff of the same name above town—did not save the town.

Lansing residents have been resilient in the face of changing economic fortunes. The town's initial growth was fueled by a booming trade in shipping grain and the Kerndt brothers (Gustav, Moritz, William, and Julius) were part of the reason. They built a warehouse in 1859 and an elevator in 1861; both riverfront structures are still are standing. Fortunes slumped for a while as the wheat harvest declined, but farmers eventually switched to dairy, livestock, and other crops. Local industry received a boost when the Chicago, Milwaukee and St. Paul railroad arrived in 1872; townsfolk threw an exuberant party to celebrate the arrival of the first train.

Lansing also profited from the lumber business in the late 1800s; during the peak years of the lumber trade, log rafts floated continuously downriver. As the great northern forests were depleted around the turn of the 20th century, Lansing developed an industry producing pearl buttons from Mississippi River mussels. As the pearl button industry declined in the 1920s, commercial fishing took up the slack. Lansing's economy today is closely tied to farming, with a boost from the tourist trade.

Tourist Information ⓘ

Tourism information is available through **Allamakee County Economic Development** (800.824.1424/563.568.2624; M–F 8:30–4:30).

Attractions

The **Museum of River History** (60 S. Front St.; 563.538.4641; no set hours, call to arrange a tour; free) is one of the best executed local history museums along the Mississippi. Housed in the Kerndt & Brothers Elevator, the collection is focused on—get out!—river history. Wow. Displays illustrate the fishing business with tools of the trade for clamming, fish processing, and ice harvesting. Heck, they even have a collection of outboard motors.

Mount Hosmer Park (N. 6th St.; 563.538.4757) is a 75-acre bluff-top park with commanding views of the Mississippi River from a perch 440 feet high. It was named after one Harriet Hosmer, a rather well-known sculptor from the East Coast in her day, who was reported to have raced up the hill in record time during a steamboat stop in the 1850s.

Our Savior's Lutheran Church (480 Diagonal St.; 563.538.4664) was founded in 1867 as Norwegian Evangelical Lutheran Church; Norwegian-language services were offered as late as the 1940s. The current building was completed around 1878. In 1946, the building was expanded when the closed Faegre Prairie Church was moved and attached to the east side (and given a matching brick façade); the art glass windows original to Faegre Prairie Church now adorn the parish hall. If you are here on a Wednesday evening, join them at the church for the Laughter Club (6–6:30), where they practice Laughter Yoga (good for people of all physical abilities); you don't need to speak Norwegian to participate.

Getting on the River

River excursions are offered by **Mississippi Explorer Cruises** (Main & Front Sts.; 563.586.4444), specialists in tours that focus on wildlife and the environment along the Upper Miss. Tour days, times, and prices from Lansing vary, so call to verify.

S & S Rentals Houseboat Rentals (990 S. Front St.; 800.728.0131/563.538.4454; M–Sa 8–5, Su 9–4 from mid-May–mid-October) can equip you with a houseboat to explore the Mississippi River; weekly rentals during the peak summer months run $2881–$4071/week but are substantially cheaper the rest of the season. If you have never piloted a houseboat, orientation will take 4–6 hours to complete; if you have experience, expect about two hours. Most of the boats have waterslides. If you want a less ambitious experience, they also rent pontoon boats ($150/half day, $200/full day) and 16' fishing boats with a 15 HP motor ($75/day).

Entertainment and Events

Lansing Fish Days (563.538.4641) is the event of the summer social season in Lansing, usually held the second weekend in August; highlights include duck races, granny basketball, and eating lots of fish.

Sports and Recreation

The **Lansing Swimming Pool** (490 Bench St.; 563.538.4343; $4/adults;) is on the west side of town.

Shopping

THE RED GERANIUM (201 Main St.; 563.538.3943; M–F 9–5 Sa 9–2) is a fun place to shop for all things floral and creative gifts for that special someone.

HORSFALLS LANSING VARIETY (300 & 360 Main St.; 563.538.4966; M–Sa 9–5, Su Noon–4) is an old-fashioned variety store—two variety stores, to be precise—where "variety" is taken seriously; wander through tightly packed aisles stacked high with toys, kitchen supplies, greeting cards, and just about anything else you can imagine. Consider leaving a trail of bread crumbs to find your way out.

FELICITY ARTS (80 S. 2nd St.; 563.538.9279; W–Sa 10–4) is a glassblowing studio and gift shop. They host occasional glassblowing demonstrations, usually in concert with local festivals.

Eating and Drinking 🍸 🍴

Head to **WALL MARKS** (197 Main St.; 563.538.9088; Tu–Su 11a–7:30p) for ice cream; a double scoop in a handmade waffle cone will cost about $3.

TJ HUNTERS (377 Main St.; 563.538.4544; daily 7a–9p, bar open later) serves up mid-American cuisine on steroids. Check out the monster burgers: 12 ounces of ground beef with toppings to match ($10). The fiesta chicken sandwich ($7) is loaded with an entire jalapeno; something to warm your innards on a cold January day. If you're looking for something more pedestrian, they also serve a range of sandwiches ($6–$8), a few Mexican staples ($9–$12), and standard steak and seafood entrées ($9–$30)

MILTY'S RESTAURANT AND BAR (200 Main St.; 563.538.4585; Tu–Th 10:30–9; F 10:30a–10, Sa

6a–10p, Su 6a–9p; bar open later) is a festive place, with friendly staff and reliable food. Entrées include the standard range of steaks, pork, and pasta ($8–$14), but Milty's also offers themed buffets on a regular basis (seafood, Mexican) and a Friday night fish fry. They also have live music on some nights.

You can't beat the views at **RIVER'S EDGE BAR AND RESTAURANT** (10 S. Front St.; 563.538.4497; M–Sa 6a–2a, Su 7a–2a; kitchen closes about 9p). Standard breakfast items run about $4–$7. For other meals, the burgers ($3–$5) and catfish ($10) won't disappoint. They also have a good selection of quality beer.

Sleeping

Camping and Cabins. RED BARN RESORT AND CAMPGROUND (2609 Main St.; 888.538.4956/563.538.4956; open mid-April thru mid-October) has 117 sites on the western edge of Lansing, most with water and electric ($18/basic, $24/full hookup); they also offer five RVs for nightly rentals ($65 + tax).

Budget. The **SCENIC VALLEY MOTEL** (1608 Main St.; 563.538.4245; WiFi) has 12 rooms ($55–$65+tax), some with a fridge, plus a cabin ($70+tax) with microwave, refrigerator, and stove. Rooms are well maintained, clean, but not big. **MILTY'S** (200 Main St.; 563.538.4585) rents a spacious, unadorned second floor apartment ($70+tax for two people, $10/each extra person). The three-bedroom, one-bathroom smoke-free apartment has a big deck, off-street parking, full kitchen, satellite TV, and washer and dryer.

Bed and Breakfast. About eight miles west of Lansing, **OUR TARA INN** (1231 Highway 9; 563.568.2665/563.380.8272; WiFi) sits atop one of the highest points in Iowa; on a clear day you can see Minnesota and Wisconsin. The four rooms and one suite are in a rehabbed, 1890s-era barn. Each is well equipped with full bath, coffee maker, microwave, fridge, and satellite TV ($70–$150).

Moderate. MCGARRITY'S INN ON MAIN (203 Main St.; 866.538.9262/563.538.9262; WiFi) is home to four impressively rehabbed, luxury suites; each unit is spacious, beautiful and loaded with amenities like exposed brick walls, wood floors, cable TV, full bath, and kitchenette ($85–$170 + tax).

Houses. UNCLE CHARLIE'S PLACE (221 Walnut St.; 319.393.1423; WiFi) is a furnished three-bedroom house loaded with amenities: full kitchen, 1½ baths, BBQ grill, garage, sauna, and great views ($187.50 per night with a two-night minimum). **MURPHY'S COVE BED AND BATH** (51 N. Front St.; 563.568.6448) offers a fully furnished riverfront house with three bedrooms, two baths, and amenities like garage parking, a BBQ grill, and cable TV in a new, immaculate house. The views are great, especially from the second floor master bedroom and deck ($190 + tax/two night minimum on summer weekends). Consider a dockside stay in a houseboat with **S & S HOUSEBOAT RENTALS** (990 S. Front St.; 800.728.0131/563.538.4454; M–Sa 8–5, Su 9–4 from mid-May–mid-October; WiFi). The houseboats are comfortable and can rock 6–10 people to sleep, depending on the model ($200/night + tax for 4 persons or $550/2 nights + tax for 4 incl pontoon boat rental).

Resources

- Post Office: 383 Main St.; 563.538.4767.
- Meehan Memorial Lansing Public Library: 515 Main St.; 563.538.4693; M 9–10:30, Tu,F 1–4:30 & 7–9, Th 1–7, Sa 8:30–Noon.

DE SOTO

(366)

De Soto is a small river town that stretches into two counties where river tourism is a big deal.

Arriving in Town

State Highway 35 skirts the western edge of town. Main Street (State Highway 82) heads east from the river.

History

Among the early settlers were two French traders named Godfrey who were employed by the Astor Fur Trading Company. Their families farmed and trapped in the area before moving to Prairie du Chien. The village was initially known as Winneshiek's Landing in honor of the Ho Chunk chief who made regular visits to trade with the French. Chief Winneshiek died in 1848 at Lansing and was reportedly buried atop a bluff just north of town that is named after him.

The village was laid out in 1854 by Moses Strong and renamed for Hernando de Soto, the Spanish explorer who, in 1541, became the first European to see the Mississippi River. The town's proprietors included several doctors who originally sought to create a village that would be settled only by people who shared their New England roots. The bustling sawmills in the mid-1850s, however, needed laborers more quickly than you can say chowdah, so they had to settle for a more varied group. Most of the new arrivals were Norwegians and Germans. Unlike some of its neighbors to the south, De Soto lacked a good spot for a steamboat landing. Using that famous frontier ingenuity, in 1867 a few dozen men from town used the cover of night to construct a wing dam, which was technically in violation of federal law. The dam, off Woodbury's Island, was meant to divert the flow of the river so it would dig a deeper channel near the village. It worked. Four grain elevators were soon built and De Soto became an important shipping point for grain, at least until the railroad reached nearby Viroqua and grain shipping shifted there. Shoemaking propelled the town into the national limelight when, in 1884, local cobbler Patrick De Lap was proclaimed the oldest shoemaker in America.

The De Soto Evangelical Lutheran Church was organized in 1896 by thirteen local residents, five of whom were named Ole. Four years later, they built a small Gothic Revival frame church atop Powers Hill on land donated by Ole Nasseth. When the basement was added in 1933, the church became a hot spot for lutefisk suppers. Services, conducted only in Norwegian until 1918, were held once a month on a Monday because of the difficulty of securing a pastor. When the Mississippi River bridge washed out in 1946, the pastor, who was serving congregations in Lansing, Ferryville, and De Soto had to cross the river in a boat—a rowboat, to be precise—which he did for a while before being worn out by the constant back-and-forth. The church was wired with electricity in 1948 but never got running water. The congregation built a new church in 1966 and sold the old church to a local farmer.

Tourist Information ⓘ

Direct your questions to the **De Soto Town Clerk** during normal business hours (115 Houghton St.; 608.648.2756).

Sports and Recreation

About three miles north of the village, **Battle Bluff Prairie State Natural Area** (608.266.5244) is the distinctive bluff with a goat prairie that takes up the entire south slope. There are no groomed trails, and it is a fairly vigorous 25-minute hike to the top, but the views are awesome and it is a great place to watch raptors catching thermals and slowly circling in front of you. From the highway, go one-quarter mile east on Battle Hollow Road; park on the road, then start walking uphill. Stay off the prairie itself; if you don't kill yourself trying to climb the steep slope, you will probably kill one of the endangered plants that live in the delicate ecosystem.

Blackhawk Park (E590 County Road BI; 608.648.3314) has a number of good spots for fishing, picnicking, and wildlife watching, plus a swimming beach.

Shopping

When the idea of a flea market pops in your head, you probably think of a place like **M & M TRADERS** (402 S. Mill Park Dr.; 608.648.3141; M,W–Sa 10–5, Su Noon–5) with shelves overflowing, aisles nearly impassable, and a very enthusiastic owner like Peggy Duncan. Search through the stash of vinyl records, Amish baskets, antiques, junk, clothing, electronics, books, and God only knows what else to find your personal treasure; bring cash.

Eating and Drinking

THE GREAT RIVER ROADHOUSE (9660 Highway 35; 608.648.2045; in summer open daily 11–10, otherwise open M,W,Th 4–close, F-Su 11–close) is a very popular stop for food and drinks along the River Road. You can get pizza in just about any form with

Battle Bluff

nearly any toppings, and it goes a long way. I got three meals from a 14" Roadhouse Special (sausage, mushroom, onion, cheese; $16). Broasted chicken is another popular choice ($9 for a ½ chicken dinner). I thought that implied some kind of oven roasting; wrong. It's just deep-fried in a pressure cooker using a "broaster" probably made in Wisconsin, so I guess that makes it local food. If you still prefer something different, they also have sandwiches ($6–$8.50) and entrées that run the gamut from seafood to ribs to pasta dishes ($8–$26). You will probably have to wait for a table on a weekend evening.

Sleeping

Camping. BLACKHAWK PARK (E590 County Road BI ; 608.648.3314) has a large campground along a backwater channel with several separate camping areas. The sites nearest the shower house are cramped and have little shade, but there are a few primitive sites at the boathouse camping area that are separated from the rest of the campground and are right next to the river with great views; bring bug spray. The sites around Peck Lake are generally more private, especially around the east side of the lake. **Mississippi Sports and Recreation** (E870 Ghelf Rd.;

The Amish Communities of the Driftless Area

The Driftless Area has a growing number of Amish families. The Amish are descended from Swiss Anabaptists, a movement founded by Felix Manz and Conrad Grebel in the early 16th century. Anabaptist means twice baptized—once as a child and once as an adult.

The Amish and the Mennonites share the same roots. The word Mennonite is derived from the name of a former Roman Catholic priest, Menno Simons, who embraced the Anabaptist movement in 1536. Jacob Amman believed that the Mennonites were straying from the theological roots of the faith, especially when it came to the practice of shunning members who had been banned for proscribed acts and had not repented. This led to a schism in 1693 with the Mennonites; his followers are therefore called Amish.

The Amish began arriving the US in the 18th century, settling first in Pennsylvania then spreading throughout the US. There are many divisions within this world, but the Amish you probably have at least some passing familiarity with are known as Old Order Amish and are perhaps the most conservative descendents of the Anabaptists.

The Old Order Amish live exclusively in rural areas. They don't use modern conveniences like electricity, phones, or cars, and they dress in traditional clothes. Worship services are held in the homes of community members;; they do not build churches. Most speak an old German dialect as their first language but are also fluent in English.

The Amish have a growing population and now number over 200,000 in the US. The population increase has created land and economic pressures which has led many Amish to migrate to new parts of the US in search of new land to farm or led some to give up farming altogether and find other forms of work (e.g., woodworking or factories) that would still allow them to maintain their traditional lifestyle.

In Wisconsin, there are large Amish communities in the west-central part of the state. Along the Mississippi River, you are most likely to encounter Amish families around Genoa and De Soto and further south to Cassville. In Minnesota, the highest concentration of Amish communities is in the southeast, especially around the village of Harmony.

The Amish are known for handmade products, especially quilts and furniture; you may see them at farmers markets, too, selling fresh bread and jams. They do not want their faces to be photographed, so please respect their wishes.

608.648.3630) has a small campground just off the highway ($12/primitive site, $15/site with water, $18/water & electric).

Budget. THE BOAT HOUSE (212 Main St.; 608.648.2269) has three basic apartments in a historic building in the business district; all units have a private bath, cable TV, stove, fridge, and coffee ($55+tax); units 1 and 2 adjoin and could be rented together by families or couples traveling together. **WINNESHIEK TRAILER RENTAL** (Hwy 35 3 miles south of De Soto; 608.317.8880) is a 1960s-era mobile home in decent shape and with few bells and whistles that is available from March through November. The trailer has two bedrooms (each with double beds), a kitchen, screened-in porch, good views of the river; and a back yard that abuts a large state natural area ($75 incl tax/4 people; 2 night minimum).

Cabins. RIVERVIEW CABINS (121 Crawford St.; 888.817.3640/608.648.3640) has five cabins and two apartments equipped with a full kitchen, cable TV, and linens; one cabin is wheelchair accessible ($80 incl tax; 2 nite min on weekends). **SCENIC VIEW CABINS** (S7602B State Highway 35; 608.648.3329) has six roomy, well-maintained cabins in a secluded location above the highway ($50-$60 incl tax); a larger stand-alone cabin ($70 incl tax), and a mobile home that is available for overnight rentals ($70 incl tax). Each unit has a refrigerator and either a regular oven or microwave. From December to mid-March they are essentially closed, but they do keep one cabin available for overnight rentals. They do not take credit cards. **MISSISSIPPI SPORTS AND RECREATION** (E870 Ghelf Rd.; 608.648.3630) has eight updated, spacious cabins that overlook the backwaters; each has a fridge, microwave, and coffee ($65+tax); no credit cards.

De Soto, Wisconsin

Houses. Women in need of a retreat (and who isn't really?), should make a call right now to **A PLACE TO SEW** (608.335.9694). Two houses are available for rentals: *The Steamboat House* (116 De Soto St.) has room for eight, and *The Cottage* (125 De Soto St.) can sleep ten ($75/person/night for 3-5, $50/person/night for 6+ incl tax). Both houses are beautiful, tastefully decorated, have spacious work rooms for whatever craft you wish to bring along (quilting, scrapbooking, etc.), a full kitchen, screened porches, and comfortable sitting rooms to chat and watch the river flow by. **MURPH'S HIDEAWAY** (65835 Chandler Rd.; 608.648.2000) has a deep woods cabin feel atop an isolate ridge but in a new building with modern luxuries: full kitchen, dishwasher, microwave, satellite TV, washer and dryer, gas grill, spacious deck, and hot tub; the cabin can comfortably sleep eight people ($199/night + tax, 2 night minimum, $75 cleaning fee).

Moderate. For something completely different, why not stay in a retrofitted railroad caboose? The **COULEE JUNCTION CABOOSE** (10414 Coulee Creek Rd.; 708.341.3255) is set on railroad tracks on five acres deep in a coulee and outfitted with nice features like a big deck, a barbeque grill (bring charcoal), a firepit, and hot tub. The interior has wood floors, a fireplace, a kitchen with a microwave; and enough room to sleep four adults, but probably best for two ($150+tax, cleaning fee of $45 waived for 2 or more night stay).

Resources

- Post Office: 207 Houghton St.; 608.648.3392.
- De Soto Public Library: 111 Houghton St.; 608.648.3593; T,W 12:30–8, Sa 8–1.

VICTORY

(Uninc)

Tiny Victory is an unlikely place to be counted among my favorite places to stop, but it is, thanks to the Red Lion Pub.

Arriving in Town

State Highway 35 skirts the western end of town; there's not really a main street, and you probably won't have much of a need to find one.

History

Ira Stevens was born near Toronto in 1819; he left home at age 20. He worked in Galena for a few years, then moved on to Prairie du Chien in 1844. Five years later he moved another 30 miles upriver and became the first settler for the village of Victory. The site had previously housed a small trading post; because of Stevens, the site became known as Stevens' Landing. When the village was platted in 1852, Judge William Terhune, one of the original landowners, suggested the name Victory because the village was near the location of the final battle in the Black Hawk War.

At the time of the plat, Victory had three houses; it only takes a casual glance to see that the village has only a few more than that today. Victory enjoyed a few years as a reasonably busy spot for buying and shipping grain because it had a good steamboat landing, but the village lost business to De Soto after its residents furtively built a wing dam to improve their own landing.

Victory had 114 residents by 1880 and has been something of a melting pot—more of a melting teaspoon, really—as there was no single nationality that dominated among the early settlers. In the 19th century, residents of Victory could take a steamboat to La Crosse and return the same day; for 50 cents, they got a full day's ride, plus two hours to shop in the city.

One of the most memorable events in the town's history was the crash of the *John Streckfus* steamer in June 1910. As the boat was returning to Lansing from La Crosse, it erupted in flames, causing panicked passengers to jump into the shallow river for safety; one young woman died from the jump. The captain ran the boat aground on Bad Axe Island, so passengers could evacuate. It took several hours to get everyone back to the mainland. Remarkably, only two of the ship's 1500 passengers died. The cause of the fire has been a source of controversy from the beginning. The evidence suggests that the fire started with John Pleen, who was the other person who died in the fire. Pleen had been thrown in the brig for disorderly conduct and drunkenness. His nearly extinguished cigar probably ignited the fire.

Attractions

Take a self-guided tour around the **Genoa National Fish Hatchery** (S5689 State Highway 35; 608.689.2605; free) for insights into the process of breeding fish.

Eating

You may think that you have no reason to stop in Victory proper; you'd be wrong, especially if you are hungry or thirsty. The **RED LION PUB AND EATERY** (608.648.3100; Tu–Th 4p-11ish, F–Su Noon–11ish; in winter, Th–Sa) has an amazing beer selection and good food—it's the only place to get Indian curries in a 150-mile radius. Check out the standout fish and chips ($11)—get them dusted, of course—or one of the many curry dishes (most about $12).

Sleeping

Cabins. THE GREAT RIVER RESORT (S5524 State Highway 35; 888.880.4092/608.689.2212) may not have the most aesthetically pleasing units you'll ever see, but they are inexpensive and outfitted with coffee, fridge, stove, and satellite TV, and you won't find a more cordial host than Don (and I'm not saying that just because we shared a beer on his deck after my tour). Choose from one of the three cabins; D has the most room ($65–$90 + tax; open May–Oct.). Don also rents out the adjacent four bedroom, 1½ bathroom house; relax in the comfy living room or on the deck ($195+tax/6 people).

✔ TIP: Cell phone reception can be a little tricky along the river because the bluffs interfere with the signal. If you are having trouble getting reception, head up to the top of a ridge and give it a try, or, just put your phone away and enjoy the quiet.

For more information and updates, visit my web site at www.mississippivalleytraveler.com.

GENOA
(263)

Genoa is a rarity in the US: a rural village with a strong Italian identity. Although that identity may be somewhat less salient today, as you explore the immediate area you will encounter plenty of tangible reminders of it.

Arriving in Town

Wisconsin Highway 35 stays west of the village; the small business district runs along Main Street, which is also Wisconsin Highway 56 through the southern two-thirds of the village.

History

A village called Genoa founded by families with names like Starlochi, Gilardi, Buzzetti, Fanetti, and Francoli obviously has a strong connection to Italy, although it didn't start out that way. Initially known as Hasting's Landing (for David Hastings) and platted in 1854 as Bad Axe City, the village's origins began in 1853 with the purchase of 296 acres in Vernon County by Guiseppe Monti, who left northern Illinois to find a location for a new settlement for Italian/Swiss immigrants unhappy with conditions in Galena. Like many of his compatriots Monti's family was grew up in Switzerland near the Italian border; one of his parents was Italian and one was Swiss. The Monti family had migrated from New York City via Cincinnati, St. Louis, and Galena before settling in Wisconsin. In 1868, the village's predominantly Italian residents changed the town's name to Genoa in honor of the hometown of Christopher Columbus.

Genoa had a busy steamboat landing for a while and developed the typical river town industries: hotels (room and board at the Monti Hotel in 1900 cost $3.50/week and included breakfast), a limestone factory, a fishery, the railroad. A pearl one inch in diameter was reportedly found near Genoa and later ended up as part of the British Crown Jewels.

Just for fun, here are a few diary entries from Genoa's St. Charles School:

> October 14, 1915: "Still one barefoot boy in school."
>
> January 15, 1918: "School closed today at 10 o'clock because of diphtheria. School closed four days."
>
> February 1, 1918: "40 below zero today"
>
> January 24, 1919: "It has been above 50 degrees nearly every noon this week"
>
> January 28, 1919: "Willie Monti was seen wearing a white summer hat yesterday. Carl Guscetti killed a mosquito Sunday."

The construction of Lock and Dam 8 in the 1930s was a boon for a few years, especially for taverns and room rentals. Genoa has also benefited from the energy industry. A coal-burning power plant was built in 1940 and the first nuclear-power plant in Wisconsin went up from 1962–66 (it closed in 1987); a steam plant was built in 1966–69. Today, many Genoa residents commute to jobs elsewhere, especially in La Crosse, and tourism is among the village's biggest industries.

Tourist Information ⓘ

If you have questions about Genoa, stop at the **Captain Hook Bait Shop** (108 Main St.; 608.689.2800; M–Sa 6a–5p, Su 6a–3p) to get them answered.

Attractions

Lock and Dam 8 (608.689.2625) was completed in 1938 and overhauled from 1989 to 2003. The lock has a maximum lift of 11 feet; the dam is 934 feet long, but it connects to an earthen dam that runs another 17,000 feet. There is an observation platform where you can watch boats locking through.

The **Old Settlers Park Scenic Overlook** (Spring Coulee Rd.) has good view of the valley, and better yet, I suppose, you can drive virtually all the way to the top. The road is open from roughly Memorial Day to Labor Day, but you can park on the road below and walk up any time.

Getting on the River

If you want to fish but forgot your boat, don't fret; head to **Clements Fishing Barge** (below Lock and Dam 8; 608.689.2800; daily 7a–6p from mid-March–late Nov.; $16/day for adults, $5/day for kids ages 6–12). Park at the lot just south of the power plant, walk across the highway (carefully), and raise the orange flag; a boat will come get you. Boats usually run on the hour but will make a special trip to get you, if needed. Just bring a fishing license, a fishing pole, tackle, and bait.

Entertainment and Events

In late May, fishing enthusiasts flock to the village for the **Genoa Lions Walleye Fishing Tournament** (608.457.2407), which gives you the chance to measure your skills against the best, if that's what you're into. **St. Charles Church** throws a party on July 4th that draws a big crowd (608.689.2646).

Shopping

CORY SMITH STUDIOS (Water St.; 800.689.2577; M,Tu,Th,F 9:30–5:30, Sa 10–3) is the gallery and workshop of gemologist and artist Paul Finch, who has been creating custom, high-end jewelry since 1971; you are welcome to drop in if the shop is open. **OLD TOOL SHED ANTIQUES** (612 Main St.; 608.689.2066; Th–M 10–5) is one of those labors-of-love. Housed in an 1867-era building, the store is a gold mine of antique hand tools, hammers, planes, fish scales, old kitchen gadgets, ice hooks, meat grinders, and many other things.

Eating

Visit **ENGH'S FISH MARKET** (N165 State Highway 35; 608.689.2394; F–Su 9–5) for smoked Mississippi River fish and catfish fillets at reasonable prices.

Sleeping

Cabins. THE CAPTAIN'S QUARTERS (108 Main St.; 608.689.2800) looks like a converted garage from the outside, which it may be, but inside it feels like a cozy place to call home for a few days. The cabin has one bedroom with a queen bed plus bunk beds in another room, with a full kitchen and a full-size bathroom; you also get to use the charcoal grill ($72 + tax, $10 for each person after two guests).

Budget. If you just want a cheap bed to crash in and aren't into amenities like a private bathroom or cable TV, check out **RUDY'S BAR AND HOTEL** (608 Main St.; 608.689.2994). There are just six rooms, all above a bar, and they are about as basic (and cheap) as they come, but are clean and well-kept; room #9 is the biggest, with two double beds and a sofa ($22 incl tax); cash only. **THE BIG RIVER INN** (200 Beaver

St.; 608.689.2339; WiFi) has 12 rooms in a variety of configurations that are clean but simple, if a little cramped. All have beds that are slightly larger than a double and come equipped with a microwave, fridge, coffee pot, and satellite TV ($44–$59; $7 for each person after 2). **THE GENOA MOTEL** (708 Water St.; 608.689.2339) is another small place, having just four units. The two motel rooms are small and simple but clean and each has a small fridge, microwave, and coffee pot ($50 + tax). The apartment, in a Civil War-era building, has one bedroom plus a loft with a queen bed and two twin beds, cable TV, full kitchen and two bathrooms ($90 + tax). The fourth unit is an apartment with a queen bed, two twin beds, fridge, and microwave ($69 + tax).

Resources

- Post Office: 501 Main St.; 608.689.2478.

For more information and updates, visit my web site at www.mississippivalleytraveler.com.

STODDARD

(815)

Unlike most other towns along the Mississippi River, Stoddard did not start its life as a river town but rather became one in the 1930s thanks to the Army Corps of Engineers. The original town was built next to a narrow slough and did not have a riverboat landing, so it grew later than its neighbors.

Arriving in Town

State Highway 35 is Main Street through Stoddard. It is a good idea to watch your speed as you drive through town.

History

Europeans began moving into the area in the 1850s, but they settled primarily in the country, growing grain and tobacco. Henry White, who arrived in 1867 from New England, is credited as the village's founder. The village site was located next to a narrow slough and did not have direct access to the Mississippi River, so the village had no river trade. Instead, it grew into a modest commercial center to meet the needs of area farmers, with businesses like a blacksmith and general stores. The village experienced some modest growth when a school was completed in 1885 and with the arrival of the railroad. When the village was platted in 1886 it was named Stoddard, probably in honor of Colonel Thomas Stoddard, the first mayor of La Crosse. Mills sprang up in the 1890s. One of these made boom plugs, the pins that were used to secure wood rafts floating downriver. Logs were floated down the Black River to North La Crosse at an astonishing rate in the late 19th century, but, the story goes, the logs ran out before the boom plugs. Stoddard residents also worked at a tobacco warehouse and at factories that made pickles, cigars, and kraut. Otto Wodzynski, a rural mail carrier and Stoddard resident, had the distinction of owning the first horseless carriage in Vernon County, so that's gotta count for something. Stoddard incorporated in 1903 when it had 329 residents; the population didn't grow until the 1960s when Stoddard evolved into a suburb of La Crosse. The completion of Lock and Dam 8 in 1937 raised the level of the Mississippi River high enough to give Stoddard its first reliable access to the main channel.

Colonel Thomas Stoddard

Tourist Information ⓘ

Contact the **Vernon County Tourism Council** (608.637.2575).

Attractions

Stoddard River Park (Forest Lane) is a small riverside park that would be a pleasant spot for a picnic.

Doug Sinniger has received accolades for his work as a taxidermist, winning several international competitions. You can view samples of his work at the **Riverland Taxidermy Studio** (103 N. Main St.; 608.457.2998; M–F 9–6, Sa,Su variable). There is always something on display but usually not much for sale; what's on display changes because most of the works are for customers. When I dropped in, I saw a brown bear, a few fish, and some small mammals in the front, plus a few big African beasts in the back. He doesn't mind if you stop in and look around.

Getting on the River

Water's Edge (201 N. Pearl St.; 608.457.2126) rents a pontoon boat ($95–$130/4 hours, $200/day), a 14-foot fishing boat ($45/4 hours, $60/day), a 16-foot fishing boat ($50/4 hours, $65/day), plus rowboats and paddleboats ($15/4 hours, $25/day). If you reach town in your own boat, they also have transient slips at their marina ($5/4 hours or $25/day).

Entertainment and Events

The village celebration is called **Stoddard Fun Days** (July) and usually includes a fishing tournament for the kids, food, and games.

Sleeping

Camping. WATER'S EDGE (201 N. Pearl St.; 608.457.2126) has 38 sites, as the name suggests, next to the river in a quiet, shaded setting ($18/primitive site, $25/water & elec, $28/water, elec, sewer; all + tax).

Budget. WATER'S EDGE (201 N. Pearl St.; 608.457.2126) has eight units that exude 1940s charm right down to the the appliances; kitchenettes have a microwave and fridge but no oven and are spacious enough to include a separate sitting room ($48 + tax, two night minimum on summer weekends). The 11 rooms at the **SAFE LANDING MOTEL** (329 N. Main St.; 608.457.2122; WiFi) are nothing fancy and small-ish, but they are clean and well-kept and equipped with a fridge; a microwave can be requested ($49–$69 incl tax).

Cabins/Houses. WATER'S EDGE (201 N. Pearl St.; 608.457.2126) has three cabins with kitchenettes ($55–$75 + tax; two night minimum on weekends; WiFi) and a cute cottage for rent that can sleep up to eight and comes with cable TV, washer and dryer, and gas grill ($85/night $10/night/extra person after two, two-night minimum on weekends; WiFi). **THE SUNSET LODGE VACATION RENTAL** (N1316 State Highway 35; 608.457.2378; WiFi) is a three-bedroom, three-bath A-frame house south of Stoddard that is loaded with amenities: full kitchen, cable TV, gas grill, washer and dryer, and a nice view of the river ($150/night + tax for 6 people; $20/extra person).

Resources

- Post Office: 115 N. Main St.; 608.457.2577.

LA CROSSE
(51,818)

I'm not the least bit objective about La Crosse, and I won't pretend to be. I went to college at the University of Wisconsin–La Crosse and feel in love with the city and the region. It's the place where I grew up, learned how to live, and learned how to love. And, its's the place I first felt the draw of the Mississippi River. Even now when I return, I feel great affection for the city and still consider it one of my favorite places. Stick around for a few days, and you're likely to feel the same way.

Arriving in Town

To follow the Great River Road through La Crosse, follow State Highway 35 (Mormon Coulee Road) to US Highway 14/61 as it changes names repeatedly (Mormon Coulee Road, South Avenue, 4th Street, Copeland Avenue, then Rose Street) and reunites with State Highway 35 on the city's north side near Interstate 90. Through downtown, the Great River Road is divided into two one-way streets: 4th Street going northbound and 3rd Street heading south.

> ✔ TIP: State law requires automobiles to stop for pedestrians in crosswalks, even if there is no stop sign or stop light. Pay attention when driving, especially downtown and around the universities.

History

When Europeans began exploring the area, they found a prairie that was a popular spot for a game that they had never seen. In 1837, the Reverend Alfred Brunson described the Native American sport this way: "The game was played with a ball, thrown by a stick some four feet in length, the outer end of which was brought round into a ring, say six inches in diameter, to which is attached a bag of network made of strong thongs of some kind of skin. The parties start at a center post. The ball is thrown into the air as perpendicularly as possible, and when it comes down each party strives to catch it in the bag at the end of their stick and throw it as far as possible against the opposite party. The ball is caught up and thrown so back and forth, and the victors are those who drive it eventually and effectually by the center post on to the side of their opponents. It is a very exciting sport, and many a one gets an unlucky blow, sometimes from friends and sometimes from foes; but as no one is supposed to design it, no offense is given or insult imagined."

Although it is not entirely clear why the French named the sport *la crosse*, it may be that the game sticks used by the Native Americans bore a strong resemblance to the crook carried by Catholic Bishops that was called *la crozier*. Regardless, the name stuck and the field where the game was played became known as Prairie la Crosse.

> **RANDOM FACT**: *You can watch a game of lacrosse in La Crosse; it is a club sport at UW-La Crosse.*

In the autumn of 1841, just six months after leaving a comfortable life in upstate New York, 18-year old Nathan Myrick was on a keelboat heading upriver from Prairie du Chien, eager to open a trading post at Prairie la Crosse. (See the sidebar on page 197 for more about Nathan Myrick.) Loaded with supplies he purchased on credit from Fort Crawford, he and his partner, Eben Weld, arrived on November 4 after five days of travel. (You can now drive this stretch in about an hour.) The little village that grew up around him was initially called Prairie la Crosse, but Myrick, as the city's first postmaster, decided to shorten the name. In October 1844, Myrick acquired some neighbors when a group of Mormons came up from Nauvoo and spent one winter in an area south and east of his trading post (that area is now called Mormon Coulee).

In 1848 when the land was finally available for sale, Myrick bought 100 acres but left town later in the year because of declining business prospects and transferred half his land to Harmon Miller. In 1850, Timothy Burns, who was elected Lieutenant Governor of Wisconsin a year later, bought Myrick's half-share claim, then sold half of that back to Myrick a short time later. Myrick, Burns, and Miller were the original three proprietors who instigated an official town survey in 1851.

When Myrick left La Crosse, the village had a handful of houses and a bowling alley where patrons used a ball made from a pine knot. Settlers began streaming to town around 1850, attracted to its location on a flat, treeless plain high enough to avoid flooding; it also helped that the area was nearly malaria-free. Among the first arrivals was Emfin Emfinson—the area's first known immigrant from Norway. By the end of 1853, La Crosse had 100 houses and five taverns. (La Crosse may still have one tavern for every 20 households.) A steady stream of covered wagons arrived from the East to cross the river via the ferry at La Crosse; 61 wagons crossed in a single June day in 1856. La Crosse incorporated as a city in 1856 and elected its first mayor, Thomas Stoddard, by a 216-215 vote.

La Crosse rapidly grew into a regional commercial center, fueled by industries like logging, banking, grain milling, and large scale manufacturing. La Crosse was also home to a high concentration of *jobbers*—whole-

Nathan Myrick

Nathan Myrick was born in Westport, New York in 1823. His father was a busy guy, running lumber mills, iron forges, and a canal, among other things. When he was 18 years old, he left for the West. He sailed on the steamer Chesapeake to Chicago (which had just 5000 residents at that time), then took a stagecoach to Galena. Two days later, a team of hired horses carried him into Prairie du Chien.

He tried to get a job with a fur trading company but was turned down by both Hercules Dousman and Alexander MacGregor because he didn't speak any Indian languages. He earned some cash by joining a commercial hunting trip with Harmon Miller. They didn't catch much, but Miller later became Myrick's business partner, so the trip wasn't a total loss.

Myrick was hired as a clerk in the post office for board but no salary. He got a tip about an opportunity to start a trading post upriver at Prairie la Crosse. Not one to waste an opportunity, he borrowed a keelboat from Fort Crawford and left on November 4, 1841 with a load of supplies he purchased on credit. He and his business partner, Eben Weld, reached the new site five days later.

They didn't find any signs that anyone else was already there, so they built a log cabin on Barron's Island. The trading post did well right away;

his customers included Chiefs Winnishiek and Decorah. The next year, Weld moved on to Fort Snelling and Harmon Miller joined Myrick.

In 1843, Myrick made a trip back east to find a wife. This hunting trip was more successful: he married Rebecca Ismon at Charlotte, Vermont. For several years, Myrick made a decent living in the area. Besides the post, he owned a sawmill on the Black River and sold wood to riverboats, even rafting logs down to St. Louis. Myrick moved to Minnesota in 1848 but kept a share of his land claim throughout his life. He died in 1903 in St. Paul.

sale businesses that supplied the retail trade and had an active ship building and repair industry. The railroads, which connected La Crosse to Milwaukee in 1858, were major employers. La Crosse also had a sizeable beer brewing industry, brewing as much product as their counterparts in Milwaukee.

La Crosse also grew through annexation. One of the most controversial moves was the annexation of North La Crosse, an incorporated city that was separated from La Crosse by a mile of swamp (and still is). North La Crosse had a number of sawmills, but the railroads and iron works were also major employers. Nearly one-third of the residents in North La Crosse were foreign-born, many of them Norwegian. The village had incorporated in 1868, but that didn't stop annexation, which La Crosse pulled off through an act of the Wisconsin legislature on March 22, 1871; there was never a public vote. Annexation added 1494 residents, many of them disgruntled, increasing the city's population to over 9000.

Settlers coming up the Mississippi found a growing city, with a busy steamboat landing. Among those early arrivals were a small number of blacks who passed through town in search of economic opportunity. Zacharias Louis Moss, who arrived in 1859, was among the few who made La Crosse home; he still has descendents in the area. George Edwin Taylor was another of those early black residents. Taylor was a strong advocate for labor, very active politically, and publisher of *The Wisconsin Labor Advocate*. He left La Crosse frustrated by racial politics and later became the first black man to receive a major party nomination for President of the US (National Liberty Party in 1904).

By the 1890s, the city's economic growth had slowed considerably. The steamboat era ended in the 1880s, La Crosse's grain milling industry was declin-

George Taylor campaign poster (Eartha White Collection, U North Flor.)

ing, and the last of the lumber mills would close in 1906. In response, the Board of Trade (a group of private businessmen) subsidized the construction of new factories to help transition lumber mill workers into new employment. They didn't take many chances with their money, showing a strong preference to fund existing businesses such as the La Crosse Rubber Mills.

Anti-German sentiment stirred up by World War I ushered in a number of changes around town: Berlin Street was renamed Liberty Street; sauerkraut became "liberty cabbage"; and the German Society rebranded as the Pioneer Club. Prohibition nearly killed the local brewing industry; only the G. Heileman Company survived, by making soda water, malt extract, and near-beer products with names like *Coney Island Beer* and *King of Clubs*. The city generally did well, however, in the 1920s. Jobs from large employers like the La Crosse Rubber Works, Trane Company, La Crosse Plow Works, and auto parts manufacturing helped put enough money in people's pockets to trigger a boom in housing construction. As the Great Depression hit, government-sponsored programs through the Works Progress Administration and the construction of Lock and Dam 7 kept many folks afloat. In the immediate aftermath of World War II, pent-up labor-management conflict led to a series of contentious strikes. A decade later, La Crosse lost a quarter of its manufacturing jobs, a national trend that accelerated in the 1970s and 1980s. Ethnic Hmong began arriving from Laos in the late 1970s; many fought alongside US soldiers in Vietnam but were left to fend for themselves when the US withdrew. Thousands migrated to the US after months or years in refugee camps.

La Crosse continues to adapt. Healthcare is now a leading employer, and education and tourism have grown in importance.

Tourist Information ⓘ

The best source for all your tourism needs (besides this book) is the **Visitors Center** in Riverside Park (800.658.9424/608.782.2366) or the one at Bridgeview Plaza on the north side near Interstate 90 (2500 Rose St.); both centers are open all year (M–Sa 10–6, Su 10–4 in summer, M–Sa 10:30–4:30, Su 10:30–4 the rest of the year).

Attractions: Central La Crosse

Riverside Park (State St.; 608.789.7533) is a great public space, popular for hanging out and watching the sun set. The **Riverside Museum** (Visitors Center; 608.782.2366; open Memorial Day–Labor Day M–Sa 10:30–4:30, Su 10:30–4, open Sa,Su in Sept.,Oct.; $2) has exhibits on Native American history in the region and interesting displays about the steamboat era, including the *War Eagle* that burned while docked in the Black River. Also check out the **International Friendship Gardens** just east of the Visitors Center.

Directly across the Mississippi from Riverside Park, **Pettibone Park** (608.789.7533) takes up part of Bar-

La Crosse (regional)

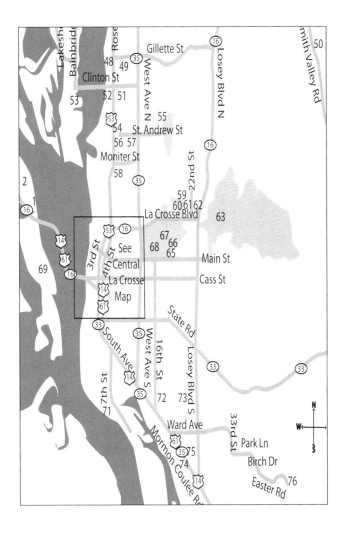

La Crosse (central)

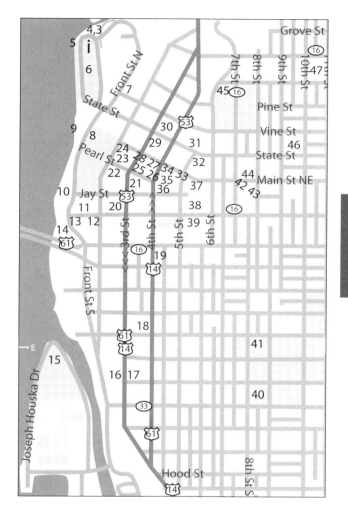

Map Key

Things to Do
48. Black River Beach
54. Buzz's Bikes and Boats
38. Children's Museum of La Crosse
44. Christ Episcopal Church
52. Copeland Park
73. Erickson Pool
30. Farmers Markets
64. Grandad Park
71. Green Island Ice Arena
76. Hass Tract
63. Hixon Forest
45. Hixon House
15. Houska Park
3. International Friendship Gardens
16. King Gambrinus
20. La Crosse Bike Rentals
32. La Crosse Community Theater
5. La Crosse Queen
40. La Crosse Symphony Orchestra
41. Maria Angelorum Chapel
66. Memorial Pool
9. Mississippi Explorer Cruises
67. Mississippi Valley Archaeology Center
19. Mons Anderson House
59. Myrick Hixon EcoPark
60. Myrick Park
49. North Side Community Pool
55. Pearl Street Brewery
1. Pettibone Beach
2. Pettibone Park
11. Pump House Arts Center
4. Riverside Museum
6. Riverside Park
43. Swarthout Museum
34. Three Rivers Outdoors
68. UW-La Crosse
17. World's Largest Six Pack

Sleeping
74. Adriatic Motel
58. Affordable Inn
50. Bluebird Spring Recreation Area
61. Bluff View House
62. The Cottage
14. Courtyard by Marriott
18. Guest House Motel
69. Pettibone RV Park
8. Radisson Hotel
75. Welch Motel

Places to Eat
25. Big Al's
27. Bodega Brew Pub
22. Buzzard Billy's
33. Cha Guan Tea Shop
29. Digger's Sting
36. Fayze's Restaurant and Bakery
7. Freight House
28. Grounded Specialty Coffee
46. Hmong Golden Eggrolls
53. Huck Finn's On the Water
26. Jules Coffee House
65. Kate's on State
24. Kate's Pizza Amore
23. The Pearl Ice Cream Parlor
39. People's Food Coop
21. Pickerman's
13. Piggy's Restaurant
70. Ranison Ice Cream
35. The Root Note
72. Rosie's Café
47. Rudy's Drive-In
51. The Sweet Shop
37. Tres Compadres
10. Waterfront Restaurant
12. Wine Guyz

Other
57. Amtrak Station
31. Downtown post office
56. Jefferson Lines
42. La Crosse Public Library

ron Island. The island was part of Minnesota when Alzono Barron sketched plans for Island City, a planned development that never happened. In 1901, lumber baron (and former mayor) A.W. Pettibone purchased the entire 200-acre island and donated it to the city for use as a park. In 1918, the US Congress approved a land swap in which Minnesota gave Barron Island to Wisconsin in exchange for an island in Pierce County. Like its neighbor across the river, the park is a popular place to picnic and hang out.

The Hixon House (429 N. 7th St.; 608.782.1980; guided tours from Memorial Day–Labor Day Tu–Su 10–5, mid-Sept–end of Oct Sa,Su 10–5; $8.50/adult) is one of the oldest residences in the area. Built for lumber baron Gideon Hixon in 1859, the Italianate mansion has been beautifully restored. The house is loaded with exquisite woodwork, a quirky Turkish sitting room, and, remarkably, has retained most of the original furnishings.

> ✔ TIP: Most parking in the downtown area is free for up to two hours, whether on-street or in one of the parking garages (Main St. between 2nd & 3rd; Jay St. betw 4th & 5th); head to the top of a garage for free long-term parking but after 5pm you don't need to worry about the two-hour limit.

The Children's Museum of La Crosse (207 5th Ave. South; 608.784.2652; Tu–Sa 10–5; Su Noon–5; $6) offers a playful and educational experience for children up to age 12; let your kids simulate controlling the flow of the Mississippi River or build a bridge. Hands-on exhibits include a 28-foot vertical wall for the future rock climber in the family.

Christ Episcopal Church (831 Main St.; 608.784.0697; office open M–F 9–1) is one of the oldest faith communities in town, with a history dating back to the 1850s. The current Richardsonian Romanesque building was completed in 1898 when the congregation hoped it would become the cathedral for the region's Episcopal population; it didn't, but locals still got a wonderful church. The spacious interior is notable for two particular art glass windows. On the south side, the luminous window called *Transfiguration of Christ* was created by the Louis Tiffany Company. On the opposite side, *The Beatitudes* was created by the Charles Connick Studio of Boston and installed in 1933; it is one of the few church windows known to commemorate those famous verses from the Bible.

The Swarthout Museum (800 Main St.; 608.782.1980; Tu–F 10–5, Sa,Su 1–5; free) is in the lower level of the La Crosse Public Library and hosts rotating exhibits about La Crosse history.

> Hey, what's that? The stone house at 410 Cass Street is the Mons Anderson House, a unique blend of Gothic Revival and Italian villa styles and the oldest building in town, dating to 1854. Anderson was born in Valders, Norway in 1830 and emigrated to the US at age 16. He settled in La Crosse in 1851 and made a very good living as a merchant; some of his business included selling boots and clothing to lumbermen. Anderson bought the house in 1861, then hired architect William Nichols to transform the house into the building you see today; the overhaul was completed in 1878. The house has a number of outstanding features, like the parquet floors and the exquisite library that is ornamented with black walnut paneling and bookshelves and a mosaic pattern in the floor. The house was operated as a bed and breakfast for a number of years but was sold in 2010 to owners who intend to open a restaurant in it.

Worlds Largest Six-Pack

In a city that loves to drink, located in a state known for its beer, it's only fitting that one would find the **World's Largest Six Pack** (1111 S. 3rd St.). These giant storage containers hold 688,200 gallons of beer—enough beer for one person to have a six pack a day for 3351 years. Walk across Third Street to check out the statue of the legendary (and possibly mythical) Flemish **King Gambrinus,** the patron saint and purported inventor of hopped malt beer. The brewery complex is now called the **City Brewery** (1111 S. 3rd St.; 608.785.4820) but was once the headquarters for the G. Heileman Brewing Company (think *Old Style* and *Special Export*). Tours of the complex used to be offered routinely but are now only available for groups of 25 or more.

Attractions: Citywide

North of downtown, **Copeland Park** (Copeland Ave. @ Clinton St.; 608.789.7533) runs along a section of the Black River; the restored steam engine *Alice the Goon* is located at the northern end.

Myrick Park (La Crosse Street between East & Hillview Avenues; 608.789.7533) is a peaceful city park that borders the La Crosse River marsh and has a few Native American burial mounds, including a rare turtle effigy. On the north side of the park where the zoo was formerly located is the new building for the **Myrick Hixon EcoPark** (789 Myrick Park Dr.; 608.784.0303; M-Sa 9-4, Su Noon-4). The center overlooks the La Crosse River marsh and has a few stuffed animals on display, but unless there's a special event, there's little reason to visit. Go hiking instead.

The **Mississippi Valley Archaeology Center** (1725 State St.; 608.785.8454; M–F 9–4; free) is located in a small brick building near the Cartwright student center on the campus of the University of Wisconsin-La Crosse. The center has been studying ancient civilizations in the Upper Mississippi Valley for decades. Their building has exhibits that showcase previous and current digs, plus displays about the cultural history of native populations, including their musical instruments and art.

Grandad Park (Bliss Rd.; 608.789.7533) has been a beloved local landmark nearly as long as the city has been in existence. In 1909, Norris Bachellor purchased a chunk of it and announced plans to quarry its stone. This did not go over very well. A group led by Ellen Hixon was formed and quickly began buying up adjacent property. They purchased land on the north and west slopes and donated it to the city; it is now called Hixon Forest. In 1912, the city acquired 533 acres atop the bluff for a park. Follow Main Street east; it will become Bliss Road as it starts to switchback its way to the top.

Maria Angelorum Chapel at St. Rose Convent is a hidden gem (912 Market St.; 608.784.2288; tours offered M–Sa 9a–10:45am & 1–3, Su 1–3; call ahead to reserve a spot). The rich Romanesque chapel, completed in 1906, has an Italian marble altar, pillars of onyx, dozens of Bavarian art glass windows and mosaics that incorporate mother of pearl and Venetian glass. The complex is the motherhouse for the Sisters of Perpetual Adoration, who have been praying 365/24/7 since 1878; lay volunteers fill in some shifts now.

Houska Park (Hood Street & Houska Dr.; 608.789.7533) is a small riverfront park south of downtown with a good view of the river bridges.

A short drive southeast of town, the **Shrine of Our Lady of Guadalupe** (5250 Justin Rd.; 608.782.5440; daily 9–4) is a new religious monument that has quickly attracted a large following. Construction began in 2001, and no expense was spared. The 100-acre site has a visitor center, votive candle chapel, outdoor Stations of the Cross, and a striking Romanesque shrine church. Go through the visitor center to begin the ten-minute gentle uphill walk to the shrine; you can ride up on a golf cart, if you prefer. Guided tours of the shrine are offered every day (M–Sa 1:30, Su 2:30).

Norwegian immigrants settled in many of the coulees around La Crosse; a typical Norwegian farmstead has been preserved at the **Norskedalen Nature and Heritage Center** (County Road PI; 608.452.3424; M–F 9–5, Sa 10–5, Su Noon–5 from May 1–Oct 31, M–F 8–4 the rest of the year, with Su Noon–4 in Nov–Dec & April; $6). The *Bekkum Homestead* will transport you back in time to the 19th century, with a period house and outbuildings like a chicken coop and summer kitchen. The visitor center has displays on the history of Norwegian immigration to the area, the tobacco plant that was the main cash crop for generations, plus some cool antique steamer trunks. If that's not enough, on the way back to La Crosse, stop at the *Skumsrud Farm* (open F Noon–6, Sa 10–5, Su Noon–5 from June–Aug) to tour another group of 19th century buildings, including a single room log cabin that is the oldest house in the county. Allow

Norskedalen's Bekkum homestead

25 minutes to drive to the Bekkum Homestead from downtown La Crosse. Follow US Highway 16 to Coon Valley, then the signs will lead down County Highways P and PI to reach the site.

Goose Island County Park (County Road GI; 608.788.7018) is a 700-acre county park with excellent facilities and numerous places for wildlife viewing, fishing, and relaxing.

Getting on the River

The **La Crosse Queen** (608.784.2893) is a replica of a 19th century paddlewheeler that cruises from Riverside Park. They offer a variety of cruising options: a 90-minute sightseeing cruise (daily 11a,1:30p,3:30p from Memorial Day–Labor Day, with a reduced scheduled in May, Sept. & Oct.; $14.50/person over age 11), weekend dinner cruises (F,Sa,Su 6p except F from Memorial Day–Labor Day cruise departs at 7:30; $33–$42/person over age 11), and a Sunday brunch cruise (11a; $27/person over age 11).

For a more intimate experience, take a ride with **Mississippi Explorer Cruises** (877.688.9260). They run narrated cruises on small boats through the backwaters with an emphasis on river ecology. From

June to August, they offer 90-minute daytime cruises (W–F 10:30a; $15), and two-hour cruises (F 6:30, Sa 2p,6:30, Su 10a; $20); in September and October, only two-hour cruises are offered (Sa 2p,5p, Su 10a). Cruises depart from the south end of Riverside Park.

Goose Island County Park (County Road GI; 608.788.7018) has a signed seven-mile canoe trail that will require some effort to complete, given that part of the route is upstream.

The **La Crosse River Water Trail** (www.ccakc.org) is an easy 3½ mile paddle on a tributary of the Mississippi. Begin at County Highway B just one-quarter mile west of its intersection with Highway 16 and follow it to a point just above the river's confluence with the Black and Mississippi Rivers in Riverside Park.

If you didn't bring a canoe or kayak with you, don't fret; you have options. **Buzz's Bikes and Boats** (800 Rose St.; 608.785.2737; M–F 10–6, Sa 10–5) will rent you a kayak (day/2-4 days/week $20/$40/$70 including paddle and life preserver). **Three Rivers Outdoors** (400 Main St.; 608.793.1470; M–Tu 10–5, W–F 10–7, Sa 10–5, Su 11–4) also rents kayaks ($20/day, $90/week) and canoes of various sizes ($20–$30/day, $90–$110/week). Neither place has a shuttle service, so you'll have to transport the boat yourself. You can also rent a canoe through **Pettibone RV Park** (333 Park Plaza Dr.; 800.738.8426/608.782.5858) and paddle the adjacent backwaters ($10/2 hours, $20/4 hours, $40/day).

Three Rivers Outdoors can also outfit you with camping equipment, skis, and snowshoes. Check with the store for rental prices.

If you'd rather have a boat with a motor, or more precisely, a floating house with a motor, **Huck's Houseboat Rentals** (920.625.3142) can set you up.

Rental rates vary depending on the size of the boat, the season, and the number of days you wish to rent, plus you pay for your own gas. Peak summer rates range from $1595–$3899 for a three-day weekend to $3140–$7999 for a week.

Mississippi River Rentals (608.793.1776) has a single houseboat for rent; it is a 15-foot by 28-foot houseboat docked at Black's Cove Marina (2003 Rose St.). The peak summer rate is $1800/3-day weekend, $3300/week; the cheapest rates are in May and October: $1150–$1250/3-day weekend, $2150–$2195/week. If you are looking for a boat of more modest size, Huck's also rents a 24-foot pontoon boat ($135/3 hours, $279/day); a 23-foot deck boat ($170/3 hours, $349/day), and a 16-foot fishing boat ($50/3 hours, $65/day); all rates are for peak summer periods.

Culture & Arts

The **Pump House Regional Arts Center** (119 King St.; 608.785.1434; Tu–F Noon–5, Sa Noon–4) hosts rotating exhibits highlighting regional art with an occasional national show; they have a theater on the second floor to showcase performing arts.

The **La Crosse Symphony Orchestra** (608.783.2121) plays several concerts a year, generally from October to April, at the Viterbo University Fine Arts Center (929 Jackson St.).

For live theater, check out the schedule at the **La Crosse Community Theater** (118 5th Ave. N.; 608.784.9292); they perform seven shows each year from September to June. And, don't forget to check the schedules for theater productions at **Viterbo University** (Fine Arts Center; 608.796.3100) and **UW-La Crosse** (Toland Theater, 16th and Vine Sts.; 608.785.8522).

Tours

You may not get a chance to tour the old brewhouse for the City Brewery, but don't fret. Head over to **Pearl Street Brewery** (1401 St. Andrew St.; 608.784.4832) on a Saturday afternoon (Noon–5; free), and they'll show you how they make beer.

Entertainment and Events

La Crosse has a three **Farmers Markets** a week in summer at (608.785.9872): Bridgeview Plaza (2500 Rose; W 8a–1p from June–Oct.); Cameron Park (5th and King Sts.; F 4p–8p from May–Oct.); and downtown (4th and Vine Sts; Sa 6a–1p from June–Oct.).

Festivals. If you're in the mood for a cold swim in early March, head to Pettibone Beach for the annual **Polar Plunge** (608.789.7596), the event where otherwise reasonable people strip down and dive into a very cold Mississippi River. At least it's for a good cause: the Special Olympics. La Crosse's major summer festival is **Riverfest** (608.782.6000), which happens the week of July 4th at Riverside Park; join the crowds for food, music, and fireworks. In August, La Crosse hosts the **Great River Jazz Festival** (608.789.7400; La Crosse Center) and the **Great River Folk Festival** (608.784.3033; UW-La Crosse). August is also the month for putting those sandcastle-building skills to work at **Sand on the Riverfront** (800.949.7380/608.784.9450; Riverside Park). Ah, but the the granddaddy of La Crosse festivals is **Oktoberfest** (608.784.3378), and it is one helluva party that is so big it spans two weekends, attracting tens of thousands of visitors. Expect to find a lot of happy people, occasionally a few that are too happy, and enjoy the pomp, parades, and bratwurst. If you are planning to visit La Crosse either weekend, book your room well in advance, or you'll be driving an hour from town to find a place to stay.

Music. In the 19th century, La Crosse residents enjoyed the music of German brass bands, a cornet band, choral music, church choirs, light opera, and a Norwegian men's choral group called *Normanna Saengerkor*. You probably won't find any of those today, but the city still has some good options to get your music fix. **NIGHTHAWKS TAP** (401 3rd St. South; 608.785.7427; M–F 4p–2a, Sa 7p–2:30a) is a cavernous bar with live blues and jazz most nights of the week. The bands at **JB'S SPEAKEASY** (717 Rose St.; 608.796.1161; M–Th 5p–2a, F,Sa 5p–2:30a, Su for football), a fun dive bar frequented by a late 20s/early 30s crowd, are a bit more varied: one night you might get a little hardcore and the next punk-rock honky tonk. For a more sedate experience, the lounges at the **WATERFRONT TAVERN** (328 Front St.; 608.782.5400) and **PIGGY'S RESTAURANT** (501 Front St. South; 608.784.4877) have live jazz on many evenings. **THE ROOT NOTE** (115 S. 4th St.; 608.782.7668; Su–W 8:30a–10p, Th–Sa 8:30a–midnight) hosts a jazz improv session on Tuesday nights and weekend concerts from regional musicians that lean toward folk/singer-songwriter types.

Drinking

La Crosse has a reputation as a hard-drinking town and, frankly, it's hard to argue the point, especially after a drive down Third Street any night after 10pm. Although downtown bars draw a wide range of people, many cater to the college crowd. Not that you wouldn't be welcome; you would. Just don't expect a lot of high-brow entertainment. Here are a few bars around town that stand out from the rest. The **PEARL STREET BREWERY** (1401 St. Andrew St.; 608.784.4832) is housed in the former La Crosse Footwear building; visit the tasting room and enjoy their beer directly from the source (Tu–F 4p–8p). The **BODEGA BREW PUB** (122 S. 4th St.; 608.782.0677; Su–Th 10a–2a, F,Sa 10a–2:30a), located in the storefront that has had a café since 1875, is a must stop if you love quality beer; they have over a dozen on tap and 400+ in bottles. **THE STARLITE LOUNGE** (222 Pearl St.; 608.796.0905; Th–Sa 4p–close) has a 1950s vibe and is the hip place for martini lovers; they host live jazz a couple of times a week. **THE EAGLE'S NEST** (1914 Campbell Rd.; 608.782.7764; daily 11a–2a) is a popular sports bar next to UW-La Crosse. Sitting at the top of the road to Grandad Bluff, the **ALPINE INN** (W5717 Bliss Rd.; 608.784.8470; Su–Th 11a–2a, F,Sa 11a–2:30a; will close earlier if slow) is a fine place to stop for a drink, especially if you brought a designated driver.

For the straight dope on the gay scene, stop into the **LGBT RESOURCE CENTER** (303 Pearl St.; 608.784.0452; M–W,F 9:30–6, Tu 9:30–5, Th 10–2, 5p–9p, Sa 11–4). Gay bars include the neighborhood taverns **MY PLACE** (3201 South Avenue; 608.788.9073; M–Th 3p–2a, F 3p–2:30a, Sa Noon–2:30a, Su Noon–2a) and **CHANCES R** (417 Jay Street; 608.782.5105; Su-Th 3p–2a, F,Sa 3p–2:30a), and the dance-oriented **PLAYERS** (300 4th St. S.; 608.784.4200; Tu–Th 5p–2a, F,Sa 3p–2:30a, Su 3p–2a), which also hosts the occasional drag show.

Sports and Recreation

It isn't quite like what you may have seen in the 1970s movie *Rollerball*, but women's flat track derby is back and La Crosse has two teams: the **La Crosse Skating Sirens** (www.skatingsirens.com; $7–$13.50) and the **Mississippi Valley Mayhem** (mississippivalleymayhem.com; $5). The action will keep you on the edge of your seat as the five-player teams roll and push and elbow their way to victory. They usually play one game a month; check their websites for the schedule.

The **La Crosse Loggers** (Copeland Park; 608.796.9553) are a member of the Northwoods League, a summer league for college players with remaining NCAA eligibility; players do not get paid, so they can preserve their college eligibility. The atmosphere feels very much like a good minor league game; prices range from just $3 for standing room to $9 for field level box seats.

New in 2010, the **La Crosse Spartans** (La Crosse Center; 608.567.4299) compete in the Indoor Football League. Single game tickets run $10 to $33.

> RANDOM FACT: *La Crosse native George Coleman Poage was a gifted track star who was the first black athlete to win a medal at the Olympic Games. He won a bronze medal in the 200-meter and 400-meter hurdles at the 1904 St. Louis games. Poage was also a gifted polyglot: he could read and write five languages.*

Hixon Forest (608.784.0303) is an 800-acre preserve with 13 miles of hiking trails that lead up and through the forest and to at least three overlooks. The trails are part of the **River to Bluff Trail**, which makes it possible to hike or bike from the Mississippi River to the bluff tops without having to cross a city street. In the winter, some of the trails are groomed for cross-country skiing or snowshoeing (rent snowshoes for $5/day through the park office).

Mississippi Valley Conservancy (608.784.3606) manages several bluff top properties that were donated to protect them from development. The most accessible is the **Hass Tract** (Easter Rd.). After a moderately difficult uphill hike, you can explore goat prairies at the top and enjoy good views of the river valley.

Human Powered Trails (608.785.0000) builds and maintains multi-use trails atop the bluffs; the trailhead is next to National Weather Service station on County Road FA. Currently, they have 11 miles of trails of varying difficulty that are used by horseback riders, joggers, hikers, and mountain bikers.

La Crosse just may be the bicycling capital of Wisconsin. If you didn't bring your own, you can rent from **Buzz's Bikes and Boats** (800 Rose St.; 608.785.2737; M–F 10–6, Sa 10–5; day/2–4 days/week $15/$30/$60) or from **La Crosse Bike Rentals** (324 S. 3rd St.; 608.782.7233), which has mountain bikes, hybrid bikes, cruising bikes ($6/hr, $18/day) and tandems ($10/hr, $38/day). Once you are equipped with a bicycle, ride it along the **La Crosse River State Trail** (888.540.8434/608.269.4123), a 21.5 mile bike trail from La Crosse to Sparta ($4/day or $15/annual pass).

If you'd rather relax with a swim, La Crosse has three public beaches: the **Black River Beach** (1400 Rose St.; 608.789.7557; open June–Aug), **Pettibone Beach** (Pettibone Park; 608.789.7557; daily 10–6), and at **Goose Island County Park** (County GI; 608.788.7018). If you'd rather swim in a pool, you're in luck. The City of La Crosse Parks and Recreation Department operates three public swimming pools: **Erickson Pool** (2412 Losey Blvd.; 608.791.8918), **Memorial Pool** (1901 Campbell Rd.; 608.791.8918), and **North Side Community Pool** (1450 Liberty St.; 608.791.8956); daily admission is $3 for adults; call for open swim times.

In winter, the city has a number of outdoor skating rinks. If you want to skate indoors, head to the **Green Island Ice Arena** (2312 7th St. South; 608.789.7199; mid-October–February; $3/adult; $3/skate rental; call for open skate hours). If you prefer

The Leona

Leona Foerster

If you were alive in 1900—and a woman—a crucial part of your wardrobe might be a piece of clothing called *The Leona*. This cutting edge garment combined a corset, slip, and camisole into a single piece. The designer was Leona Foerster, born 1872 in La Crosse. She worked as a seamstress from an early age and was teaching others to sew when she was still a young girl. She became a designer for Chicago's Gossard Corset Company and traveled throughout Europe as a sales agent for the company. She returned to La Crosse in 1905 and patented *The Leona*. In 1907, she founded The Leona Garment Company and kept it going until 1920 when changing fashions reduced demand.

something more vertical, take your skis or snowboard to **Mount La Crosse** (N5549 Old Town Rd.; 800.426.3665/608.788.0044; M–F 10a–9p, Sa,Su 9–9). At press time, an all-day lift ticket was $46 ($24 for 4p–9p); an all-day ski rental package was $28 ($19 for 4p–9p); and all-day snowboard rental was $34 ($25 for 4p–9p).

> **RANDOM FACT:** *From January 17 to the end of February, 1936, La Crosse had exactly two days with a temperature above 0° F. A few months later, residents suffered through nice consecutive 100° F days in July. This is what you call a highly variable climate.*

Shopping

Indulge your shopping urges in downtown, home to boutique clothing stores, jewelers, hair salons, and many specialty stores. **GALLERY LA CROSSE** (320 Main St.; 608.782.4278; W–Sa 11–6) is a retail gallery for local artists; you'll find jewelry, photography, folk art, paintings, and other fun stuff. I think you can figure out that **FINNOTTE'S NUT & CHOCOLATE SHOP** (535 Main St.; 608.782.3184; M–F 9:30–5:30 Sa 10–3) sells gourmet chocolates and nuts, purchased from top-notch producers. **MAY'S COMMUNITY CAMERA** (425 Main St.; 608.782.1535; M–F 10–5:30, Sa 10–2) is an independent camera shop specializing in customer service and equipped with 21st century toys; they can clean the sensor of your digital camera in a day or two. **PEARL STREET BOOKS** (323 Pearl St.; 608.782.3424; M–Th 10–8, F 10–9, Sa 10–5, Su Noon–5) sells mostly used books but some new ones, too; they have a good selection of books about the river and by local and regional authors (like me). At **GENEROUS EARTH POTTERY** (221 Pearl St.; 608.484.1902; W,Th 11–5, F 11–6, Sa,Su 11–4), potter Karen Bressi might be throwing pottery in the front window when you walk by; you will find beautiful pieces at very reasonable prices. **SATORI ARTS** (201 Pearl St.; 608.785.2779; M–F 10–6, Sa 10–5, Su Noon–4) has a rather quirky collection of hand-crafted jewelry, fine art, and imported art from China. If you really want quirky, though, step in to the **CHEDDARHEADS GIFT GALLERY** (215 Pearl St.; 608.784.8899; M,W 11–5, Th 10–5, F 10–9, Sa 10–5 Su Noon–4) and buy something with a Wisconsin theme, like a cheese-shaped beer cozy or even real Wisconsin cheese. If you like old-time record stores, then you don't miss **DEAF EAR RECORDS** (112 S. 4th St.; 608.782.7829; M–Th 9–7, F,Sa 9–8, Su 11–6), an independent music store that has been in business for over 30 years; they sell new and used music across genres and formats including vinyl. The **ANTIQUE CENTER OF LA CROSSE** (110 S. 3rd St.; 608.782.6533; M–Sa 9–5:30, Su 11–5:30) has three floors of glassware, collectibles, old cameras, post cards, vinyl, and more in an antique building.

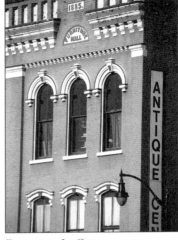

Downtown La Crosse

On the city's north side, **GIFTED HANDS** (1200 Caledonia; 608.784.4500; M–F 9:30–5, Sa 9:30–4) sells crafts that your grandmother might have made, which makes sense because all of the items are made by local residents who are at least 50 years of age: doilies, quilts, woodwork, clothing.

Random Weird Fact: *On July 8, 1938 an invasion of June bugs piled 18-30" deep under the lights on the Mississippi River wagon bridge; the city used snowplows to clear them.*

Eating ✘

La Crosse has surprisingly few ethnic restaurants—given the number of college students—and putting Canadian bacon on a pizza is considered a sign of culinary diversity.

Coffee shops. It's a college town, so there are good places to catch a caffeine buzz. **JULES COFFEE HOUSE** (327 Pearl St.; 608.796.1200; M–Sa 7:30a–midnight, Su 7:30a–11p) also has good soup, beer, and wine and the added bonus of being connected to Pearl Street Books. At **GROUNDED SPECIALTY COFFEE** (308 Main St.; 608.784.5282; M–Sa 6–6, Su 8a–3p), it's not just the coffee that's perky; smiles abound from the friendly staff. **THE ROOT NOTE** (115 S. 4th St.; 608.782.7668; Su–W 8:30a–10p, Th–Sa 8:30a–midnight) has quickly become my personal favorite. Besides offering the standard coffee drinks, they have a vegetarian menu that emphasizes sustainable food products ($5–$8 for mains), local wine and beer, and a funky atmosphere in an historic downtown commercial building that is decorated with the work of local artists.

Breakfast. FAYZE'S RESTAURANT AND BAKERY (135 S. 4th St.; 608.784.9548; breakfast served M–F 6:30a–11:30a, Sa,Su 6:30a–1:30p) is a long-time local favorite. The extensive breakfast menu includes familiar items but also surprises like the Santa Fe Scrambler with eggs, grilled peppers and onions, pepper jack, and jalapeño bacon atop grilled jalapeño cheddar sourdough bread ($4.29); I'm salivating just thinking about it. You can eat a hearty breakfast for about $5. For a traditional diner breakfast, head to deep south La Crosse for **ROSIE'S CAFÉ** (2225 16th Street S.; 608.788.9004; M–F 5:30a–2p, Sa,Su 7a–1p) where you can fill up on a breakfast skillet, cinnamon roll, and waffles (most breakfast entrées $4–$7).

Light fare. PICKERMAN'S (327 Jay St.; 608.782.7087; M–Sa 10:30–7:30) is a good choice for freshly made soup and sandwiches on bread baked in-house ($5 for a sandwich; $7 for combo meal); they have at least six soups available every day. **CHA GUAN TEA SHOP** (400 Main St.; 608.448.5378; M–F 8–6, Sa 10–6, Su 10–4) is a new place offering dim sum like ShaoMai ($2.50 for 5), shrimp dumplings ($2.50 for 5), and mini pork buns (0.75¢), plus bubble tea and traditional Chinese tea; they are hidden behind the Three Rivers Outfitters store. The **BODEGA BREW PUB** (122 S. 4th St.; 608.782.0677; Su–Th 10a–2a, F,Sa 10a–2:30a) makes lighter fare like sandwiches and soup ($4–$8.25) and is a good late-night option. **THE PEOPLE'S FOOD COOP** (315 5th Ave. S.; 608.784.5798; daily 7a–10p) specializes in organic and locally-produced foods but they also have a number of delicious ready-to-eat foods prepared fresh every day; the impressive salad bar may be the best bargain in the store ($4.99/lb). If you'd like to sip some wine while snacking, check out the **WINE GUYZ** (122 King St.; 608.782.9463; M 11–8, Tu-Th 11–10, F,Sa 11–11) where you can get wine by the glass or flights for about $7. On the food front, you can snack on pizza or cheese plates ($8–$10), or choose from among the Panini and other sandwiches ($5–$6.50). **PIGGY'S RESTAURANT** (501 Front St. South; 608.784.4877) is a local landmark, and, while many folks opt for an evening of expensive dining, I think the best bet is to go there for lunch (11a–2p) and go hog wild at the impressive salad bar, which is loaded with fresh ingredients, plenty of green lettuce and spinach (not a hint of iceberg to be found), and made-from-scratch soups and salad dressings ($9); add a half-sandwich for just $2 more and take it with you for your next meal. Reservations are a good idea.

Hearty options. RUDY'S DRIVE-IN (1004 La Crosse St.; 608.782.2200; daily 10–10 from March–Oct.) is a classic and still a local favorite and not just for the servers on rollerskates. You can splurge on a big burger made to order for about $4 and add a basket (fries and cole-slaw) for $2 more; wash it down with a draft root beer. **BIG AL'S** (115 S. 3rd St.; 608.782.7550; Su–Th 11–11, F,Sa 11a–midnight) is housed in a fun and quirky setting decorated with transportation-themed mobiles. Go there for the pizza, though—a thin and crispy crust generously topped with quality ingredients. You can get an 8-inch pizza with cheese for about $6 or load up a 16-inch monster with all the fixins for $29. While many folks insist Big Al's has the best pizza in town, fans of **KATE'S PIZZA AMORE** (212 Main St.; 608.782.6673; Tu–Su 4p–10p) would beg to differ. Inside the sleek, modern décor outfitted with chandeliers made of colored wine bottles, you can delight in gourmet pizza from the same person who owns the standout Kate's on State. Pizza sizes run from individual (8"/$10–$14) to large (16"/$21–$33) with creative topping combinations like the Mediterranean (shrimp, chorizo, chick peas, sun-dried tomato pesto, spinach, olives, feta cheese, pine nuts). **BUZZARD BILLY'S** (222 Pearl St.; 608.796.2277; M–Th 11:30–10, F 11:30–11, Sa 11–11, Su 11–10) serves Cajun food that is tasty and usually has a nice kick. Choose from traditional dishes like red beans and rice, jambalaya, or blackened catfish ($6–$14) or go with a po'boy for a more affordable option ($7). **TRES COMPADRES MEXICAN GRILL**

& CANTINA (115 5th Ave. S.; 608.782.2021; daily 11a–10p) has an interior designed like a courtyard in a Mexican country village. The wide-ranging menu goes beyond standard Mexican-American restaurant fare, with several varieties of steaks ($12–$13), two types of mole ($10), and many other opportunities to try something other than a burrito, although they have that, too (most entrées $8–$11). **HMONG GOLDEN EGGROLLS RESTAURANT** (929 State St.; 608.782.0096; M–Sa 11–9) is about the only place in town to get decent food with a Southeast Asian influence (pho, curries, etc.). Everything is under $10 and most items are $6–$8; they have many vegetarian options. The namesake eggrolls are delicious, the size of zucchini, and a good value ($1.35).

 Fine dining. THE FREIGHT HOUSE (107 Vine St.; 608.784.6211; Su–Th 5p–9p-ish, F,Sa 5p–10p-ish) is a popular choice for high quality steaks and seafood in a historic 1880-era railroad warehouse that can get a bit loud; steak entrées (10 options!) are mostly around $25; pork chops, chicken, and vegetarian entrées run a little less ($17–$20) while seafood entrées like king crab legs, salmon, and lobster can be ordered as half ($17–$34) or full orders ($22–$48). **THE WATERFRONT RESTAURANT AND TAVERN** (328 Front St. South; 608.782.5400; M–Th, 5–9:30, F,Sa 5–10:30) offers a number of sophisticated entrées that change with the seasons; a recent winter menu was seafood-heavy and included coconut-curried mussels, a meat-free Corsican linguini, prosciutto-wrapped pork tenderloin, steaks, and lamb (entrées from $15–$32); lunch is served during the week (M–F 11–2:30) with a wide selection of sandwiches, salads, and soups for under $10. **HUCK FINN'S ON THE WATER** (127 Marina Dr.; 608.791.3595; Su–Th 11–9, F,Sa 11–10) is set on a bay on the Black River, with something of a Key West vibe, next to a marina where you can stare at the big boats and wish you had one. The menu includes steak and fish like catfish and walleye (entrées $14–$19). The lunch menu has a number of more affordable options, mostly sandwiches for about $7. When I walked into **DIGGER'S STING** (122 3rd St. N.; 608.782.3796; M 11a–9p, Tu–Th 11a–10p, F 11a–10:30p, Sa 4p–10:30, Su 4p–9p in winter), I expected to bump into Vito Corleone; the dark interior suggests 1940s gangster chic. Locals love the prime rib ($21 for 10 ounces) but they prepare a range of other meat-centric entrées like beef tenderloin, baby back ribs, and chicken marinara (mostly $20–$25) or you can opt for the less expensive salad and sandwich options ($9–$14). Did I mention the mushrooms? Oh, those mushrooms…

★**Author's Pick:** In a city with more than its fair share of fine dining, **KATE'S ON STATE** (1810 State St.; 608.784.3354; Tu–Su 5–9) has set a new standard. Ched Kate Gerrard takes classic Italian cuisine and ramps it up until the flavors explode in your mouth. Sure, the portion sizes are generous but dishes like pesto prawns with tortellini will open your eyes and satisfy your belly in new ways (entrées $18–$29). Even the side salad is rich with flavor, with mixed greens, grapefruit, hearts of palm, fresh mozzarella, red onion, soy nuts, and beans. Kate's is a small place; if you are serious about eating here (and you should be), make a reservation; you won't get in on a weekend without one.

Ice cream. La Crosse can help you with that ice cream fix, too. **THE SWEET SHOP** (1113 Caledonia St.; 608.784.7724; M–F 9–7, Sa 9–6, Su Noon–5) is an old-fashioned ice cream parlor, the kind where they still make their own ice cream and have since 1921 and you can get one of those old-fashioned

Rivertown Brothels

Brothels were a common feature of frontier towns, and Mississippi River towns were no exception. In La Crosse, the red light district was along the riverfront, roughly between Jay and King Streets.

Brothels were technically illegal but that didn't stop the city from regulating them. Prostitutes needed a license and routine health inspections to get that license. Arrests were rare but did occur. Typically, the madam would get a $50 fine, while the working girls might be fined $10.

In 1913, La Crosse had upwards of 50 brothels in operation. In that year Ori Sorensen ran for mayor vowing to clean things up; he won but didn't get too far and his successor, John Langdon, was rumored to have a brothel operating above his butcher shop.

The Mississippi House was a well-known brothel that operated from 1856 to 1889 and was a regular stop for rivermen with a reputation for being a bit rougher than the other places. Anna Bennett was one of the best known madams; she ran the European Hotel (216 N. 2nd Street) from 1925 to 1946. The normal rate for services at that time was $2 ($1 for the madam and $1 for the working girl); Ma Bennett charged $5. And, just so you don't think I'm picking on La Crosse, Winona (Minnesota) had brothels into the 1990s, when El Cid's finally closed.

sodas with fizzy water. Oh, they also make chocolates. **THE PEARL ICE CREAM PARLOR** (207 Pearl St.; 608.782.6655; Su–Th 9–9, F,Sa 9a–10p) is another old-fashioned soda fountain where they make their own; get a double scoop in a waffle cone for $2.85, a root beer float for $3, or a banana split for $4.20. And, let's not forget **RANISON ICE CREAM** (706 16th St. South; 608.782.1987; M–Sa 9a–10p, Su 10a–9p), a charming neighborhood shop with deep roots in the area that also makes it own ice cream.

Sleeping

Reminder: If you are going to be in La Crosse for OktoberFest, you should book a room well in advance.

Camping. Well off the beaten path, **BLUEBIRD SPRING RECREATION AREA** (N2833 Smith Valley Rd.; 608.781.2267) has a number of primitive sites ($18+tax) and electric only sites ($28+tax) at the back end of a coulee; many of the primitive sites are in an open field with little shade. **GOOSE ISLAND COUNTY PARK** (W6488 County Road GI; 608.788.7018) packs in the campers in its 400 sites; don't expect spacious, private sites, but the area is beautiful and many sites are next to the river ($18/tent to $24/water & elec). **PETTIBONE RV PARK** (333 Park Plaza Dr.; 800.738.8426/608.782.5858; WiFi) is another large campground, this one in the floodplain along the backwaters; sites have plenty of shade but not much space ($19/primitive site, $33/water & elec).

Budget. THE GUEST HOUSE MOTEL (810 S. 4th St.; 800.274.6873/608.784.8840; WiFi) has 39 well-kept, quiet rooms in a very convenient downtown location ($60–$76+tax). **WELCH MOTEL** (3643 Mormon Coulee Rd.; 608.788.1300; WiFi) has a 1950s vibe, especially on the exterior, with 16 tidy rooms that have been updated ($65–$110 + tax).

View from Riverside Park

THE MAPLE GROVE MOTEL (5212 Mormon Coulee Rd.; 608.788.0353) has 26 small, simple rooms with cable TV that are in good shape; some rooms have a kitchenette ($55–$65 incl tax). The 22 rooms at the **AFFORDABLE INN** (614 Monitor St.; 608.784.2278; WiFi) are larger than other budget places and in decent shape but won't win any awards for style ($55+tax). **THE ADRIATIC MOTEL** (3438 Mormon Coulee Rd.; 608.788.1811; WiFi) is set back from a busy road. The 10 rooms got a top-to-bottom overhaul in recent years and have a modern feel; they are moderately sized, all have king-sized beds, fridge, microwave, and cable TV ($55+tax).

Bed and Breakfast. The **FOUR GABLES BED & BREAKFAST** (W5648 Highway 14-61; 608.788.7958; WiFi) has two guest rooms with private baths, ($90–$100 + tax, incl full breakfast) in a Queen Anne house built in 1906; they have an overflow room for parties of three ($60+tax); rooms are comfortable and furnished with antiques but not overflowing with them; no credit cards.

Cabins/Houses. THE COTTAGE (756 N. 22nd St.; 608.317.4311; WiFi) is a 600-square foot converted garage that is set back from the street; it has two bedrooms, satellite TV, a kitchen with full-size appliances, and a bathroom with shower ($125 + tax for 4 guests; $15 for each additional guest). **THE WILSON SCHOOLHOUSE INN** (W5718 Highway 14-61; 608.787.1982; WiFi) is another distinctive place to stay. The former brick schoolhouse, built in 1917, has been converted to a gorgeous and comfortable inn, with a spacious living room bathed in generous amounts of natural light and some original features left intact (like part of the a chalkboard). The inn has two bedrooms, two bathrooms, and a modern kitchen and could sleep up to eight guests ($155 +tax/double; $30/each additional person). The inn is easy to miss, because it is shielded by a row of evergreen trees.

Moderate. There are two chain hotels that have rooms on the downtown riverfront. **THE RADISSON HOTEL** (200 Harborview Plaza; 800.333.3333/608.784.6680; WiFi) is a high-rise hotel with 169 rooms that is popular with wedding parties; the rooms on the west side have river views ($179–$246+tax). The **COURTYARD BY MARRIOTT** (500 Front St.; 800.321.2211/608.782.1000; WiFi) is further south in a cluster of newer riverfront buildings; the hotel has 78 rooms, some with river views ($179–$209+tax).

★ **Author's Pick:** You won't find a more unique place to stay than the **BLUFF VIEW HOUSE** (751 22nd St. N.; 608.317.4311; WiFi). Built in 1949, this is one of only 2499 Lustron pre-fab all-metal houses built in the US and one of about 1600 left. The two-bedroom house has a full bath, full kitchen, washer and dryer, garage, and bicycles available for guests ($125+tax for 4 guests; $15 for each additional guest).

Resources

- The *La Crosse Tribune* (608.782.9710) is the local daily newspaper. The *Second Supper* (608.782.7001) is the alternative weekly paper and has a good guide to local live music scene.
- Downtown post office: 425 State St.; 608.791.8100.
- La Crosse Public Library: 800 Main St.; 608.789.7100; WiFi; M–Th 9–9, F,Sa 9–5,Su 1–5.
- Public Radio Station: 90.3, WHLA.

Getting To and Out of Dodge ✈

La Crosse is one of the stops along **Amtrak's Empire Builder** route. The train station is on the north side under the Rose Street viaduct (601 Caledonia; 800.872.7245; office open daily 8:30a–11:30a, 6p–8:30p); westbound trains depart La Crosse at 7:14p for destinations along the Mississippi River that include Winona (36 minutes), Red Wing (1 ½ hours), St. Paul/Minneapolis (3 hours 15 minutes), and St. Cloud (5 ½ hours) before continuing on through the western United States to Seattle. Eastbound trains depart La Crosse at 10:47a ending at Chicago (5 hours). Fares are based on the number of available seats and therefore vary considerably; in general, the earlier you book, the cheaper the ticket will be.

Jefferson Lines (800.451.5333) operates regional bus service with once daily eastbound connections to Tomah, Madison, and Milwaukee (4½ hours to Milwaukee; M–Th,Sa 12:05p, F,Su 5:20p) and once daily westbound connections to Winona, Rochester, Minneapolis (3 hrs 10 min to Mpls; M-Th,Sa 3:20p, F,Su 5:20p). Schedules and fares are so damn confusing and change so often, you are better off just calling them directly for the most current info. What I can tell you is that the cheapest rates are for 21-day advance purchase, especially for travel Su–Th. The bus stops at the Amtrak station (601 Andrews, M–Th,Sa 11a–4p, F 1p–5:30p) and at UW-La Crosse (Whitney Center, 1451 Badger St. from Aug–May; buy tickets at the Cartwright Center information desk). If you are buying tickets at the last minute, check fares for Amtrak, too.

The **La Crosse Municipal Airport** is north of downtown on French Island (608.789.7464); it is served by American Eagle and Delta. Short-term parking is $1.25/half-hour. There is no taxi stand; use the phones across from the rental car counter to call for one. There is also bus service to the airport through MTU bus route #7, but it is not very convenient. Busses only run M–F (service from 6:08a–5:38p) and to reach downtown La Crosse, you must transfer at the Clinton/Caledonia stop to route #6.

Getting Around

Bus service is provided by the **La Crosse MTU** (608.789.7350; operating hours generally M–F from 5a–10p Sa, Su 7a–7p but exact times vary by route; standard adult fare is $1.25 incl transfer). Each bus has a bike rack with space for two bikes (no additional charge). Buses run every half hour or hour, depending upon the route; after 6p, you can ask to be dropped off at a location other than a designated stop. Later at night, free rides are offered from the downtown bars to campus locations (Th 10p–3a, F,Sa 9p–3a).

Rental cars. Three companies have counters at the airport: **National/Alamo** (800.227.7368), **Hertz** (800.654.3131), and **Avis** (800.331.1212). In town, you can rent from **Enterprise** (227 3rd St. South; 608.785.7400) or **Hertz** (600 4th St. South; 608.782.6183).

FRENCH ISLAND

(4,376)

Bounded by the Mississippi River on one side and the Black River on the other, French Island is an unincorporated part of the La Crosse region that has some of the best waterfront views.

Arriving in Town

The only routes onto the island are from Interstate 90 in the middle and Clinton Street on the south. The main north-south routes are County Highways B (Bainbridge St., then Dawson Ave., then Fanta Reed Rd.) and County Highway BW (Lake Shore Dr.).

History

French Island (technically the Town of Campbell) gets its name from the presence of early French Canadian settlers on the island. One of the earliest arrivals was Montreal native Xavier Goyette, who arrived in 1849 after living in Dubuque for a while. Another major figure was Moses Jolivette, also from Montreal; he settled on the island in 1852. Then again, maybe the island is named for the Englishman Joseph French, who arrived in 1851 and farmed 360 acres on the island. I found sources that attributed the island's name to both stories, so pick your favorite.

French Island had a few sawmills but farming was the main industry for generations. When North La Crosse was annexed in 1871, the Town of Campbell was split in two (it used to go much further west). Because state law requires that townships be contiguous, the section east of North La Crosse became the Town of Medary. The township lost some land when the lock and dam system was built and a bit more to the expanding cities of La Crosse and Onalaska. La Crosse has tried many times—unsuccessfully—to annex the entire township. Residents have made a few attempts to incorporate as a village (as recently as 2002), but there just hasn't been a lot of enthusiasm for the idea.

Tourist Information ⓘ

Contact the **Visitors Center** in Riverside Park (800.658.9424/608.782.2366) or the one at Bridgeview Plaza on the north side near Interstate 90 (2500 Rose St.); both centers are open all year (M–Sa 10–6, Su 10–4 in summer, M–Sa 10:30–4:30, Su 10:30–4 the rest of the year).

Attractions

On the northwest part of the island, quiet **Nelson Park** (Lakeshore Dr.; 608.789.7533) is a great place to picnic next to Lake Onalaska. Follow Lakeshore Drive until it ends.

The **Upper Midwest Environmental Sciences Center** (2630 Fanta Reed Rd.; 608.781.6398; M–F 8a–4p; free) is part of the US Geological Survey and home to unheralded scientists who are doing important work to improve water quality and reduce the impact of invasive species. There are exhibits in the lobby describing their work; you can also sign in at the desk and walk down to the outdoor classroom, which is along the backwaters and has a hiking trail through three ecosystems: oak savanna, prairie, and bottomland forest. Tours of the rest of the facility (including the tanks where they breed fish for their research) can be arranged for groups of at least 10 people with advance notice.

If you take County Highway B to Fanta Reed Road and follow it around the east side of the airport, it will become **Fishermans Road** and wind around the airport to the north; this narrow strip of undeveloped land has boat ramps and many places to stop and enjoy Lake Onalaska (daily 5a–10p).

For more information and updates, visit my web site at www.mississippivalleytraveler.com.

ONALASKA

(14,839)

A community with old roots that began because of a chain of logs floating down the Black River, Onalaska today is a bedroom community that has evolved into a haven for chain stores.

Arriving in Town

The River Road enters town as 2nd Avenue; Main Street (State Highway 157) runs east.

History

Thomas Rowe, a native New Yorker, arrived in the area in 1851, apparently with the idea of opening a tavern to serve the lumberjacks working along the Black River, which seems like it must have been a good idea, given their numbers in the area. Mr. Rowe was a fan of Thomas Campbell whose poem *The Pleasures of Hope* references a town in the Alaskan Aleutian Islands that provided the inspiration for the town's name:

> "Now fore he sweeps, where scarce a summer smiles,
>
> On Behring's rocks, or Greenland's naked isles;
>
> Cold on his midnight watch the breezes blow;
>
> From wastes that slumber in eternal snow,
>
> And waft across the waves' tumultuous roar,
>
> The wolf's long howl from Oonalaska's shore."

William Carlisle, a lumberman by trade, was so taken with the name that after he left the area, he used it three more times to establish communities in Arkansas, Texas, and Washington.

Back to lumber. The first sawmill went up around 1853, and by 1856 there were three sawmills in operation and two more under construction. Most of the workers were immigrants from Germany and Norway. From 1855 to 1899, over six billion board feet of lumber floated down the Black River to Onalaska. That's enough lumber to build two million three-bedroom, 1000-square-foot ranch houses. That's a lot of lumber. During the early years, the mills kicked out a lot of sawdust as a byproduct; for a while, the sawdust was dumped on roads to make them more passable, which turned out to be not such a good idea, because sawdust is, of course, flammable and, while flaming streets might be really cool effect in a video game, they aren't so good for a town trying to convince people to stick around. The lumber business peaked in 1892; 10 years later it was essentially done, as the forests had been depleted. Employment at the Black River mills fell from 1785 in 1899 to 39 just six years later.

Now back to Onalaska. Onalaska grew more slowly than its neighbor because La Crosse had a more favorable river port and a railroad station 12 years earlier. After the mills closed, Onalaska dipped into a recession; light manufacturing and agriculture gradually turned the economy around. One of the light manufacturers was the Onalaska Pickle and Canning factory, which occupies 12 pages in the local history book. They packed pickles, cabbage, peas, and corn beginning in 1906, shipping sauerkraut around the world until closing in 1958. Onalaska was a favorite ending point for sleighing expeditions; arriving sleighers would throw a big party, drinking and sometimes fighting, although this activity probably had less of an economic impact than light manufacturing and agriculture.

Onalaska expanded to the north and east in the

Logs floating down the Black River (Area Research Center, UW-LaCrosse)

1960s but this growth was mostly residential. In 1982, the city annexed land in the Town of Medary around Valley View Mall after a lengthy legal dispute and promptly licensed developers to build the strip mall hell that you see today.

> **Random Fact:** *Onalaska is the hometown of the Gullikson brothers (Tom and Tim), professional tennis players who excelled at doubles play in the 1980s. Tim also achieved fame as the coach who helped Pete Sampras to 14 Grand Slam titles before a brain tumor cut his life short in 1996.*

Tourist Information ⓘ

You can find out everything you need to know about Onalaska and the surrounding area at the **Onalaska Center for Commerce & Tourism** (1101 Main St.; 800.873.1901/608.781.9570; May–Oct open M–F 8–Noon & 1–5, Sa 9–3 Su 9–2; the rest of the year open M–F 8-Noon & 1–5).

Attractions 💡

The wide expanse of water to the west of town is known as **Lake Onalaska**, although it is obviously part of the Mississippi River. The lake was formed when Lock and Dam 7 was completed in the 1930s.

The lake flooded low-lying sections of French Island and obscured what was once the Black River channel along the east side of French Island. By the 1970s sedimentation was causing the lake to fill in. A 1976 report found that the lake had lost 31% of its volume since being created. Local folks organized the Lake Onalaska Protection and Rehabilitation District to push for more effective management policies. The lake is very popular with folks who like to fish; in winter ice fishing shacks spread out across the section between French Island and Brice Prairie.

The **Sunfish overlook** on State Highway 35 is a great place to look out over the lake. (I honestly don't know the name of this overlook, but it has a two-ton sculpture of Onalaska's sunfish mascot, Sunny, hence my name.) It's a popular place for sunset watching (and for speed traps).

The **Onalaska Area Historical Museum** (741 Oak Ave. S.; 608.781.9568; W–F 2p–4p, Sa 9a–Noon, plus M 6p–8p from Oct–March) uses a room at the Onalaska Public Library to display Native American artifacts and exhibits about the lumber history, and local schools, plus an occasional rotating exhibit.

Entertainment and Events ♫

Onalaska hosts a **Farmers Market** (Festival Foods, 1260 Crossing Meadows Dr.; 608.781.2278) on Sunday mornings (8a–1p) from June through October.

Festivals. **Sunfish Days** (608.781.9570) was not held in 2010, but, when it resumes in 2011, you can expect live music, a carnival, a parade, and a kids fishing tournament. Hmong refugees began moving into the area in the 1970s and now have a community that counts several thousand. Join them in October for the **Hmong New Year's Celebration** (608.781.5744) in Veteran's Park (on Highway 16 near West Salem). You can sample food that is not widely available in the region and take part in events that celebrate Hmong culture ($15/car).

Sports and Recreation

The **Great River State Trail** is a 24-mile multi-use trail of crushed limestone that runs from Onalaska to Trempealeau; the trailhead is on the west side of Highway 35 at Main Street. The Great River Trail connects to the **La Crosse River State Trail**, which runs about 22 miles from La Crosse to Sparta. For both trails, persons 16 years old and up must have a trail pass ($4/day; 800.873.1901/608.781.9570). A convenient place to buy a pass is at **Blue Heron Bicycle Works** (213 Main St.; 608.783.7433; M–F 10–6, Sa 10–4), which is just one block from the trailhead of the Great River Trail. At Blue Heron, you can also rent bicycles ($15/day).

Onalaska has a public swimming pool at the **Onalaska Aquatic Center** (250 Riders Club Rd.; 608.781.9560; open Memorial Day–Labor Day with open swim M–F 12:30–4:30, 6:30–8:30, Sa Noon–7, Su Noon–5; $4/day for non-residents).

> **RANDOM FACT:** *In 1886, a 52-pound boy caught a 44-pound catfish in the Black River.*

Eating and Drinking

The **SEVEN BRIDGES RESTAURANT** (910 2nd Ave. North; 608.783.6103; daily 4p–close; happy hour daily 4p–6p) has a large patio with expansive views of the river and is a good spot to enjoy a cocktail. **NUT BUSH CITY LIMITS BAR & GRILL** (3264 George St.; 608.783.0228) is about as local as it gets. Breakfast is their best meal (6a–3p) and is affordable and hearty. You can easily fill up on eggs, pancakes, waffles, hash browns, etc. for about $6. The **BLUE MOON SALOON AND ROADHOUSE** (716 2nd Ave. N.; 608.781.6800; Su–Tu, Th 6a–9p W,F,Sa, 6a–10p), part intimate restaurant and part sports bar, seems like it is always busy. There has been a restaurant on this site for decades; one operated a speakeasy. The views are always good view, especially from the small patio. The menu is rather steak-heavy ($11–$20) but the Cajun catfish is a nice alternative for the meat weary ($13); on the lighter side, sandwiches and burgers run about $7.

For a fine dining experience that emphasizes seasonal ingredients and high-end cuts of meat, head to **TRADITIONS RESTAURANT** (201 Main St.; 608.783-0200; Tu–Sa 5:30–10). The cozy restaurant is housed in a former bank and offers one of the best fine dining experiences in the area. The seasonal menu has entrées favoring lean cuts of quality meat (beef tenderloin, pork tenderloin, yellowfin tuna); when I looked at a menu, entrée prices ranged from $23 to $30. **MANNY'S COCINA** (301 Hampton Court; 608.781.5601; Su–Th 11–9:30, F,Sa 11–10:30) is conveniently located hear Home Depot and Wal-Mart, so the atmosphere is more strip mall chic, but the menu is heavy on seafood and fish prepared with Mexican flavors (most entrées are around $20 but specials can run much higher). I had seafood cooked in parchment paper (mahi mahi, shrimp, lobster, scallops, peppers, spices/$22) and thoroughly enjoyed it.

Sleeping

Budget. THE EDGEWATER MOTEL (N5326 State Road 35; 608.783.2286) is along the highway but set back far enough from the road, so there's not much traffic noise. The seven rooms are small and

Life in a Logging Camp

Logging was a winter activity that required men (and boys) to live in camps for months. This took some planning and preparation.

In late fall, the pinery boys, as they were known, gathered supplies for their families to use while they were gone. They bought staples from the general store—on credit—and paid for them when they returned from the camps in the spring with cash in hand. The men would pack their belongings in a bag (clothes plus items to mend them, medicines, paper and pencil, winter wear like gloves and overalls), then wrap the bag in a heavy wool coat called a mackinaw.

Each camp housed about 100 men. Camp life had few comforts. Men might have to spend a few nights in tents before the cabins were ready. Clothes often failed to dry from one day to the next. Lice were a common problem.

They worked in crews, usually with four or five other men: two *sawyers* who cut the trees down, a *swamper* who trimmed branches and marked the tree with the name of the company, a *skidder* (aka, a *skidding teamster*) whose job was to drag the logs (with the help of oxen or horses) to the spot where they were gathered, and a *chainer* whose job was to attach a chain to the logs and then to the oxen so the skidder could get his job done.

Logs were loaded onto a sled and transported to the river; 20 tons was a normal load. A *road monkey* helped keep the pathways in good shape for the sleds; he sometimes had to work through the night to pour water over tracks so they would freeze and improve the route for the sleds the next day. Logs were unloaded on an ice-covered river. In spring, as the ice melted, the logs would be caught in the current and carried downriver to the mills. Men called *drivers* would sometimes guide the logs from shore, but often they would ride the logs (with the aid of spiked

Winter camp construction (Area Research Center, UW-La Crosse)

shoes) to keep them from getting hung up.

Spring meant getting paid, and a raucous return to town to share their money with tavern owners and their families (and probably with a few professional women, too).

simple but in good shape; each has a microwave, fridge, and cable TV ($45+tax); no credit cards. **THE ONALASKA INN** (651 2nd Ave. South; 888.359.2619/608.783.2270; WiFi) has 12 well-kept rooms all with identical features: fridge, microwave, cable TV ($55+tax). **THE LAKE INN** (926 2nd Ave. North; 608.783.3348; WiFi) has nine tidy rooms, many recently updated, right on the River Road ($60+tax). **THE SHADOW RUN MOTEL** (710 2nd Ave. N.; 800.566.0798/608.783.0020; WiFi) has 22 rooms with 22 personalities accented with homey touches like quilted pillow cases. Each room has a microwave and fridge, access to decks and patios, and comfy bedding; second floor rooms have good views of Lake Onalaska; four rooms have a stove ($70+tax).

Bed and Breakfast. THE LUMBER BARON INN (421 2nd Ave. North; 608.781.8938; WiFi) is right on the River Road and overlooks Lake Onalaska. The East Lake Victorian home, built in 1888 for lumber baron C.H. Nichols, is more elegant on the inside than the outside. All six rooms have a private bath but not every room has a shower; the third floor suite has a Jacuzzi tub and fireplace ($99–$149+tax incl full breakfast). If you prefer more of a country experience, **RAINBOW RIDGE FARMS** (N5732 Hauser Rd.; 888.347.2594/608.783.8181; WiFi) is a hobby farm that does double duty as a B&B. Guests are welcome to help with chores like feeding the goats, sheep, llamas, ducks, and chickens, or not. Each of the four guest rooms has its own bathroom and overlooks a pond ($94+tax). Located in a quiet setting deep in a coulee, you are just a 20-minute drive to restaurants and entertainment in La Crosse. Guests are served a full breakfast on weekends, expanded continental during the week.

Resources

- The local newspaper is the weekly *Onalaska Holmen Courier-Life* (608.786.1950).
- Post Office: 304 11th Ave. North; 608.781.8777.
- Onalaska Public Library: 741 Oak Ave. South; 608.781.9568; M,W,Th 9–9, Tu Noon–9, F 9–5, Sa 9–2.

Getting To and Out of Dodge ✈

MTU route 9 runs between Onalaska and La Crosse on MTU (6:55a–5:25p, weekdays only).

Getting Around 🚌

The **Onalaska/Holmen/West Salem Public Transit** (OHWSPT; 608.784.0000; operates daily 6:30a–7p) operates a van service that is only available by reservation. The fare is $3/adult within the service area; a ride to the airport will cost $6.

HOLMEN

(6,200)

Holmen is another small town that has evolved into a bedroom community for La Crosse.

Arriving in Town

State Highway 35 skirts the south and western edge of town. To get into Holmen proper, stay on Business 35, aka Holmen Drive (aka County Highway HD). To get to the business district, follow County DH (Gaarder Rd.) at the stoplight and turn left on Main Street.

History

Settlers began filing into the area around 1850, with the Jenks family perhaps being the first to call Holmen home, before it was Holmen. The area was initially called Frederickstown in honor of the village blacksmith, Frederick Anderson, then the name Cricken (Norwegian for creek) caught on. The origin of the town's name is a bit of a mystery, but there are two theories: 1) in 1851, a surveyor passed through whose name was Holmen and who went on to win election as a State Senator in Indiana; the postmaster may have suggested naming the town after him; or 2) the name has a Norwegian origin based on the word *Holm*, which means something like a projection of low, level, rich land extending into the water. (Or it might mean island. The town once had a large pond in the middle of town created by backup water from a dammed creek. There was an island in the middle of that pond that was a favorite recreation site. All you Norwegian speakers out there, let me know.) The second one is more likely.

Holmen was never a thriving industrial center, but it had its share of goings-on: the Casberg Mill opened in 1876, grinding corn, wheat, rye, and buckwheat into flour. Holmen also had a factory that made the pins that held log rafts together, a sorghum mill, and an ice harvesting operation. Most of the early settlers were Norwegian and many of the customs they brought with them were practiced by generations of Holmen residents. One of those was a Norwegian Christmas tradition called *jule bakking*. To participate, one had to dress up in a funny, tacky costume and don a mask, then gather with a big group of friends in similar attire. Once assembled, all would head to the neighbors' houses to see if they could guess who's who. Once identities are revealed, everyone celebrates with food like lefse, lutefisk, rosettes, and grog. This custom seems to have died out in recent years; I think it should be revived.

Tourist Information ⓘ

You can pick up brochures at the **Village Hall** (421 S. Main St.; M–F 8–4:30) or library (see below).

Attractions

The **Holmen Historical Center** is in the Village Hall (421 S. Main St.; M–F 8–4:30) and includes a window display with a few old pictures, plus a display cabinet full of Native American arrowheads.

Entertainment and Events ♪

The **Holmen Farmers Market** (Festival Foods, 600 N. Holmen Dr.; 608.526.3339) is on Wednesday afternoons (3p–7p) from June through October.

Festivals. Holmen's major festival is called **Kornfest** (mid-August; 800.873.1901/608.526.4444) where you can eat all the corn-on-the-cob you desire, then enjoy the swap meet, parade and music.

Sports and Recreation

Just outside of town, **Holland Sand Prairie** (McHugh Rd.; 608.784.3606) preserves 61 acres of native sand prairie and natural dunes which you can hike around.

Halfway Creek Bike Trail is a 3.4 mile paved multi-use path that connects to the Great River Trail via a mile stretch on a county road. If you didn't bring a bicycle with you, **River Trail Cycles** (Holmen Square, 500 N. Holmen Drive; 608.526.4678; M,W,F 10–8, Tu,Th 10–5:30, Sa 9–5, Su 11–4, reduced hours from Sept 1–mid-April), can set you up with a rental ($15/day, $25/weekend including helmet and lock). They are also good folks to ask about bike routes through nearby country roads.

The public swimming pool is the **Holmen Area Aquatic Center** (315 Anderson St.; 608.526.6092; open from early June–late August with open swim M–F 1p–6:20p, Sa Noon–7, Su Noon–5; $4/day for non-residents).

Shopping

HOLMEN BERRY CORNER (608.526.9321; open daily June–Oct) is three miles north of Holmen at the State Highway 35 exit from US Highway 53; stock up on fresh fruit and produce in season.

Eating

When you walk in the door of the **HOLMEN LOCKER AND MEAT MARKET** (412 N. Main St.; 608.526.3112; M–F 8–6, Sa 8–3) be prepared to be knocked off your feet with the scent of smoked meats. This place is a traditional butcher shop fused with a boutique grocer: fresh and smoked meats, plus local

God's Country

You may have noticed that the La Crosse region likes to call itself *God's Country*. The now-defunct G. Heileman Brewing Country helped to advance the slogan when every can of *Old Style* beer was labeled with the phrase "Pure Brewed in God's Country." You may think this is because of the natural beauty of the area—the rivers, bluffs, forests, hills. You would only be partially right.

Van Slyke statue
Galesville., Wis.

The origins of the slogan actually go back to the 19th century, to a Methodist minister, the Reverend David Van Slyke, who believed that Trempealeau County was the actual location of the Biblical Garden of Eden. The combination of the rich agricultural lands and the configuration of its rivers convinced the Reverend that the area's first residents were actually Adam and Eve, not Nathan Myrick or Judge George Gale.

Van Slyke detailed the rationale in a book called *Found at Last: The Veritable Garden of Eden, or a Place that Answers the Bible Description of That Notable Spot Better than Anything Yet Discovered*. Catchy title. While he attracted few believers to this theory, he does get at least some of the credit for the God's Country slogan.

You can detour off the River Road to Galesville and visit a statue of the good Reverend. From Holmen, take US 53 north about 11 miles to Galesville. The statue is on Main Street/US 53 just south of business district; you may even be able to buy a copy of his book at a store in Galesville.

artisanal food items like jams, flour, and Wisconsin cheese. They also have a good selection of regional beer and wine and host wine tastings twice a week (W,F 6p–9p). You can find bargains here for a picnic lunch, but many of the specialty food items, while good quality, might bust your budget.

Sleeping

Camping. WHISPERING PINES CAMPGROUND (N8905 US Highway 53N; 800.526.4958/608.526.4956; open mid-April–mid-Oct.) has several overnight sites in a field with no shade (at least for a few years until the saplings mature), plus a few overnight sites among the seasonal campers in an older section of the campground that is more pleasant ($21+tax/primitive, $32+tax/water & electric).

Budget and up. The **PRAIRIE INN & SUITES** (3913 Circle Dr.; 888.841.3480/608.781.4490; WiFi) is located at the intersection of County OT and Highway 53 in a new Prairie Style-inspired building. The 38 rooms are spacious and look great; each is equipped with a microwave, fridge, and cable TV ($79 + tax for 1 queen bed, $89 + tax for 2 queen beds, $125 + tax for whirlpool suite; incl expanded continental breakfast).

Resources

- The local newspaper is the weekly *Onalaska Holmen Courier-Life* (608.786.1950).
- Post Office: 1111 Linden Dr.; 608.526.4055.
- Holmen Area Library: 103 State St.; 608.526.4198; WiFi; M,W,Th 10–8, Tu 1–8, F 10–5, Sa 9–2.

Getting To and Around Holmen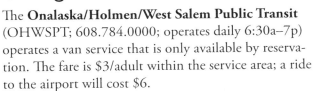

The **Onalaska/Holmen/West Salem Public Transit** (OHWSPT; 608.784.0000; operates daily 6:30a–7p) operates a van service that is only available by reservation. The fare is $3/adult within the service area; a ride to the airport will cost $6.

BRICE PRAIRIE

(Uninc)

Brice Prairie is both a natural feature and a small, unincorporated community that bends around Lake Onalaska and is popular with recreation seekers.

Arriving in Town

The main route through the area is County Highway Z, but County Highways Zb and Zn also provide access to some areas. None of these roads connect to State Highway 35, so you'll need to backtrack to get to the River Road.

History

Brice Prairie was home to a Ho Chunk winter camp in the 1800s known as White Oak Spring; they made a living by trading furs and selling maple syrup. Logging along the Black River generated some commerce, but the area was mostly home to dairy farms. Alexander and Lucy Brice moved to Wisconsin in 1843 from New England and settled in La Crosse County in 1855. Alex was a veteran of the War of 1812. They had 10 children, one of whom, George, went on to some success selling farm implements and in local politics. The prairie once had a track for training sulky racers and an airfield used to train pilots during WWI. Today, the area is dotted with subdivisions but no incorporated community.

For more information and updates, visit my web site at www.mississippivalleytraveler.com.

Tourist Information ⓘ

Direct your questions to the **Onalaska Center for Commerce & Tourism** (1101 Main St.; 800.873.1901/608.781.9570; May–Oct open M–F 8–5, Sa 9–3 Su 9–2; the rest of the year open M–F 8–5 only).

Getting on the River 🚤

Schafer's Boats and Bait (W7221 N. Shore Lane; 608.781.3100; daily 6a–8p in summer and fall; daily 7a–5p in winter) sells bait and tackle year-round and rents boats after the ice melts: pontoon boats ($30–$40/hour but $100–$140 min; $200–$250/day + gas), canoes, rowboats, tandem kayaks ($5/hour w/$15 min or $35/day), and 16' fishing boats ($8–$10/hour w/$25–$30 min or $50–$60/day + gas), single kayaks ($10/3 hours or $20/day).

Entertainment and Events ♪

Brice Prairie Time Trials (last Saturday in June) is a 40-kilometer bike race around the prairie; indulge in a carb-fest the Friday evening before at the all-you-can-eat spaghetti dinner ($7). The event actually began as a canoe race; you can still paddle around with fellow canoeists the morning of the bike race; meet the group at Lytle's Landing at 6:30am prepared for a 2-3 hour paddle through the backwaters of the Black River (www.briceprairiecanoerace.org).

Sports and Recreation ≋

The **Great River Trail** passes through Brice Prairie (see page 239).

Eating and Drinking

RED PINES BAR & GRILL (W7305 County Road Z; 608.779.2800; kitchen open daily 11a–9p) sits along the backwaters with a good view of the lake; dine on the patio and enjoy walleye cheeks (chunks of deep-fried walleye; $8), stringer of sunfish or catfish ($11–$12) or pizza (14" w/ 2 toppings for $14). On the lighter side, get a sandwich $8–$10) and pair it with chips made on-site.

MIDWAY
(Uninc)

Arriving in Town
The little village is at the intersection of County Highways OT and ZN.

History
Initially called Midway Station, Midway originated in the 1870s as a station for the Chicago and Northwestern Railroad. The village got a post office in 1872, but it was closed in 1934. In 1881, the village boasted a blacksmith shop, a hotel, a store, and an elevator that could store 10,000 bushels of grain. That's about as good as it got.

Attractions
The **Great River Trail** passes through Midway; see page 239.

NEW AMSTERDAM
(Uninc)

Another small, unincorporated village, New Amsterdam was founded by a group of Dutch settlers—an ethnic group called Friesians, technically—who endured an epic journey to start a new life on this small patch of prairie near the Mississippi River.

Arriving in Town
County Highway XX will get you into and out of the village.

History
On February 26, 1853 Oepke Bonnema led a group of 90 Friesians from Harlingen on a journey to a new life in the United States. After a storm-wrought crossing of the English Channel took two days, the group arrived in Lowestoft, England, only to learn that the ship for which they had booked passage was full. They were forced to wait three weeks for the next one, finally leaving Europe on March 22 on the *William and Mary*.

The ship carried 86 passengers from the Netherlands and 100 from Ireland and England. Early in the voyage, 13 passengers died from disease or storms. On May 2, the crew spotted land, but it was the North Bahamas where there was no port. Captain Stinson risked passing through a channel that was only 20 feet deep (the ship had a 17-foot draw) and, predictably, hit a sandbar. The *William and Mary* took on water and was blown back to sea. The crew, including Captain Stinson, ditched the ship and her passengers and took as much cargo as they could grab. The captain was hoping to collect insurance on the cargo.

The remaining passengers of the *William and Mary* continued to man the pumps and tried to signal for help. A big storm on May 4 created some tense moments, but they weathered it. Ultimately, the ship was lost and the passengers lost all their wealth; they had invested their money in goods like blankets rather than bringing cash. At least they had their lives. They were rescued by a group of Bahamians who helped them travel on to Nassau where their story engendered more sympathy. Islanders rallied to outfit them with new supplies and arranged onward travel.

On June 1st, the Friesians boarded a boat for New Orleans (the English and Irish traveled on a different boat) and reached the city one week later. When they arrived, they heard the news that the *William and Mary* sank and that they were all dead.

A German relief society heard their story and helped the Friesians resupply, even paying for their fare on a steamboat up the Mississippi River. The group reached St. Louis on June 21. They finally reached this part of Wisconsin on July 15, 1853, nearly five months after leaving home, and bought 800 acres. They were the first settlers in the township, creating a village they initially called Frisia. Many endured their first winter in hillside dugouts (holes were dug and the tops covered with sticks and grass) before building more permanent structures the following spring and attending to the more mundane tasks of building a new life.

In spite of the hard work and sacrifices of those early settlers, the village didn't grow substantially and never attracted much industry. It has remained a small village with a farm-based economy.

New Amsterdam Presbyterian Church

Tourist Information ⓘ

Contact the **Onalaska Center for Commerce & Tourism** (1101 Main St.; 800.873.1901 or 608.781.9570; May–Oct open M–F 8–5, Sa 9–3 Su 9–2; the rest of the year open M–F 8–5 only).

Attractions

The simple Gothic Revival **New Amsterdam Presbyterian Church** (N7383 John St.; 608.526.3992) was built from 1873 to 1879. Early services were in Dutch. In 1905, a bell tower and bell were installed; an annex was built in 1916. Art glass windows were installed in the 1930s. The interior has been remodeled several times, most recently in 1995 with the installation of new wood paneling and crosses behind altar, new wainscoting in the rest of the church, and the removal of the barrier between the sanctuary and the annex.

Sports and Recreation

The **Van Loon Wildlife Area** (Amsterdam Prairie Rd. North; 608.266.2621) is a serene and mystical 4000 acres along the marshy Black River floodplain. The area is best known for the six rare bowstring arch truss bridges built between 1905 and 1908 for McGilvary

Road but the peaceful preserve also has good birding and easy hiking. Allow 60-90 minutes to explore it. To get there from the US 53/WI 35 split: Go north on WI 35 for one mile to Amsterdam Prairie Road North and turn right (north); go 1.6 miles to the parking lot on the left.

For more information and updates, visit my web site at www.mississippivalleytraveler.com.

TREMPEALEAU
(1,319)

I was going write that Trempealeau has an old-fashioned charm and is oddly picturesque, then I realized that I could just call it quaint. So, Trempealeau is quaint.

Arriving in Town

On the east side of town, State Highway 35 is East 3rd Street; on the north side of town, it is Main Street.

History

The town was named after a distinctive, conical land mass just upriver that is completely surrounded by water. Local Native Americans referred it as mountain soaking in the water, which French explorers translated as *la montagne qui trempe a l'eau*.

The village of Trempealeau stirred to life in the 1840s as Reed's Landing (James Reed was an early settler), a small port and fur trading outpost inhabited by a few migrants from Prairie du Chien and French Canada. Platted in 1852 as Montoville, then quickly replatted as Trempealeau, the village was formally called Montoville-Trempealeau but many still called it Reeds Landing. Finally, in 1856 the confusion ended and the village became just Trempealeau. Settlers began arriving in 1856, many coming upriver by steamboat and others overland in covered wagons. A commercial district developed rapidly along the riverfront to serve increasing river commerce and the burgeoning agriculture in surrounding areas.

Land speculators, many of them East coast residents trying to make a quick buck, fueled dramatic inflation in the cost of land. Prices for choice lots that sold for $40 were listed for many times that amount just a few months later. Even with cheaper land available in neighboring areas, Trempealeau land owners continued to demand high prices. As a result, many would-be settlers moved on to other settlements in Red Wing, Winona, and St. Paul.

The waning role of river transportation in favor of rail traffic plus declining wheat production after the Civil War also slowed Trempealeau's growth. Even with the arrival of a second railroad line in 1887 the village's economic fortunes changed little. The town's economic hopes went up in flames in 1888 when a large fire wiped out most of the riverfront commercial district on Front Street (now First Street). When the town rebuilt its commercial district, new construction was concentrated along the current Main Street, two blocks from the riverfront, reflecting the declining importance of river commerce for the village. This two block stretch has remained the center of a stable but small population ever since.

Tourist Information ⓘ

If you are planning your trip from home, contact the **Trempealeau Chamber of Commerce** with your questions (24436 Third St.; 608.534.6780; M–F 8–4:30). Once you get to town, however, your best bet is to stop in at the **Trempealeau Hotel** to get the lay of the land (11332 Main St.; see hours below); you may as well grab a beer while you're here.

Attractions

Lock and Dam 6 (608.534.6774) was completed in 1936 and the latest rehab was finished in 2002. The lock has a maximum lift of 6.5 feet; the dam is 893 feet long.

Perrot State Park (W26247 Sullivan Rd.; 608.534.6409; $7/Wisc resident, $10/non-resident) is

Trempealeau before the 1888 fire

another jewel along the Mississippi River and another one we can thank John Latsch for (see sidebar on page 119). The river is much narrower along this stretch because the main channel used to run to the north until sand and silt from glacial melt blocked the flow and diverted water into this channel; from Perrot Ridge you can see where the channel used to flow. The park has some good hiking, scenic vistas, camping, and a canoe route through the backwaters. The dramatic vistas are best from Brady's Bluff; the East Brady's Bluff trail is a relatively easy hike with switchbacks and a gradual ascent until you reach the top, while the West Brady's Bluff trail is more vertical and harder work; give yourself at least an hour to get up, enjoy the view, and get back. Oh—you probably won't see any—but be aware that rattlesnakes live in the area. Trempealeau Mountain is a 390-foot landmark that has long been a place of great spiritual meaning for Native Americans. The mountain is not off-limits but be mindful of its spiritual significance; there are no developed trails, and you can only reach it by boat.

Trempealeau Community Heritage Museum (Village Hall, 24455 3rd St.; 608.534.6780; Sa,Su 1–3 in summer or by appt.; free) has exhibits that will interest locals more than visiitors, but the small display of old photos are fun and the applehead dolls (carved from dried apples) are kinda interesting, in a creepy way.

Getting on the River

Perrot State Park (608.534.6409) has a 3.4 mile canoe trail through Trempealeau Bay. The park rents canoes on a first-come, first-served basis ($10/4 hours); make arrangements through the park office. You can also experience the backwaters on the **Long Lake Canoe Trail** (608.783.8405), an easy 4.5 mile loop; access is 1.5 miles south of Lock and Dam 6 at the Long Lake Boat Landing.

If you'd like to paddle area waters but don't have your own boat, contact **Al's Canoes** (608.792.2886). He can arrange a trip on the Black or Trempealeau River or on the backwaters of the Mississippi between Memorial Day and Labor Day ($20/day w/o shuttle service; $26/day w/shuttle service; call to make a reservation).

For those without a boat, you can get on the river at the **Tremplo Fishing Float** (608.385.7337; Sa,Su,holidays 7a–5p), a fishing platform below Lock and Dam 6; raise the red flag for a boat ride to the float ($15/day).

Through Chuck of **Chuck's Cabins** (608.790.3277), you can rent a 14-foot fishing boat with a 25-hp engine ($45/4 hours or $75/8 hours), a pontoon boat ($115/4 hours or $200/8 hours + gas), a jet ski ($75/hour + gas), or inflatable kayaks ($10/day).

Entertainment and Events

Festivals. Trempealeau Catfish Days (608.534.6780) is a good weekend party that includes bicycle tours, a motorcycle run, and a fishing tournament. Yes, it also includes catfish cooked in many forms—just not on a stick. Try a burger made from locally-caught catfish and stick around on Sunday for the parade and fireworks.

Music. The **Trempealeau Hotel** (11332 Main St.; 608.534.6898) hosts live music, primarily on weekends. The **Elmaro Vineyard** (608.534.6456) hosts special events like wine tastings from around the world paired with live music. Check their website for details (www.elmarovineyard.com).

Sports and Recreation

The **Great River State Trail** (see page 239) ends at Perrot State Park; if you rode your bike here, it's time to turn around and go back. If you didn't bring a bicycle with you, you can rent one through the **Trempealeau Hotel** (11332 Main St.; 608.534.6898; $12/day).

If you'd rather swim in a pool than the Mississippi River, head to the **Trempealeau Village Swimming Pool** (23924 4th St.; 608.534.6606; open swim daily 1p–5p, 6p–9p; $2.50).

Eating and Drinking

The historic **TREMPEALEAU HOTEL** (11332 Main St.; 608.534.6898; May 1–Oct 31 Su–Th 11–9, F,Sa 11–10; Apr,Nov,Dec W–Su 11–9, Jan–March F,Sa 4p–9p) opened in 1871 and managed to survive the 1888 fire, in spite of its wood construction. Good thing, otherwise you might never have had the chance to try a Walnut Burger ($8 a la carte at lunch or $13 as a dinner entrée). If that's not your thing, they have plenty of other options like catfish and bluegill fillet sandwiches for lunch ($7–$10) or dinner entrées of grilled meats, steaks, pasta, and fish ($14–$27).

The **HUNGRY POINT BAR AND GRILL** (W23797 Lake Rd.; 608.534.7771; M–F 11a–10p,

Sa,Su 6a–10:30a, 11a–10p) serves great burgers in quarter-pound (<$5), half-pound ($5–$7.50), and—good God—full pound portions ($9–$10), plus fries that put McDonald's to shame, all of which you can enjoy from the large riverside patio; it can get loud inside when busy. They also have a dock with transient slips.

At **SULLIVAN'S SUPPER CLUB** (W25709 Sullivan Rd,; 608.534.7775; M,Tu,Th–Sa 5p–close, Su 11:30a–close) you can enjoy an Irish Handshake (tenderloin tips and scallops), the Dublin Delight (shrimp and barbeque pork ribs), or a number of other Irish-named combo entrées (most about $17), or you can just select a standard steak or seafood entrée and enjoy good food with a great view, especially from the riverside patio (entrées mostly $15–$20 except king crab and lobster which are $35+).

Sleeping

Camping. PERROT STATE PARK (W26247 Sullivan Rd.; 608.534.6409) has 102 sites (38 with electric); if you are into the privacy thing when you camp, sites 87–95 (electricity available only at sites 94,95) are more remote than the rest and heavily shaded. There are a handful of sites on the water ($3 extra for the water view). To camp in the park, you must pay the daily fee ($7/Wisc resident, $10/non-resident); sites are $12 for Wisconsin residents, $14 for non-residents and electricity is $5/night extra. **MULBERRY MEADOWS** (23828 Lake Rd.; 507.429.1667) is a compact campground near the lock and dam with plenty of shade but geared to RV campers ($16/water & elec).

Budget. The **TREMPEALEAU HOTEL** (11332 Main St.; 608.534.6898) has eight simple rooms above the bar in the space that was the original hotel; the rooms share a bath and a common sititing area

($40–$49 + tax; WiFi). The hotel also has four motel-style units in a building near the lock and dam (the Kingfishers) that have good river views, especially from the decks ($60–$70 + tax). The **LITTLE BLUFF INN** (11451 Main St.; 608.534.6615; WiFi) has 16 rooms in many configurations, including six kitchenettes and a large suite ($58–$74 + tax with continental breakfast).

Bed and Breakfast. Some B&Bs feel like museums, and some feel like homes; the **LUCAS HOUSE BED & BREAKFAST** (24616 2nd St.; 608.534.6665; WiFi) feels like a home. The house has several common rooms where you can spread out and relax. The six guest rooms are furnished with comfort in mind and share three bathrooms; some rooms are slightly larger and three have river views ($75–$85 + tax, incl continental breakfast).

Cabins. CHUCK'S CABINS (608.790.3277) includes three exceptional, rehabbed cabins decorated with a guy's touch: the *Eagles Nest*—on the Mississippi River—that can sleep four ($135/4 people, two night min); *Whispering Willows*, on a backwaters lake, that can sleep four in the cabin plus it has a separate bunkhouse for an afternoon escape or to hide the in-laws in tow ($160/4 people, 2 night min); and the *Round Lake Hilton* that can sleep 8–10 ($235/6 people, $20/extra person, two night min); the cabins are loaded with amenities like flat screen TVs with satellite channels, full kitchens, private docks, and outdoor patios with gas grills. **3 LAKES CABIN** (10288 Birch Lane; 608.534.6729) sits on stilts in a quiet spot by the Long Lake boat ramp; there is a screened-in porch below the house; the upstairs has a number of quality touches like the glass block shower wall and generous use of tile, a full kitchen, satellite TV, fireplaces, and a Jacuzzi tub ($125+tax, two night min). **THE CABIN BY**

THE RIVER (W25448 Sullivan Rd.; 608.534.6510; open Apr. 1–Dec. 1) overlooks the main channel of the river; it has two bedrooms, a full bath, and a full kitchen. The cabin is well-maintained and a clean, pleasant place to vacation within walking distance of Perrot State Park ($110/4 people incl tax, $20/night for each extra person); bring your own towels.

Moderate. THE TREMPEALEAU HOTEL (11332 Main St.; 608.534.6898) also has three suites on offer, all with WiFi. *The Doc West House* consists of two beautiful suites in a completely renovated building; each suite has a Jacuzzi tub and good river views ($130 + tax). *The Pines Cottage*, a petite riverside house comes with a Jacuzzi tub, kitchenette, and good river views ($130+tax). The **INN ON THE RIVER** (11321 Main St.; 608.534.7784; WiFi) has 12 pleasant rooms, all with a view of the river and all with fridge, coffee, and microwave ($90+tax; two night min); they also offer a suite with a Jacuzzi tub ($130+tax).

Resources

- Post Office: 11421 Main St.; 608.534.6571.
- Shirley M. Wright Memorial Library: 11455 Fremont St.; 608.534.6197; WiFi; M–Th 11–7, F 11–6, Sa 9–Noon.

CENTERVILLE

(Uninc)

A small crossroads town with a couple of surprises surrounded by a bounty of fresh local produce.

Arriving in Town

Centerville is the crossroads of state highways 35, 54, and 93 and only has two roads. If you get lost here, you shouldn't be driving.

History

Initially called Martin's Corners, presumably because some guy named Martin lived here, someone eventually realized that this little unincorporated village was right in the middle of Trempealeau Prairie and about halfway between Trempealeau and Galesville. Thus was born Centerville.

Attractions

The **Trempealeau National Wildlife Refuge** (W28488 Refuge Rd.; 608.539.2311; open during daylight hours only) has 6220 acres of splendid isolation. Instead of the jarring sound of trains or cars, you'll just hear distant echoes from across the river. The refuge has a varied topography like sand prairies and bottomland forest with wildlife to match. If you arrive around dawn or dusk, you are more likely to see wildlife, like the beaver that swam in front of me one spring evening. The refuge has a visitor center (M–F 7:30a–4p), an observation deck overlooking the backwaters, a 4½ mile auto route, and three hiking trails.

Sports and Recreation 〰

The **Centerville Curling Club** (608.539.3651; Nov–March) has been active since 1947 but the sport has been popular in these parts since the 1850s. Visitors are welcome to drop by and watch the action, especially on weekends when bonspiels (tournaments) fill the ice. Most events are free.

Shopping

Fresh produce abounds around Centerville. Four generations of Eckers have run **ECKERS ORCHARDS** (W27062 State Road 54/35; 608.539.2652; daily 10–6 Aug–Dec.). They grow about a dozen varieties of apples; you can sample before you buy, and get homemade apple pie, to boot ($3/slice or $11/whole pie). **THE BERRY PATCH** (N16414 Kriesel Lane; 608.539.5541; daily 7–7 in season) is a great place for fresh, seasonal fruits and vegetables, including some that you can pick yourself: strawberries, blueberries, snozberries, tomatoes, squash. **SACIA'S ORCHARDS** (N16545 Kriesel Lane; 608.582.2511; daily 9–5 in season) has strawberries and asparagus in spring, plus apples in the fall.

Eating ✕

BEEDLES BAR AND RESTAURANT (W24966 State Highway 54/93; 608.539.2251; Tu-Th 4-9:30, F 4-11, Sa 11-11, Su 9:30-9:30) is a pleasant surprise with its upscale cafeteria ambience. The menu is loaded with steak and seafood entrées ($15-$21); you can get a full pound ribeye steak for $21, if you dare. On the lighter side, the salad bar has a nice range of items including lettuce that is actually green ($9).

MARSHLAND

(Uninc)

Marshland is the surprising home to a restaurant that has been a local favorite for fish and seafood for a century and a half.

Arriving in Town

If you got lost in Centerville, don't worry; Marshland has only road you need concern yourself with, and it's the one you are on (State Highway 35).

History

Marshland began as a railroad town, its growth fueled by the commerce generated from two rail lines and its proximity to the railroad bridge to Winona; fish and fur were two items that shipped in large quantities. The town's name rightly suggests that the area once had extensive marshes, but these were drained in the early 1900s. During Prohibition, the Marshland Hotel was an important supply station for bootleggers; local folks made the alcohol that the bootleggers sold. Like the marshes, the town's population has been drained away and today Marshland is a small, unincorporated community.

Eating ✗

THE HILLSIDE FISH HOUSE (W124 State Highway 35; 608.687.6141; M–Th 5–9, F,Sa 4:30–10; Su 4:30–9) offers consistently good, if unspectacular, fish and seafood entrées in an unlikely rural location far from the salty seas. The restaurant opened in 1855 as the Marshland Hotel to serve railroad workers and

Get your fish to go or eat inside at the Hillside Fish House

passengers when Marshland was a (relatively) important junction. In 1900, the new owners renamed it the Hillside Tavern and ran it for nearly a century. The fish tradition began when local Native Americans brought in freshly-caught fish to trade for goods. Among the fish and seafood entrées ($10–$20), walleye is a popular choice ($16). Consider a combo meal, opting for the modest cod and shrimp or scallops ($14) or the luxurious New York Strip with lobster tail ($42); reservations are a good idea on weekend nights.

BLUFF SIDING

(Uninc)

Located on a narrow strip of land slightly elevated above the highway, Bluff Siding has a few liquor stores and houses but not much else.

Arriving in Town

Bluff Siding Road runs above the highway and through the village.

History

Early maps labeled this area Atlanta Station but its current name comes from the railroad siding built by the Chicago and Northwestern railroad, so its cars could load lime from the local lime plant.

For more information and updates, visit my web site at www.mississippivalleytraveler.com.

FOUNTAIN CITY
(983)

Fountain City is a laid back rivertown with a few quirks and some cool old saloons. My kind of place.

Arriving in Town

Highway 35 in Fountain City is Main Street on the south end of town and Shore Drive on the north end of town; the primary east-west road is State Highway 95, also known as North Street (just to confuse you).

History

Thomas Holmes showed up in the fall of 1839 with a small party of 13 people and established a trading post; this gave the site its first name: Holmes Landing. He ended up staying until 1846, at which time he felt civilization was getting to close to him, so moved further west, founding about 30 other communities including Helena, Montana before retiring in Culman, Alabama.

After Holmes left, Holmes Landing became known by the Native American name *Wah-mah-dee*, but it was changed to Fountain City in 1852, inspired by one of the many springs oozing from the bluffs that resembled a fountain. The busiest period of settlement was from 1847 to 1862; the city had a modest amount of success as a trading and shipping center, aided by a ferry connection to Winona. Early businesses included a cigar factory, lumber yard, foundry, brickyard, rock quarry, planing mills, agricultural implement dealers, commercial fishing operations, and a boat yard.

Most of the early settlers were German or Swiss. In 1860, Judge Gale described Fountain City as feeling very much like a German village. The town officers were all German, the primary language used around town was, yes, German, and a number of social clubs organized according to German traditions: Der Turnverein (gymnastic society); Gesangverein (singing society); Schutzenverein (shooting society); and Biervery (drinking society)—just kidding on that last one.

Fountain City has maintained a strong connection to the river to this day. The construction of Lock and Dam 5A in the 1930s provided some much needed work for residents. In addition, the Army Corps of Engineers has had a boatyard at Fountain City since the 19th century. The yard is used for maintenance and to store dredges and other equipment used by the Corps to maintain the shipping channel.

Tourist Information

Your best bet is to visit **Lefse Time** and chat with Gwen (see below).

Attractions

Lock and Dam 5A (507.452.2789) went operational in 1936 and was rehabbed from 1989 to 2000. The lock has a maximum lift of six feet; the dam is 682 feet long. It was not part of the original plan but had to be built when someone figured out that building Lock and Dam 6 as planned would have flooded Winona's sewers. You can reach the viewing area by passing through a concrete-lined walkway under the railroad tracks, but you are across the river from the locks and don't get a close-up look. On the other hand, standing in the pedestrian underpass when a train rumbles over your head is a wild experience.

The **Fountain City Area Historical Society** (7 Main St.; 608.687.7481; F,Sa 11–4; free) maintains an interesting collection of displays on steamboats and

Sports and Recreation

The **Mississippi Thunder Speedway** (2895 State Highway 35; 608.687.3282) roars to life on Friday nights with the sound of racing stock cars and something called USRA modifieds and B-Mods; I hope that means something to you. Races begin at 6p and 7p from April through August ($18). The track is three miles north of Fountain City.

Merrick State Park (S2965 State Highway 35; 608.687.4936; $7/Wisc resident, $10/non-resident) is another park that exists because of John Latsch (see page 119), who donated the land and had it named for George Merrick, a steamboat historian and cub pilot. The park's main attractions are camping and fishing, but there are some easy hikes, too.

If you need a quick fix for your bicycle or a new one altogether, head to **Brone's Bicycle Shop** (615 S. Main St.; 608.687.8601; M,W,F,Sa 10–5, Tu,Th 10–6). They are also a good source of information on where to ride in the area.

Shopping

LEFSE TIME (115 North Shore; 800.687.2058/608.687.4299; W–Su Noon–5 in summer; Th–Sa Noon–5 the rest of the year) offers Scandinavian-themed gifts, including the thin pancakes known as lefse. They don't sell ludefisk, though, and they don't think it's funny anymore when fools like me ask. **SEVEN HAWKS VINEYARDS** (17 North St.; 866.946.3741; M–Sa 11–7, Su Noon–5 in summer, W–Su 11–7 the rest of the year) makes a variety of wines of good quality at reasonable prices; you can sample before you buy.

Eating and Drinking 🍸 🍴

Just north of town, **BAY'S END** (S2931 Indian Creek Rd.; 608.687.8216; Tu–Th 1p–2a, F,1p–2:30a, Sa 11a–2:30a, Su 11a–2a) is a friendly watering hole; they host live music a few times during the summer.

The **GOLDEN FROG SALOON** (112 N. Shore Dr.; 608.687.3335; daily 11a–2a), known originally by its German name *zum golden frosch* is a long-time local watering hole and still a good place to enjoy a drink.

At **NANA J'S JAVA JUNCTION** (2 S. Main St.; 608.687.3313; Tu–F 9–5, Sa 9–3:30 in the summer; reduced hours the rest of the year) grab a seat at the lunch counter and enjoy coffee and ice cream with local residents ($1.50/single scoop), all while washing your clothes in the adjacent laundromat

The **WING DAM BAR & GRILL** (1 N. Shore Dr.; 608.687.4144; kitchen open M 11a–9p, Tu–F 7a–10p, Sa 6a–10p, Su 9–9; bar open later) is the only spot in town that serves breakfast (mains from $3–$8).

If you like Irish pubs (if you don't, don't talk to me), you'll love the **MONARCH PUBLIC HOUSE** (19 N. Main St.; 608.687.4231; F,Sa 11a–10p, Su–Tu 11a–9p, W,Th 4p–9p, bar open later). Housed in an 1894 building that has been a tavern from the start, the pub still has many original furnishings, including the impressive bar. They serve a couple of local beers, but they are not brewed on-site. The menu includes Irish stew, Galway pot pie, and many other dishes inspired by the Emerald Isle (entrées $7–$11, sandwiches and salads $4–$9).

Sleeping 🛏

Camping. **DRIFT INN RESORT** (S2945 Indian Creek Rd.; 608.687.9581) is a small fishing resort that has a campground next to the backwaters occupied primarily by seasonal campers but might have a site or two available for overnight rental ($20/water & elec); call first to find out if they have a site. **MERRICK STATE PARK** (S2965 State Highway 35; 608.687.4936) has three different areas to camp. The sites at the north campground are shaded and close to the shower house but packed in tightly. The island sites are primitive walk-in sites that are more private and on the water (sites 49 and 50 are the most private). The south campground sites are all primitive and a bit of a hike from the shower house but not as crowded and many are close to the water (sites 51 and 52 are walk-in sites that are on the water and have no neighbors). Mosquitoes can be very active here in summer ($12/Wisc resident, $14/non-resident + $5/elec + daily fee of $7/Wisc resident, $10/non-resident).

Budget. The **FOUNTAIN CITY MOTEL** (810 S. Main St.; 608. 687.3111; WiFi) is a bargain, with 13 moderately-sized rooms in good shape that have been going through a gradual overhaul. All rooms have cable TV, fridge, microwave, and coffee; some rooms are decorated with a theme, like the Harley room ($65–$70 + tax).

Cabins/Houses. DRIFT INN RESORT (S2947 Indian Creek Road; 608.687.4936) has four cozy, simple cabins, two of which are kitchenettes ($45–$65 incl tax). For something completely different, consider a getaway at **ROOM TO ROAM** (W656 Veraguth Dr.; 608.687.8575), a 300-acre farm where you can participate in the daily activities of farm life and connect with your food source or just kick back and relax. The century-old, four-bedroom farm house is at the end of the road atop a bluff with views of the river valley toward Winona. While the house is not loaded with amenities, it does have a full kitchen and air conditioning and includes a chance to learn about farm life ($100+tax). On the other hand, the **HAWKS VIEW LODGES** (320 Hill St.; 866.293.0803/651.293.0803; WiFi) is the choice for a relaxing weekend in a luxurious setting. The folks at Seven Hawks have an eye for dramatic locations, and the two lodges are no exception. *The Osprey* is a two- story, two-bedroom house set on a hillside in a heavily wooded location at the top of several dozen steps. It has good, partially obstructed views of the river, a unique outdoor shower, and plentiful deck space. Inside, there is a full kitchen and several fireplaces ($225+tax, $25/per person extra). The *Blackhawk Lodge* is a four-bedroom house atop a ridge with expansive, unobstructed views of the Mississippi Valley and surrounded by vineyards. The house is loaded with amenities like fireplaces, a full kitchen, whirlpool tub, and easy access to a ridgetop hiking trail ($290+tax/4 persons, $25/person extra). The five houses that are the **HAWKS VIEW COTTAGES** (320 Hill St.; 866.293.0803/651.293.0803; WiFi) are built into the hillside and feel more than just a little like treehouses; all but one require climbing several steps to reach. Each cottage has a comfortable, modern décor and is flush with niceties like fireplaces, a full kitchen, and a whirlpool tub ($175–$200 + tax).

Moderate and up. The **HAWKS VIEW SUITES** (17 North St.; 866.293.0803/651.293.0803; WiFi) are above the wine store and have a full kitchen, air-jet tub, fireplace, king bed, and views of the river ($135–$160 + tax).

Resources

- The local newspaper is the *Cochrane-Fountain City Recorder* (608.248.2451).
- Post Office: 1 S. Main St.; 608.687.6851.

COCHRANE
(435)

Cochrane is one of the world's largest producers of oatmeal, thanks to the La Crosse Milling plant. Thought you might like to know that.

Arriving in Town

The business district is along Main Street, which parallels State Highway 35. Fifth Street connects the highway to Main Street.

History

Peter Shnugg owned some property in an area that some folks called Petersburgh. He sold part of it to the Chicago, Burlington, and Northern railroad, which promptly sold some of it the St. Paul Land Company to build a town around their new station. The land company platted a village in 1886 and named the village Cochrane after a railroad conductor who was popular in the area. J.L. and G.M. Rohrer, local farmers, bought the first parcels of land. They sensed a chance to make a few bucks and built a hardware store, reflecting an early trend where land owners were more concerned with developing commercial interests than building houses.

The new town had a busy livestock depot for a while, as well as a cheese factory. Folks finally got around to incorporating in 1910 and promptly built a village hall. The La Crosse Milling Company relocated to Cochrane shortly after its founding in La Crosse and has been busily churning out products like oatmeal since that time.

Tourist Information ⓘ

You can contact the **village clerk** (102 W. 5th St.; 608.248.2737) but the office has limited office hours.

Attractions 💡

The **Prairie Moon Museum and Sculpture Garden** (S2921 County Road G; 608.685.6290) makes many lists for quirky and/or odd attractions, and it's on mine, too. When farmer Herman Rusche retired in 1952, he needed something else to do, so the self-taught artist began creating sculptures out of stone and concrete, eventually making about 40. In 1979, at age 94, he retired again, auctioning his pieces so he could spend more time fishing. He died in 1985, just a few days after his 100th birthday. Interest in his work grew, and in 1992, The Kohler Foundation bought and restored the site, bringing back most of the original pieces to create a sculpture garden, then donating it all to Milton township to maintain as a public art site. Since that time, the collection has grown with the addition of pieces from John Mehringer's *Fountain City Rock Garden* that he created in the 1930s. The grounds are open all year.

Threatened with demolition when State Highway 35 was being realigned, the death sentence for the **Cochrane Village Hall** (Goose Lake Park, 4th St.; 608.685.6290; by appt only) was commuted when Dallas Dworschack began an effort to save it. Built in 1911 to serve as the focal point of civil life (voting, village board, fire department) but replaced with a more modern building in recent years, the fate of the old village hall looked grim. In the face of much opposition, he rallied enough support and private funds to move the village hall from its original location to a new home in Goose Lake Park in 2001. With the help of volunteers and more private donations, the building was renovated and reopened for the community's use. Inside, there are pictures of Cochrane through the years, and articles about the preservation of the building. It is usually open only for special events, but you can arrange a private tour.

Prairie Moon artist Rusche's self-portrait

Eating ✗

If you're the type of person who detours for locally sourced and produced food, or if you just love a good pizza, head to **SUNCREST GARDENS** (S2257 Yaeger Valley Rd.; 608.626.2122). This small farm transforms into a boutique pizza joint on Thursday evenings from May through Labor Day (4:30-9), putting together pizzas made with their ingredients grown on site. All pizzas are 16 inches and cooked quickly at high temperatures in a wood-fired oven ($18–$24; cash only). They only supply the pizza, so when you bring your friends to eat here, don't forget to bring utensils, drinks, and something to sit on, then relax and savor your pizza in a scenic coulee. To get there from Cochrane, take County Highway O east to State Highway 88, go left, and follow it to Yaeger Valley Rd; go left and then left again at the Y, and you're there.

Resources

- The local newspaper is the *Cochrane-Fountain City Recorder* (608.248.2451).
- Post Office: 108 N. Main St.; 608.248.2650.

Kenny Salwey

Kenny Salwey has lived intimately with the Mississippi River for most of his life. For 30 years, he made his living from the backwater area known as Whitman Bottoms, living in communion with the flora and fauna, taking just what he needed to meet his needs.

He is a dying breed, perhaps the last of his kind to live off the river so completely. In fact, he doesn't do it anymore. He has moved into a village next to the river and makes his living writing and telling stories about the river and his relationship to it.

In *The Last River Rat*, he and co-author J. Scott Bestul describe the life cycle of the river through a series of chapters that detail the monthly changes in the bottomlands ecosystem, along with the tasks that Salwey had to tackle to adapt and survive. Through these chapters, Salwey and Bestul bring to life the amazing richness and diversity of a world that is invisible to most of us.

Salwey's other books continue the storytelling tradition with tales about life along the backwaters and other people who lived like he did (*Tales of a River Rat* and *The Old Time River Rats*). Kenny was also the main character in the Emmy-award winning documentary *Mississippi: Tales of the Last River Rat*, produced by the BBC.

BUFFALO CITY

(1,040)

Buffalo City, like Minnesota City across the river, is a place that began with the grand ambitions of folks from the East, that (again like Minnesota City) failed to materialize, leaving us with a pleasant river town instead.

Arriving in Town

County Road OO loops around from the River Road and into Buffalo City. It snakes along the river for much of its length, so naturally it is called River Road. Tenth Street (County Road O) will also get you to Cochrane and back to the River Road.

History

Buffalo City owes it origins to the Colonization Society of Cincinnati, a group of Germans who were looking for places to resettle newly-arriving immigrants from their home country. In 1854, they looked to Kansas for a new settlement, but violence between abolitionist and pro-slavery forces persuaded them to look further north. In 1856 they bought land in western Wisconsin and platted a village they called Buffalo City.

At first, the new village attracted a good number of settlers, including many from Cincinnati. It soon became apparent, however, that river access was only going to be possible during periods of high water; the rest of the time, the main channel was too far away or simply inaccessible from the village. The town didn't attract much business, and many settlers left in disap-

View from Buena Vista Park, Alma, Wis.

Maria Angelorum Chapel, La Crosse, Wis.

Alma, Wis.

Fall gourds

Marina at La Crosse, Wis.

Land of the bluffs

Stockholm, Wis.

Trempealeau National Wildlife Refuge

pointment. Folks plodded on. Buffalo City incorporated in 1859, when it had fewer than 200 residents. With incorporation out of the way, local folks made an effort to get the county seat in 1862 by erecting a small building that could be used as a courthouse; their effort failed, so the building was used for a while as a jail and city office. The building is still around (in Buffalo City Park) and is the oldest existing jail in Wisconsin. Buffalo City never attracted much business. Once the early grand plans failed, the city developed into a residential community of retired farmers and seasonal residents, and that is still pretty much the case today.

Tourist Information (i)

If the **village clerk's office** (608.248.2262) isn't open, just ask around town.

Sports and Recreation

Whitman Dam Wildlife Area (608.685.6222) is a diverse backwaters area that is popular with birders. An easy walk along the two-mile long dike will give you a good sense of the area. To get there, follow the signs to Buffalo City; when County OO makes a sharp turn at the south end of town and you see a dead end sign, continue south on River Drive for 1.2 miles to the parking area for the lower Spring Lake boat ramp.

Eating

THE COVE (175 S. River Rd.; 608.248.2683; Su–Th 7a–9p, F,Sa 7a–10p) is a popular restaurant near the Mississippi River. Breakfast is served until 2pm with the standard egg and pancake options ($3–$8). Dinner entrées include pasta, shrimp scampi, walleye, and steaks (most $14–$16), with a selection of the usual burgers, sandwiches, and salads ($6–$8).

Sleeping

Cabins. WARD'S RIVERSIDE CABINS (389 W. 20th St.; 608.248.3702) are surrounded by peace and quiet (there are no railroad tracks nearby) and have been through an expert top-to-bottom overhaul. The six cabins are bright, cozy, and comfortable; each has a kitchenette and most have screened porches; they share a common area that is equipped with a sheltered picnic area and gas grills ($65–$105 + tax, + $5 if paying with credit card).

> For more information and updates, visit my web site at www.mississippivalleytraveler.com.

ALMA

(942)

One of the more scenic river towns along the Upper Mississippi River, Alma has attracted new residents in recent years, including many artists, who are bringing the town a new energy, at least in the summer months. Many businesses close or dramatically reduce their hours after the fall foliage season but don't let that dissuade you from visiting any time of year.

Arriving in Town

Wisconsin Highway 35 enters town as Main Street; the only other north-south street is 2nd Street, which is east of Main and higher up. The two streets are connected by a few roads and a dozen sets of concrete steps that have also been given street names. Most of the parking spots are on River Street; they fill quickly on summer weekends.

History

River pilots named this spot Twelve Mile Bluff because of a rock formation that was visible from the mouth of the Chippewa River 12 miles north of the bluff. Sadly, the rock outcropping that gave the bluff its distinctive shape collapsed in 1881, sending a giant boulder rolling down hill. No one was hurt, but a couple of buildings were damaged and the town lost its most distinctive landmark.

Settlers began arriving in 1848. The first to set up stakes were Swiss immigrants Victor Probst and John Waecker; they made a living selling cordwood to passing steamboats. And the Swiss just kept coming, supplemented by a smattering of Germans. The village was platted in 1855 with the name Alma, suggested by W.H. Gates.

Alma's growth began with the usual things—hotels, a general store, and a brewery—but the very first business in town was supposedly a saloon opened by a guy who came upriver from Keokuk. The town's economy got a boost when Alma won the county seat election in 1860. Zany county seat shenanigans often found on the frontier ensued. Fountain City challenged the election results, but the Wisconsin Supreme Court wouldn't play along. In 1861, Charles Schaettle led a group of Watergate-quality burglars from Buffalo City in an attempt to steal the county papers from Alma and bolster Buffalo City's claim. They failed, and, according to one account, the bungling burglars were chased from town while a fiddler played the tune *Wender nit bald heigo, ihr Chaiba*, which means something like "Won't you please decamp, you rascals." Alma beat Buffalo City in the 1861 county seat election and never looked back. Many of the disappointed settlers from Buffalo City relocated to Alma in the 1860s; probably not the same ones that tried to steal the county papers, though.

The single most important reason for Alma's early growth was logging. Beef Slough, an area just north of the village, was the site of a major operation where, from 1867 to 1889, logs coming down the Chippewa River were sorted and assembled into log rafts. The Beef Slough Manufacturing, Booming, Log Driving, and Transportation Company was founded in 1867 and grew into one of the largest operations in the US. The company later merged with the Mississippi River Logging Company, which chose Frederick Weyerhaeuser as its leader in 1873.

Alma had a couple of sawmills of its own, plus ice

harvesting, lime kilns, boat manufacturing, and a robust cigar manufacturing sector. The Martin Exel Company rolled nearly 60,000 cigars a year in the 1870s, mostly for the local market. By 1897, Alma counted three cigar factories that produced a collective 138,000 cigars every year; the factories closed by 1928.

One of the most celebrated local residents was Gerhard Gesell, an early photographer and contemporary of Ansell Adams (his studio operated from 1876-1906). Gesell was a gifted photographer who spent a lot effort documenting daily life in and around Alma (see sidebar on page 298). He made a composite photo called *Pioneers of Buffalo Co., Wisconsin* that was created from 156 individual portraits of folks who settled in the area prior to 1857; it is on display in the courthouse.

The last of the logging-related businesses shut down in 1905. Alma began attracting artists for the summer in the 1920s but only recently have more made Alma their year-round home. Lock and Dam 4 was built in 1932, which ended Alma's days as a port of call for riverboats but provided employment during the Depression.

Tourist Information ⓘ

Get your information fix at **Wings Over Alma** (312 N. Main St.; 608.685.3303; M–Sa 10–5, Su 11–5), which also doubles as an art gallery (see below).

Attractions 💡

Buena Vista Park (Buena Vista Rd.; 608.685.3330) has one of the most dramatic overlooks along Upper Mississippi. From a vantage point some 540 feet above the river, you can see the Whitman Bottoms, the area that Kenny Salwey once called home (see the sidebar on page 283). You can drive to the top via County

Great Alma Fishing Float

Highway E and Buena Vista Road, or, alternatively, you can hike to the top; go to the trailhead at 2nd and Elm.

The **Alma Area Historical Society** (505 S. 2nd St.; 608.685.6290; Th–Su 1–4 from Memorial Day–Oct 15; free) is housed in a former two-story schoolhouse and therefore has a lot of space to use, which they use well. My favorite displays are on the second floor, which has fun, historic photos (including some by local son Gerhard Gesell), an informative display about logging tools and logging camps, and a touching display about the 1940 Armistice Day blizzard.

With a scheduled grand opening in Spring, 2011, the **Castlerock Museum** (402 S. 2nd St.; 608.685.4231; call for hours) is destined to be a hot attraction. The museum is the brainchild of Gary Schlosstein, who began his life as a collector at age 10 when he bought a Civil War-era musket and has not stopped since. He and his partners do a phenomenal job of telling a good story about the evolution of arms and armor from the Roman Empire to the cusp of the gun powder era. The museum has a number of impressive pieces, like the 16th century German Maximillian-era armor—rare for being a complete set.

I especially like the way the museum uses art to illustrate how the pieces were worn.

The current **St. Lawrence Catholic Church** (206 S. 2nd St.; 608.685.3898) was built in 1956 for a parish that traces its roots to 1868. Normally, I wouldn't include a church that is only 50 years old, but I like the story behind the windows in this building, which were built in Innsbruck, Austria and installed in the 1960s. One window is called *Christ of the Mississippi* and was designed by the priest at that time, Father Thomas Ash, who was an avid fisherman. The window depicts Jesus with a fishing pole standing in a boat on the Mississippi with Lock and Dam 4 in the background.

Here's one for the architecture geeks. The building at **101 North Main** is the oldest structure in town—the top half, anyway. The previously mentioned W.H. Gates built it in 1855 as a general store. In 1872, a lower addition was built by excavating the ground under the upper level, so the upper half is nearly 20 years older than the lower half.

Lock and Dam 4 (608.685.4421) opened in 1935 and went through rehabilitation from 1988 to 1994. The lock has an average lift of 10 feet; the dam is 367 feet long.

Riecks Lake Park (North Highway 35; 608.685.3330) is just north of town and is a good spot to enjoy a picnic; this spot attracted thousands of migrating tundra swam a few years ago, but the lake's ecosystem has changed in recent years and become a less attractive spot for them to rest and snack.

Getting on the River

Brothers Tim and Jim Lodermeier have spent every summer since 1986 running the **Great Alma Fishing Float** (608.685.3786/608.685.3782; daily 6a–6p from mid-March–Oct), a good place to do some fishing if you don't have a boat with you. A boat will pick you up at a small dock across the tracks at the foot of Pine Street; lift the board to signal you need a ride. The shuttle runs frequently until 11am, then only runs hourly. It costs $15 for a day's worth of fishing from the float; don't forget your fishing license. You are welcome to ride the shuttle and hang out without fishing ($5 for the shuttle ride).

If you want to captain your own boat, you have a few options. **Fun 'N the Sun** (Great River Harbor, S2221 State Highway 35; 888.343.5670) rents houseboats in a variety of sizes; peak rates are from late June to late August: 3 day/4 day/7 day for the smallest (12' x 32') to the largest houseboat (18' x 60'): $650–$3095/$700–$3295/$1275–$5895; rates can be hundreds of dollars less the rest of the year. You can also rent pontoon boats ($220/day on weekends, $180/day on weekdays) or a fishing boat ($45/day). **Alma Marina** (125 Beach Harbor Rd.; 800.982.8410/608.685.3333; Su–Th 8–5, F,Sa 8–8) also has some rental boats: a 40' Skipper Liner that can sleep 6–8 (1 day/3 day weekend/7 days for $350/$875/$1325) or the 52' Skipper Liner that can sleep up to 11 (1 day/3-day weekend/7 days for $500/$1525/$2275); they also rent a pontoon boat ($175–$225/day on weekends, $150–$200/day on weekdays). For something human-powered, turn to **Riverland Outfitters** (1008 S. 2nd St.; 608.385.4351) to rent a kayak (1 hour/half-day/full-day: $10/$20/$25) or canoe (1 hour/half-day/full-day: $10/$25/$30).

At press time **Johnny Elliott** was planning to offer boat tours through the backwaters beginning in spring, 2011; give him a call for details (608.685.4090).

Culture & Arts

Wings Over Alma (312 N. Main St.; 608.685.3303; M–Sa 10–5, Su 11–5) displays the work of local artists.

Stump Town Gallery (109 S. Main St.; 414.630.5954; by appt) hosts curated exhibits of local and regional art.

Tours

At the visitor center, pick up a self-guided walking tour of Alma's historic buildings.

Entertainment and Events

The **Big River Radio Wave** (Big River Theatre, 121 Main St.; 608.685.4859; $10) is an old-time variety show that tapes a few times a year in Alma for later broadcast on Wisconsin Public Radio.

Festivals. The **Alma Music and Arts Festival** (608.685.4975) brings together local art and local music on Labor Day weekend. The Buffalo County Historical Society sponsors a **driving tour** of historic sites around the county in late September (608.685.6290).

Sports and Recreation

The **Mossy Hollow Trail** (South Highway 35; 608.685.3330) is a splendid network of trails through the woods and up the back of a bluff. You can stick to the main trail, which is wide and regularly mowed but won't get you to the top of the bluff unless you scale a short, steep hill near the end of it. The side trials are more rugged. Give yourself at least an hour to get up, take a side trail, lose the trail, get lost, and find your way back down, like I did.

The Gesell Family

The Gesells are a family of high achievers who did not shun the limelight. Patriarch Gerhard was a gifted photographer; son Arnold was a well-known psychologist; and grandson Gerhard a respected federal judge.

Gerhard Gesell emigrated to the US from Germany in 1863 and settled in Minnesota where two of his brothers were already living. He enlisted in the Army during the Civil War, serving with Brackett's Battalion in the West. When the war ended, he moved back to Reads Landing, first working in a saloon, then opening up his first photography studio in 1873. Three years later, he moved to Alma. He married Christine Giesen in 1879, and they had five children.

Their oldest child, Arnold (1880-1961) got a PhD in 1906 from Clark University when its President was the distinguished psychologist G. Stanley Hall; not one to rest on his laurels, he got an MD from Yale in 1915. Arnold specialized in child development and was tremendously influential in the field. He was the first person to identify age-appropriate signs to mark developmental progress and advanced research techniques in the field. He was also highly scrutinized for what appeared to be an early embrace of eugenics, a controversial theory that advocated selective breeding for humans in order to advance more desirable genes over less desirable ones. Proponents of eugenics believed that genes were far more important in human development than environmental factors; they advocated the idea that the poor had less desirable genes and should not be allowed to reproduce (and, in fact, many low-income people were sterilized without their consent in the early 20th century). Some took it a level further by advocating the genetic superiority of whites over everyone else. It seems clear that Arnold embraced eugenics early in his career. In a 1913 article called *The Village of a Thousand Souls*, he detailed rates of undesirable traits such as alcoholism, mental illness, and "feeble-mindedness" in his home town, arguing that selective breeding could reduce such undesirable outcomes. The folks back in Alma were not amused. Over time, as the full political and human implications of eugenics became clearer, Gesell's views evolved away from eugenics and toward a view that recognized a more subtle interaction between nature and nurture.

Arnold's son, Gerhard (1911-1993), also could not escape controversy, although he was not usually the cause of it. He was appointed to the federal judiciary in Washington, D.C. in 1967 by President Johnson and took a strong stand against the abuse of power. He was the presiding judge for a number of high profile cases related to Watergate, the *Pentagon Papers,* and the Iran-contra scandal. In the 1971 *Pentagon Papers* case, he was the only judge (of 29 involved in the case) who refused to issue an injunction to stop the *New York Times* from publishing the infamous documents, writing: "It should be obvious that the interests of the Government are inseparable from the interests of the public. These are one and the same, and the public interest makes an instant plea for publication."

Hey, what's that? When you are near the Dairyland Power Cooperative plant on the south end of town, look up. About 450 feet above the ground on the stack closest to the highway, you can see a nesting box for peregrine falcons. Like bald eagles, peregrines were on the verge of extinction in the 1970s because DDT caused the shells of their eggs to be too thin. A concerted captive breeding and release program brought them back from the brink, and they are no longer endangered. They are remarkable birds. About the size of a crow, a peregrine on the hunt folds its wings back and dives at speeds over 200 miles an hour.

The **Alma Beach and Recreation Area** (North Highway 35; 608.685.3330) is just north of town by Alma Marina.

Riverland Outfitters (1008 S. 2nd St.; 608.385.4351) can help with your winter outdoor exploration by renting you a pair of snowshoes (half-day/full-day: $5/$10).

Shopping

Alma has a good range of locally-grown shops. Take your time to look around.

At **DANZINGER VINEYARDS & WINERY** (S2106 Grapeview Rd.; 608.685.6000; daily 10–6) enjoy five free tastings or sample all ten of their wines for $2 at their scenic blufftop location. **THE BUFFALO TRADING COMPANY** (200 S. Main St.; 608.685.4555; daily 10–5) has knickknacks, books of local interest, wine, and other items to feed your appetites. **WHITE OAK GALLERY** (117 S. Main St.; 608.685.6200; Th–M 10–5) has an impressive inventory of items produced by local and regional artists, including photographers, painters, sculptors, and wood carvers. **ALMA LEATHER** (121

N. Main St.; 608.685.4775; Th–M 11–5) is the source for handmade hats, belts, and gloves. **MISSISSIPPI RIVER PEARL JEWELRY COMPANY** (125 N. Main St.; 651.301.1204; daily 10–5) sells exquisite jewelry with pearls harvested from the Mississippi River. **ART & SOUL** (303 N. Main St.; 715.448.2049/715.456.3977; Th–M 11–5 from June–Oct., Sa,Su 11–5 in April, May, Nov.) has original paintings and jewelry plus fair trade imports. **GYPSY WAGON STUDIO** (307 N. Main St.; 612.423.3653) sells the work of local and regional artists who work in a variety of media. **THE WEAVING STUDIO** (411 N. Main St.; 608.685.4151; open in summer F–Su 11–5 or by appt.) sells handmade fiber products and mosaic art.

Eating and Drinking

Get your caffeine fix at the **COFFEE GROUNDS** (202 S. Main St.; 608.685.4555; daily 10–5) or **FIRE AND ICE** (305 N. Main St.; 612.423.3653; daily 11a-9p from Memorial Day–Labor Day; F 4–9, Sa 11a–9p, Su 11–6 in Sept., Oct.); the latter also a beautiful garden in back where you can sip your coffee or slurp a scoop of ice cream ($2 for a single scoop).

For something completely different, head out to the **GREAT ALMA FISHING FLOAT** for breakfast (café open 7a–3p). *The Mess* is a wild combination of flavors that work surprisingly well together: eggs, bacon, ham, sausage, potatoes, cheese, tomatoes. But, to really make it work, you need to go all way and get it with sauerkraut ($8.75/full mess; $5.50/half mess). See the entry under Getting on the River for more details on the float.

Relax at **KATE AND GRACIE'S RESTAURANT** (215 N. Main St.; 608.685.4505; W,Th,Su 11–9, F,Sa 11–11) and enjoy a break from bar food in this casual bistro setting, where good food comes with views of the river. Local ingredients are used as much as possible to create a good selection of sandwiches and salads ($5–$10), pasta dishes ($10), and filling dinner entrées like pork or beef tenderloin ($17–$22); if the weather is nice, try to grab a table on the garden patio.

Apparently you don't have to go all the way to Memphis for good barbeque; you can enjoy it at the **PIER 4 CAFÉ AND SMOKEHOUSE** (600 N. Main St.; 608.685.4964; W–M 6a–2p); get it as a platter with two sides ($8–$10) or in a sandwich ($4–$7.50) and watch boats lock through from the screened porch. They also serve a very popular breakfast (6a–1p; most items <$6).

Sleeping

Camping. Most of the sites with services at the **GREAT RIVER HARBOR CAMPGROUND AND MARINA** (S2221 State Highway 35; 608.248.2454) are occupied by seasonal campers so call ahead to find out if any of the overnight sites are available ($35/full hookup); if you just need a place to pitch a tent, though, they should have room for you ($20/primitive site). **RIECKS LAKE PARK** (608.685.3330) has 20 sites with electricity, shared water, and coin-op showers on a narrow strip of shaded land between the highway and a backwaters lake ($15).

Budget. Alma has some unique lodging options for folks on the smallest of budgets; buyer beware. The **FELICE PATRA INN** (609 N. Main St.; 608.685.4512; WiFi; generally open April–January) has two bunk beds in a room that feels like a closet that are available for overnight rentals ($20); they share a bathroom. There are additional rooms upstairs in a rambling warren of dusty spaces that haven't been updated in a while and might remind you of your grandparent's house. One guest room has a private bath; the other three rooms share one bath. Guests have use of a full kitchen upstairs and spacious, shady decks ($58–$68 + tax). Another cheap option is the **ALMA HOTEL** (201 N. Main St.; 608.685.3380; WiFi); the 12 sleeping rooms don't get more basic—just beds in rooms without AC and with shared baths ($28 incl tax, $39 incl tax for the one room with its own bathroom). Hey, the place started life as a brothel, so a bed in a small room was good enough. Ever slept on a fish float? I bet not. Now's your chance at the **GREAT ALMA FISHING FLOAT** (608.685.3786/608.685.3782); accommodations are not luxurious unless you consider plywood walls fancy but, hey, you're on the river, and you can fish. They have two rooms with four bunks in each; you will need to bring a sleeping bag and pillow, and there are no showers ($38/person based on quad occupancy in March, April, & October; $30/person the rest of the summer; reservations required). The **LAUE HOUSE INN** (1111 S. Main St.; 608.685.4923; open mid-April–mid-December) is an adorable 1863-era home with a casual atmosphere. Adorned with period furnishings but not stuffiness, the Laue is a throwback to an earlier era when a B&B was more like a homestay and not a fancy inn. Guests can use the player piano in the parlor. There are five guest rooms, including a large room in front with good river views; they share a bathroom ($40–$45 incl tax and continental breakfast). **THE HOTEL DE VILLE** (305 N. Main St.; 612.423.3653; WiFi in some units) offers a variety of lodging options in tastefully rehabbed historic buildings along Main Street. In the main building, they have three lovely second floor rooms that are a good budget option; they share a bath ($55+tax; WiFi). The **HILLCREST MOTEL** (240 State Highway 35 North; 608.685.3511) has seven moderately-sized rooms with cable TV in good shape and with views of the river ($60+tax). **REIDTS MOTEL AND CABINS** (S1638 State Road 35; 608.685.4843; open mid-March–December) has five cozy motel rooms ($50+tax) just off the highway a few miles north of Alma.

Bed and Breakfast. The **TRITSCH HOUSE BED AND BREAKFAST** (601 S. 2nd St.; 507.450.6573; WiFi; open April–November) is a 1902 Queen Anne mansion redone top-to-bottom in impressive fashion by owner Johnny Elliott. The five guest rooms have private baths, four with Jacuzzi tubs, and flat screen TVs that are hooked up with cable TV ($95–$135 + tax incl continental breakfast); you can pass the time sitting on the deck or screened porch or playing pool in the billiard room.

Cabins/Houses. GREAT RIVER HARBOR CAMPGROUND AND MARINA (S2221 State Highway 35; 608.248.2454) has one cabin for rent that manages to feel like a houseboat in its configuration. The cabin is narrow but in good shape and clean and can sleep six comfortably; it has one full bath, a fireplace, and a full kitchen ($150+tax). As you may have noticed above, Great River Harbor also rents houseboats; if any of those boats have not been claimed, you may be able to rent one overnight for dockside lodging (from $150 + tax); call a day or two in advance of your stay to find out if one is available. A mile north of Alma, the **HILLCREST MOTEL** (240 State Highway 35 North; 608.685.3511) rents three cabins of varying sizes that are equipped with microwave, fridge, and coffee ($60–$100 + tax, two night minimum); guests have access to a shared kitchen. **REIDT'S MOTEL AND CABINS** (S1638 State Road 35; 608.685.4843; open mid-March–December) has four cabins in very good shape; all have cable TV, microwave, small fridge, and coffee; the cabins are large, two bedroom units with a full kitchen ($100+tax). **AUDREY'S RIVERVIEW INN** (101 Orange St.; 715.495.8880) is a bright space with big windows to enjoy one of the best views in town from a hillside building rehabbed from top to bottom ($100+tax for up to seven people); the house has a full kitchen, two bedrooms, and a pleasant deck.

Moderate. The **ALMA TOWN HOUSE** (104 S. Main St.; 715.926.5743/608.685.4555) is a two-bedroom, one-bath apartment on the riverfront, with a full kitchen, washer and dryer, cable TV, screened porch, and rotary phone that could sleep six comfortably ($95+tax/2 people, $110+tax/3 or more people); it is only available from May–November. **THE HOTEL DE VILLE** (305 N. Main St.; 612.423.3653; WiFi in some units) is the most exclusive place in town according to Dan, one of the owners. All units have pillow-top mattresses and French-inspired décor in tastefully rehabbed historic buildings along Main Street. The suites and cottage all have a private bath and full kitchen or kitchenette: the two-bedroom *Garden Suite* is above the art shop ($140+tax; WiFi); the two-bedroom *Falcon Cottage* is next door ($140+tax); and the *Swan* and *Eagle* suites are across the street and along the riverfront ($95–$140 + tax).

Resources

- Post Office: 205 S. Main St.; 608.685.3561.
- Alma Public Library: 312 N. Main St.; 608.685.3823; WiFi; M,W,F 10:30a–7p.

NELSON

(395)

Nelson is another crossroads town that most people zip through, although they might stop at the cheese factory. There are other reasons to get out of your car and explore, too.

Arriving in Town

State Highway 25 is the primary north-south route through town and State Highway 35 is the main east-west route.

History

Englishman James Nelson settled near the mouth of the Chippewa River in the 1840s, thus giving the area the name Nelson's Landing. The area had a ferry connection to Read's Landing for a while, although the sloughs on the Wisconsin side could make for a challenging trek. Madison Wright arrived in the township in 1848 and is generally acknowledged as the first permanent settler. He lived in the bottomlands but did most of his trading in Wabasha. When he died, Wabasha sent a bill for his burial to the Fairview-Nelson Town Board, which replied that if he died poor, it was because he spent all his money in Wabasha, so Wabasha should bury him.

Nelson's Landing was a busy place; at least it had a lot of people passing through on the way to or from the logging camps. More permanent settlers began arriving in the mid-1850s, but the village wasn't platted until 1884 when the railroad surveyed a depot site.

Tourist Information ⓘ

You can contact the **village clerk** (715.673.4804), but the office has limited hours; the folks at the Nelson Cheese Factory are your next best bet.

Entertainment and Events ♪

The village celebrates its heritage with **Good Old Nelson Days** (second weekend in August; 715.673.4804) with food and music.

Sports and Recreation ≋

Between the 12,000 acre **Tiffany Wildlife Area** and the 4,000 acre **Nelson-Trevino Bottoms State Natural Area** (State (State Highway 25; 608.685.6222), outdoor enthusiasts have much to explore around Nelson. Both areas encompass the Chippewa River delta, one of the largest in the Upper Midwest. It is a vast landscape of sloughs, marshes, and dense bottomland hardwood forest, abundant with wildlife, and very popular with folks who like to fish. The area is probably best explored by boat (a canoe or kayak would be ideal), but you are welcome to hike anywhere in the wildlife area, just be aware that there are no developed trails and it can be very wet. In winter, this is a great spot for cross-country skiing.

Shopping

The **NELSON CREAMERY** (S237 State Road 35; 715.673.4725; Su–Th 9–6, F,Sa 9–7 from April–Oct, daily 9–5:30 the rest of the year) dates to 1911 when it was called the Nelson Co-op Creamery and they actually made cheese. It is now a retail store selling an impressive selection of cheese from Wisconsin and around the world, plus wine and gourmet food items. **THE GIFT** (S310 Highway 35; 715.673.4838; F,Sa 10–5, Su 11–4 or by appt) specializes in handmade art like gemstone jewelry and the photographs of the late Gary Rodock, a gifted nature photographer who spent his life taking pictures along the Mississippi River. The photographs are remarkably affordable; bring cash. **PEELING SHUTTERS** (S210 State Highway 35; 715.673.4299; Tu–Sa 10–5, Su 10–4) sells handmade jewelry and unique home furnishings.

Eating ✗

Nelson has surprisingly good food for a village of just 400 people. If you're in the mood for something light, the **NELSON CREAMERY** (S237 State Road 35; 715.673.4725; Su–Th 9–6, F,Sa 9–7 from April–Oct, daily 9–5:30 the rest of the year) makes a good sandwich for about $6; you can follow that up with ice cream for a dollar a scoop.

For a heartier, sit down meal, head to **BETH'S TWIN BLUFF CAFÉ** (S286 State Road 35; 715.673.4040; Su–Th 6:30a–8p, F,Sa 6:30a–8:30p in summer). They serve everything from breakfast (mains <$7) to dinner (sandwiches and burgers <$8, dinner mains $9–$15) but your best bet is to try one of the daily specials. Or, you can just go there for a danged good piece of pie ($3). I had a slice of Amish Oatmeal Pie, which was rich and yummy and big enough to be my dessert for two meals.

I'm a self-professed barbeque snob. I can't help it. My family roots are in Kansas City, so I know what good barbeque is supposed to taste like. I'm not picky about the style of 'cue, I just want it done well. All this is my way of saying that I can't say enough about the quality of the barbeque at the **NELSON GENERAL STORE** (N208 N. Main St.; 715.673.4717; Tu,Th 10:30–6, F–Su 10:30–7). They make a southern-style barbeque that is tender, moist, and so full of flavor that you can eat it without any sauce and not feel the least bit deprived. My favorite is the BBQ beef but the pulled pork is savory goodness, too ($5 for a large sandwich and chips, $6 for sandwich with two sides; baby back ribs are $9/half-rack, $18/full rack). There are only four tables inside, so you may want to get it to go and have a picnic.

About nine miles outside of town, **THE STONE BARN** (S685 County Road KK; 715.673.4478, F–Su 5p–9p) is housed in the partially reconstructed ruins of a 19th century stone barn on an isolated farm; the atmosphere alone is something special. The thin crust, 16" artisanal pizzas are made from local ingredients and cooked at a high temperature in a wood-fired oven and pack great flavor ($18–$23); they also have a selection of regional beers and wine at reasonable prices.

Sleeping

Camping. You can pitch a tent within **TIFFANY WILDLIFE AREA** but you need a permit (608.685.6222); no services.

Cabins. CEDAR RIDGE RESORT (S1376 State Highway 35; 608.685.4998; WiFi) rents six attractive log cabins and cottages of various sizes with cedar siding that are nestled into a hillside overlooking the river. Cabins range from an 1860s log home (totally rehabbed, of course) to new large log homes that can sleep 12; all come with amenities like satellite TV, a full kitchen, and modern bathrooms ($75–$200 incl tax; two night minimum on weekends).

Resources
- Post Office: E200 Cleveland St.; 715.673.4025.

PEPIN

(878)

Pepin might look like a sleepy village but don't be fooled. This small river town is a big draw for fans of both Laura Ingalls Wilder and good food.

Arriving in Town

State Highway 35 is Third Street in Pepin and runs through the north part of town; most of the places you'll want to visit are along Second Street; the riverfront is along First Street.

History

The first settler in the township was John McCain, born in 1814 in Pennsylvania, who arrived in 1846, built a cabin, and later became a US Senator from Arizona and presidential nominee. McCain was involved in the logging industry and piloted boats on the Chippewa and Mississippi Rivers. He bought hundreds of acres of land and platted a village called Lakeport.

The first claim at the present site of Pepin was made by McCain's cousin, William Boyd Newcomb, thus supplying the villages first name, Newcomb's Landing. In 1846 Newcomb gave up a job as a school teacher and traveled upriver from Fort Madison (Iowa). Like his cousin, he worked initially in the lumber industry, and then became a river pilot, but was never a US Senator from Arizona.

When the village was platted in 1855, it was called North Pepin. The Pepin name may be derived from early explorers Pierre Pepin and his brother, Jean Pepin du Cardonnetes who spent time around here in 1679, because their father (Guillaume dit Tranchemontagne) and uncle (Etiene Pepin de La Fond) had a land grant from King Louis XIII. Virtually all of the village's initial growth was driven by the logging industry.

The typical businesses cropped up amid great optimism about the village's future, but the national financial panic in 1857 put the brakes on everything. A bigger problem for the village of North Pepin, however, was low river levels in 1857-58, as the village didn't have the best steamboat landing and low water made it nearly impossible for boats to dock. North Pepin also began losing business to the Beef Slough rafting operation in Alma and lost the county seat to Durand as that town boomed with its railroad business. Folks slogged on, even incorporating in 1860, but the incorporation was abandoned just four years later.

The village found new life with the growth of the local farm economy and reincorporated in 1882 with 340 residents. The Chicago, Burlington, and Northern railroad arrived in 1886, which helped provide connections to markets for the fishing industry. Commercial fishing picked up at the end of 19th century, supplying markets primarily in New York and the South. The peak fishing season was in winter when nets could be dragged under the ice, hauling in large caches of fish. Many of the fishermen worked the warmer months on the river as pilots, captains, or engineers.

Pepin was also home to the Pepin Pickle Company (1904-1937), sawmills, a creamery, a pearl button factory, and a bobsled factory. After the railroad came through, many businesses moved from First Street to Second Street because the noise from the trains scared their horses. The first automobile owned by a local resident appeared in 1908; by 1917 there were 66 in town. There are a few more than that today, as most residents commute to jobs elsewhere.

Tourist Information ⓘ

The **Pepin Visitor Center** (306 3rd St.; 800.442.3011/715.442.2142; daily 10–5 from May–Oct.) is the best source for the scoop on the area, plus it has a few displays about Laura Ingalls Wilder.

Attractions 💡

Laura Ingalls Wilder was born in rural Pepin township on February 7, 1867. Her family moved away shortly after she was born but returned around 1871 and stayed for three years. Her first book, *Little House in the Big Woods*, was based on her time in Pepin County; she was 65 years old when she wrote it. She went on to write seven more books about life on the prairie and these books were the inspiration for the 1970s-erea TV show Little House on the Prairie. Folks in Pepin have worked hard to preserve her memory and to honor her connection to the region. The **Laura Ingalls Wilder Museum** (306 3rd St.; 800.442.3011/715.442.2142; daily 10–5 from May–Oct; free) recreates the feeling of the kind of log cabin that inspired Wilder and has a store where you can buy her books.

The **Laura Ingalls Wilder Wayside and Cabin** (N3238 Cty Rd CC; 800.442.3011; 24/7/365) is about seven miles outside of town, but unless you are doing the Laura Trail, your life won't be diminished if you skip this re-creation of a log cabin on the land where she was born.

The **Pepin Depot Museum** (800 3rd St.; 715.442.6501; F–Su from May–Oct; free) is another case of a few dedicated volunteers stepping up to save a piece of local history in the face of criticism and head-scratching from the majority. Volunteers raised money to move the depot from the lakefront to its new location in 1985 when the Burlington Northern

Railroad decided it didn't want the building anymore. The 1875-era depot has some fun railroad artifacts like the 20-pound "portable" phone, a crossing bell, and assorted tools used by the rail workers.

Getting on the River

On-Deck Seminars & Charters (400 1st St.; 715.442.4424) will take you out on Lake Pepin on a two-hour cruise in a 31-foot sloop captained by David Sheridan, a man who is doing exactly what he was meant to do. This is a fine way to relax and have a more personal experience on the water than you'll get on the larger cruise boats (F-Su 11,1:30,4,7,9:30 from mid-May–Aug, F-Su 10, 12:30, 3,6,8:30 in Sept, Oct.; $50/adult).

✔ TIP: Ice boating on Lake Pepin is increasingly popular. If you'd like to learn more about it check with David of On-Deck Seminars (see above).

Culture & Arts

The **Lake Pepin Art and Design Center** (408 2nd St.; 715.442.4442; gallery open F 2–5, Sa Noon–7, Su Noon–4) has a small gallery and also hosts a number of cultural events throughout the year; check their website for a current schedule (pepinartdesign.org).

Entertainment and Events

The **Pepin Farmers Market** is at the Art and Design Center on Fridays.

Festivals. The **Pepin Lighted Boat Parade** (weekend of July 4) is an impressive spectacle as boats are decorated with bright lights and show off in a promenade around Lake Pepin. The town's major event, though, is **Laura Ingalls Wilder Days** (800.442.3011;

second weekend in Sept). The weekend includes a fiddle competition, tales from pioneer days, an essay contest, traditional crafts, and a parade. The town turns to cinema in October for the **Flyway Film Festival** (715.442.4442), a celebration of independent film.

Sports and Recreation

Five Mile Bluff Prairie State Natural Area (Cross Rd.; 608.685.6222) has three goat prairies that, if you can find them, have good views of the confluence of the Mississippi and Chippewa Rivers. I made the mistake of following an old service road, which is not a bad hike, but it won't get you to the goat prairies, and, dear God, bring mosquito spray. I spent 45 minutes hiking around, stubbornly refusing to give up, even with a cloud of mosquitoes following me the entire time. You, however, can learn from my mistake. When you park at the end of the road, ignore the old service road and hike up the hill in front of you. Let me know how the view is. And, watch out for timber rattlesnakes; you aren't likely to see any, but, then again you might. To reach this natural area, follow County Highway N from Pepin for 2.7 miles, then head east on Cross Road (a gravel road) for another 2.7 miles until the road ends.

There is a **swimming beach** on Lake Pepin just behind the yacht club by the marina.

Shopping

BNOX GOLD AND IRON (404 1st St.; 715.442.2201; M,Th 11–7, F,Sa 11–9, Su Noon–7) has beautiful handcrafted jewelry and other fine art from local and regional artists. The **DOCKSIDE MERCANTILE** (304 First St.; 715.442.4009; open mid-March–Dec, with peak hours of M,Th 11–6, Sa 10–8, Su Noon–6) is a general store for the 21st century: t-shirts, clothing, books, gourmet food items, and more! **THE SMITH BROTHERS LANDING** (200 E. Marina Dr.; 715.442.2248; daily mid-March–Oct) is the metal and glass studio for Dave Smith, who is descended from an early pioneer family and is well-versed in local history. He also makes some cool (and inexpensive) metal sculptures. **T & C LATANÉ METALWORKS** (412 2nd St.; 715.442.2419; F,Sa Noon–6) is a blacksmith shop producing traditional Scandinavian designs and locks, plus tin cookie cutters beloved throughout the region. **PAUL AND FRAN'S GROCERY** (410 2nd St.; 715.442.2441; M–F 9–6, Sa 8:30–6) makes sausages from scratch that have a big fan base.

Eating

At **GREAT RIVER ROASTERS** (415 3rd St.; 715.442.4100; M,W,Th 7a–4p, F–Su 7a–5p in summer; WiFi) you can get a fresh cup of coffee from the folks who roast the beans that supply many area coffee shops.

The **HARBOR VIEW CAFÉ** (314 First St; 715.442.3893; Th 11–2:30, F 11–2:30 & 5–9, Sa 11–2:30 & 4:45–9, Su 11:45–7:30 from mid-March–mid-November; additional hours: Th 5–9 from April–Oct, M 11–2:30 & 5–8 from Memorial Day–Labor Day) is a destination restaurant with a wide-ranging reputation for creating great food without snootiness. The restaurant is housed in an 1880s-era waterfront building and keeps everything low key. The menu is written on a chalkboard and changes depending upon what ingredients are available, but you can assume that most entrées will be in the $18–$22 range. The day I went, I had a rich, flavorful summer cassoulet with lamb sausage, pork tenderloin, grilled vegetables, and white beans, preceded by a surprisingly complex

The author pretending he can sail

cold cucumber soup. Bring plenty of cash, because they do not take credit cards.

✔ TIP: People line up early for dinner at the Harbor View (they do not take reservations) which can lead to a long wait for a table. They have the exact same menu at lunch, however, and far fewer people showing up, so you will probably get right in.

If you're in town for the day, have dinner at the Harbor View and lunch with Judith at the **THIRD STREET DELI** (1015 3rd St.; 715.442.3354; M,Th,F 7a–5p Sa 8–5 Su 8–3). Judith prepares exceptional food from scratch and serves it with sass, using local, seasonal ingredients. And I'm not just saying this because she kept calling me "handsome stranger." On my first visit, I had the whole earth breakfast, a mix of grilled vegetables—including a tomato fresh from her garden—plus sausage that is made using her recipe. Most items run a reasonable $6–$8.

If that's still not enough for you, the **HOMEMADE CAFÉ** (809 3rd St.; 612.396.5804; Th,Su 7a–2p, F,Sa 7a–9p) is yet another Pepin restaurant that specializes in cooking from scratch. Breakfast is served all day ($6–$8). Save room for pie ($3/slice); cash only.

Sleeping

Camping. The **LAKE PEPIN CAMPGROUND** (1010 Locust St.; 715.442.2012) is a large campground on the inland side of the highway ($12/tent only, $24/sewer, water, elec) with many sites that are in the open.

✔ TIP: If you're not a registered camper, you can use the campground's showers for $2.

Budget. THE GREAT RIVER AMISH INN (311 Third St.; 715.442.5400; WiFi) has seven simple but lovely rooms decorated with quilts and Amish furniture, equipped with microwave, fridge, coffee pot, and cable TV ($65–$75+tax). **THE PEPIN MOTEL** (305 Elm St..; 715.442.2012; WiFi) has 16 large, new-ish rooms with cable TV that are sensibly furnished ($71 incl tax), plus two whirlpool suites ($110 incl tax).

Bed and Breakfasts. The **HARBOR HILL INN** (310 Second St; 715.442.2324/763.300.6018; WiFi; open April–Dec.) has three homey rooms in a 19th century cottage; guests are served a full English breakfast ($120–$140 + tax); they also have a two-bedroom guest house above the garage with a full kitchen and room to sleep six ($200 + tax, no breakfast). Nancy, the genial host at **A SUMMER PLACE B&B** (106 Main St.; 715.442.2132; WiFi; open Th–M from mid-March–mid-Nov), is a professional decorator, so you know you can count on quality. The house was built in 1994 specifically as a B&B but meant to resemble an older house, so the three rooms have modern amenities like private baths with Jacuzzi tubs and are bright and uncluttered ($160+tax).

Cabins/Houses. PEPIN COTTAGE (401 W. Main St.; 651.204.0505) is a small home bathed generously with natural light that is nicely outfitted for a large family or group of friends traveling together. It has a full kitchen, two bathrooms, and enough bed space to sleep up to 10 folks ($200+tax; + $40 cleaning fee; three night minimum in summer, two nights the rest of the year). **PEPIN EAGLE'S NEST** (1480 First St.; 952.237.5210), another whole house rental, has more character than you might expect given the nondescript exterior. The house can sleep 6–8 comfortably and is equipped with a full kitchen, two bathrooms, a fireplace, a kids' playroom, and a big deck with a grill ($195+tax/4 people, $20/person extra; two night minimum). Get a taste of the good life at **MARIPORT** (734 Scenic Lane; 715.210.0073; WiFi), a modern, four-bedroom luxury home with an expansive view of Lake Pepin that is furnished as you would expect a luxury home to be: gourmet kitchen, a master bedroom with a whirlpool tub overlooking Lake Pepin, a swimming pool, satellite TV, and large decks with a gas grill; the house can comfortably accommodate nine people ($500 incl tax). Just across the pool from the main house, a two-bedroom cottage is also available for overnight rentals. The cottage has amenities like a full kitchen, two bathrooms, washer and dryer, and abundant natural light and is decorated with a big game theme ($300 incl tax). You can rent either the house or the cottage, but if you rent the house, it costs $100/night extra to keep the cottage unrented.

Resources

- Post Office: 420 2nd St.; 715.442.4961.
- Pepin Public Library: 510 Second St.; 715.442.4932; Tu–Th 10–7, Sa 9–Noon.

STOCKHOLM
(97)

Stockholm is, no surprise, a town that has deep Swedish roots. It is also home to a surprisingly large colony of artists, who have given the village new life.

Arriving in Town

State Highway 35 is the main road through town. Take Spring Street to the west to reach Lake Pepin or go east to find the small business district.

History

In 1849, Erik Peterson and two brothers left Karlskoga, Sweden to prospect gold in California. Erik changed his mind in Chicago. His brothers continued on to California, while he went south for a few months, then back north to work in a logging camp along the St. Croix River. Along the way, he passed the location of the future village site, liked it, and filed a claim in 1851. He sent a letter to another brother in Sweden, Jakob, encouraging him to come. When he didn't get a reply, he went back to Sweden only to find that Jakob had already left. Jakob had a tough voyage to America. His ship captain died en route, leaving his green son in charge; the ship rammed into an iceberg before turning south to warmer waters. Jakob's group wintered in Moline (Illinois) in 1853, where one of his daughters died. He finally reached Stockholm in the spring of 1854.

While in Sweden, Erik got married and organized a party of 200 to go to America with him. Erik was quite a cad, though. He booked the cheapest, least

Stockholm's Peterson clan

comfortable passage from Liverpool to Quebec for his fellow Swedes, keeping the extra cash as profit. After they reached North America, they traveled to Chicago by train but Erik booked them in cattle cars where a cholera epidemic killed nearly one-third of the group, including his own mother. He tried to claim he didn't know her, so he wouldn't have to pay for her funeral. When he finally arrived in Stockholm, only 30 of the original group were with him (some opted to stay in Moline rather than continue upriver).

With that inauspicious beginning, the proprietors platted the village in 1856 and called it Stockholm on Lake Pepin. Perhaps because of bad karma, the village grew very slowly, centered primarily on the farm sector. In the 1870s, Paul Sandquist made a living selling lemon beer, and John Gunderson did the same by brewing and bottling spruce beer. By the time the village incorporated in 1903, it had 300 residents but would soon enter a period of steady population loss until reaching bottom in the 1940s with fewer than 100.

On July 18, 1938, Stockholm was visited by Swedish royalty: Crown Prince Gustaf Adolf, Crown Princess Louise, and Prince Bertil. They were touring the US to mark the 300th anniversary of the founding of the first Swedish settlement in the US (at Delaware). The town was notified on a Friday that the royals would be stopping on the following Monday, so they spent the weekend busily prettying-up the town and the rail station. Nearly 700 people turned out for the 15-minute whistle-stop speeches. Prince Gustaf told a Swedish newspaper that the stop in Stockholm on Lake Pepin was one of the top three highlights of his months-long tour of the US.

The village's fortunes began to turn around when artists began moving to town in the 1970s. Most made Stockholm their year-round home and opened shops and galleries that continue to attract visitors from throughout the region.

Tourist Information ⓘ

For tourism info, head to the Internet (www.stockholmwisconsin.com) or call **Stockholm General** (715.442.9077).

Attractions

Stockholm Village Park (Spring St.) is a quaint, peaceful lakeside park, perfect for a picnic lunch. There is also an old pier that extends far into the lake, offering panoramic views.

The village's history is preserved at the **Stockholm Museum** (Spring St.; daily 10–5 from May–Oct, otherwise by appt through A Sense of Place next door). Housed in the former post office, the museum has an informative timeline of the town's history, some old photos, and a bunch of old records for genealogy enthusiasts.

> For more information and updates, visit my web site at www.mississippivalleytraveler.com.

Culture & Arts

The **WideSpot Performing Arts Center** (Stockholm Opera House, N2030 Spring St.; 715.307.8941) is in the old opera house and hosts regular concerts and performing arts; check the schedule online (www.widespotperformingarts.org).

The Palate (W12102 State Highway 35; 715.442.6400; Tu–Sa 9–5, Su 10–5) hosts a monthly cooking class at the end of which you get to eat the class assignment (www.thepalate.net; $75).

Linda Harding also offers cooking classes through **The Kitchen Sage** (www.thekitchensage.com; 612.964.9050;); lessons emphasize using seasonal, sustainable ingredients.

Entertainment and Events

The Stockholm Art Fair (mid-July) is an art fair the way an art fair oughta be, which is probably why it is insanely popular. The juried fair includes a variety of media like zipper paintings, pottery, fiber, photography, painting, wood carving, and jewelry, but, based on my entirely unscientific method, the single most popular item was a giant bag of kettle popcorn. Even the food is better than your average fair food fare: salmon ceviche, wild rice bratwurst, and portabella burgers, but, lest you forget you are in Wisconsin, you can also get deep-fried cheese curds. In between shopping and eating, you can listen to live music or wander along the shore of Lake Pepin. This being home to many artists, it is only right that they offer more than one art-centered festival. In fact, the **Fresh Art Tour**, held in May and again in October, attract crowds directly to artists' studios in the region (www.freshart.org).

✓ TIP: Parking in Stockholm for the Art Fair is an exercise in patience, and it is good exercise. My advice: bring comfortable shoes and be prepared to walk a few blocks. It's good for you, anyway. Parking is available in the park, but it will probably take a while to get in and out. You should be able to find a spot along Highway 35, especially if you don't mind a bit of a stroll.

Sports and Recreation ≋

The famed cliff from which Wenonah is reputed to have jumped rather than marry a man she didn't love (see page 328) is preserved as **Maiden Rock Bluff State Natural Area** (Long Lane; 715.235.8850). A short 1½ mile round trip hike passes through several areas of goat prairie, each with great views, so don't stop after you reach the first one. From Stockholm, go north on County J for 0.7 miles to County E and turn left (northwest); after 0.7 miles, turn left on Long Lane and follow it until it ends at a parking lot.

If you want to swim, there is a **beach** in Stockholm Village Park (Spring St.).

Shopping

My, oh my, Stockholm has a surprising number of shopping options for a town of fewer than 100 people, and, even better, all are interesting boutique shops. While I could justifiably list every single one of them, doing so would take away the fun of exploring on your own. If you need an enticement to stop, here are some of my favorites. Keep in mind that many stores may close or have reduced hours from November until spring.

A SENSE OF PLACE (N2037 Spring St.; 715.442.2185; M,Tu,Th–Sa 10–5, Su 11–4) is a store on a mission to encourage us all, but especially children, to get outside and explore the natural world.

Pick up a book or one of the many items aimed directly at children with Nature Deficit Disorder: kites, animal-themed toys; nature guides, etc. They also carry a nice selection of books about local and regional history. A village named Stockholm has to have a store with a Scandinavian theme; **INGEBRETSEN'S AV STOCKHOLM** (12092 State Highway; 715.442.2220; Th–Tu 10–5:30 from March–Oct, F–Su 10–5:30 in Nov,Dec) fits the bill, selling items like fine glass and fiber products, candy, and books. There are a number of shops and galleries showcasing the work of local artists. **STOCKHOLM POTTERY AND MERCANTILE** (N2020 Spring St.; 715.442.3506; F,Su Noon–5, Sa 11–5 from May–Dec.) obviously specializes in local pottery, but they also sell the work of artists working in other media. **ABODE STOCKHOLM** (N2030 Spring St.; 715.442.2266; daily 10–5) has a handsome space that is uses to showcase fine art. **STOCKHOLM GENERAL** (N2030 Spring St., #4; 715.442.9077; hours vary by season) has a good selection of Wisconsin-made cheese, beer, and wine. A short drive from the village, the **MAIDEN ROCK WINERY AND CIDERY** (W12266 King Lane; 715.448.3502) grows several types of apples, which are available in the retail store in late summer. What really sets them apart, though, are the ciders they create from their own apples. This is not the sweet, cloudy non-alcoholic cider that you see in every store in the fall, but a refined, hard cider that packs a bit of a punch. There is no charge to sample the ciders, but I bet you will have a hard time walking out empty-handed (Tu 4p-7p, W-Su 10–6 from April–Dec).

Eating ✖

BOGUS CREEK CAFÉ AND BAKERY (N2049 Spring St.; 715.442.5017; café open F 10–4, Sa,Su 9–4; bakery open M–Th 11–4, F,Sa 9–5; both open Apr–Dec; WiFi) is a pleasant courtyard café serving tasty, fresh food using seasonal ingredients, but the prices are high (most items, including breakfast and sandwich options are $11-$13); cash only.

THE STOCKHOLM PIE COMPANY (N2030 Spring St. #1; 715.442.5505; Th–M 10–5, Tu Noon–6; reduced hours in winter) makes pie like you wish your grandma made ($4.25/slice or get a whole 10" pie for $18); on any given day they should have eight or more types of pie, including one or two savory pies. If you'd rather have a cinnamon roll, they make those, too ($2.25).

A TO Z PRODUCE (N2956 Anker Lane) is another rural gourmet pizza joint that uses ingredients produced or grown on their farm ($20–$26). They only serve on Tuesday evenings (4:30p–8p from mid-February–Thanksgiving); bring your favorite picnicking supplies, a snack, something to drink and be prepared to wait a couple of hours for your pizza and to pack out what you brought with you.

Sleeping 🛏

Stockholm has several excellent boutique lodging options, but the only budget option is the campground.

Camping. STOCKHOLM VILLAGE PARK (Spring St.) is lovely place to camp; the sites are shaded and virtually all have views of Lake Pepin ($12/tent; $15/camper); no showers.

Houses. Inspired by Scandinavian country home décor **LILLA HUS** (N2089 Spring St.; 612.275.1227;

WiFi) embellishes a rustic cabin with elegant touches like chandeliers; the cottage is light and airy and has one bedroom, two bathrooms, a walk-out basement with patio, and a spiral staircase to the basement ($150+tax). The **GREAT RIVER BED & BREAKFAST** (State Highway 35; 800.657.4756; open mid-March–Dec.) is in the original 1870s-era home of Jakob Peterson, one of the founders of the village. Relax in the screened porch or next to the fireplace or take a hike on the extensive grounds. The house has a lively décor accented with original art and stylish furniture from different periods ($175+tax; cont breakfast; two people maximum occupancy; no credit cards). **TANSY HUS** (W12066 Second St.; 626.523.8910; WiFi) is a cute century-old home that has a Victorian farmhouse feel. The four-bedroom house has lovely oak floors, a modern kitchen, two bathrooms and room to sprawl; it is a good place for a large group or a family ($220+tax/4 people, $20/person extra, two night min + $80 cleaning fee). **A COTTAGE IN STOCKHOLM** (W12224 Highway 35; 715.448.2048) is a warm, elegant place that feels like a home and not a rental property. The house has a modern kitchen, full bathroom, a deck, and good views of Lake Pepin; it can comfortably sleep four ($250+tax/4 people).

Moderate and up. THE SPRING STREET INN (N2037 Spring St.; 651.528.9616; WiFi) is one of the older buildings in town. The cozy apartment has a rustic feel, and is furnished with Amish furniture; it has a kitchenette, full bath, and a sitting room ($125+tax; cont breakfast); no credit cards. Located a few miles from the village, **MAIDENWOOD** (N447 244th St.; 715.448.4001; WiFi; open May–Oct.) is set in a peaceful area far from the intrusions of modern life. All three rooms have a private bath and plenty of country comfort; the treehouse room is above the garage and has copious natural light; the other two rooms have amenities like a steam shower or Jacuzzi tub ($144+tax; cont breakfast). If you forgot to bring something to read, the house is filled with 8000 books, so, odds are pretty good you'll find something to your liking. **THE RIVER ROAD INN** (W12360 State Highway 35; 612.306.2100; WiFi) is a distinctive multi-gabled building, clearly visible from the other side of Lake Pepin. The two luxury suites each have an elegant spa shower, outdoor deck, wet bar, bed with pillow tops, and a great view of Lake Pepin ($220+tax; cont breakfast). The carriage house room is rich in natural light, with a fireplace, deck, satellite TV, and a shower you won't want to leave ($255+tax).

Resources

- Post Office: W12117 Highway 35; 715.442.5169.

Getting Around

Normally this is about public transportation, but Stockholm, ever eager to please visitors, has two ways to ensure your comfort as you explore the village. The **Blue Bikes of Stockholm** provide an easy way to get around town, if walking a few blocks is too much for you; pick one up and drop it off at designated locations, like the corner of Spring and State Highway 35. On a rainy day, the **Blue Umbrellas of Stockholm** will keep you dry as you explore the shops; look for them in front of local businesses and, when you are done, leave them in front of the last place you visited.

MAIDEN ROCK
(121)

A long and skinny town wedged between Lake Pepin and the bluffs, Maiden Rock has a few surprises that make it worth a stop.

Arriving in Town

State Highway 35 dips and rolls through town like a rollercoaster; the small business district is along the highway. Chestnut Street will get you to the river.

History

Maiden Rock village and bluff get their names from a long-standing legend about a young, Native American girl called Wenonah (first born daughter), who jumped to her death from the bluff rather than agree to an arranged marriage to a man she didn't love who was from a rival Indian nation, or he could have been a French voyageur, or possibly an English trader. The story has many versions, something noted sarcastically by Mark Twain in *Life on the Mississippi*. Whatever the true story, the legend has been around for generations, at least since the 18th century, and it undeniably resonates with our romantic ideals: this story inspired Perry Williams to compose a libretto for an opera and Margaret A. Persons to write an epic poem.

The first folks to settle at the future village site were brothers Amos and Albert Harris and John Trumbell. The village was initially called Harrisburg but after Trumbell bought them out and platted a village in 1857, he changed the name to Maiden Rock. Trumbell was pretty much the go-to guy in early Maiden

Rock. He tried to start a number of businesses and was probably the first European to sail on Lake Pepin. Maiden Rock did not have a regular steamboat stop because the main channel was on the Minnesota side; this was a major factor in the town's slow early growth. Early businesses included a sawmill, a shingle mill, a grist mill, a lime kiln, and a ship yard that built boats ranged from 16-foot sailboats to steamboats. Trumbell moved to Albany, Oregon in 1899 when the town had about 300 residents.

Maiden Rock lacked road connections to nearby communities for many of its early years, prompting someone to call it "a good place to live but a hard place to get out of." The village got a boost in 1886 when railroad connections to St. Paul and La Crosse were completed, but repeated fire disasters were not helpful; six fires ravaged the community just between March, 1911 and August, 1912.

This small village knows how to throw a big party, though. The town's centennial festival drew a large crowd, especially for the 55-unit parade. The centennial celebration included a beard judging contest with categories including best full beard and best trim. The major industry today is the Wisconsin Industrial Sand Company, which has an underground mine where they dig out sand for the oil and gas exploration industries in the Southwest.

Tourist Information ⓘ

Contact **Pierce County Partners in Tourism** (800.474.3723/715.273.5864) or on the web (www.travelpiercecounty.com).

Attractions

Maiden Rock Village Park (W3535 Highway 35; 715.448.2205) is a pleasant location for a picnic.

Entertainment and Events ♪

The local **Farmers Market** is on Saturday mornings near the art galleries on Highway 35 (9–Noon).

Festivals. Maiden Rock Summerfest (third Saturday in June) includes a parade and tours of the sand mine.

Sports and Recreation ≋

Rush River Delta State Natural Area (608.685.6222) is a 341-acre floodplain hardwood forest, with no groomed trails that can be soggy, but is still a fun place to explore. Park at the lot at the junction of Highway 35 with County A; the natural area is south of Highway 35.

Shopping

The **SECRET HEART GALLERY** (W3553 State Highway 35; 715.448.2005; F,Sa 10–5, Su Noon–5) is where B.J. Christofferson sells her hand-crafted dioramas that fuse mysticism with humor. Next door, the **SWAN SONG GALLERY** (W3557 State Highway 35; 715.448.2244; F–Su 10–5) has a good collection of contemporary art from several local and regional artists whose work has an ecological focus. When you walk into **BASIL'S** (W3583 State Highway 35; 715.448.3039; Th–Su Noon–5), you may feel like you walked into a quirky collectibles store on a back street in London; sort through an eclectic collection of prints, knicknacks, glassware, and veils. Located just outside of the village, **DENEEN POTTERY** (W3706 110th St.; 715.448.3300; open by appt.) is the home, studio, and gallery for potters Peter and Mary Deneen.

Eating and Drinking 🍴 🍽

The **SMILING PELICAN BAKE SHOP** (W3556 County Highway 35; 715.448.3807; F–Su 8–5 from mid-March–Dec.) is reputed to have fine breads, torts, pies and other baked goods that inspire otherwise sensible people to drive hours on end to get their fix.

The **MAIDEN ROCK INN** (N531 County Road S; 715.448.2608; open weekends, call ahead at other times to find out if they are open), housed in the former schoolhouse just one block inland from the River Road, has a small café that uses local ingredients for the freshly-prepared dishes. The Inn also has a wine bar serving their exclusive collection of Alsatian wines.

For something completely different, dine at **VINO IN THE VALLEY** (W3826 450th Ave.; 715.639.6677; Th 5p–10p, Sa 4p–10p, Su Noon–7 from mid-May–late Sept), where you will enjoy fine Italian food al fresco in a scenic rural setting among the grapevines. The menu typically includes dishes like rigatoni rustica, antipasto salad, and pasta caprese ($15–$21; Sunday buffet $19); enjoy it with a glass of their wine.

Sleeping 🛏

Camping. MAIDEN ROCK VILLAGE PARK (W3535 State Highway 35; 715.448.2205) has a few primitive sites next to the river, and a few electric sites next to the woods; no showers ($10/primitive site, $15/electric site).

Bed and Breakfast. THE JOURNEY INN (W3671 200th Ave.; 715.448.2424; WiFi) is a 21st century country inn built in 2006 to have a minimal impact on the surrounding environment. The inn is located on property that borders a large state natural area, so there are many nearby places to hike or snowshoe or meditate (try the labyrinth). The three nature-themed rooms in the house each has its own bathroom and patio ($165+tax w/breakfast buffet). There is also a two-bedroom cottage on-site that has a full kitchen, spa tub, and wood-burning stove that can sleep up to six ($165+tax; $25/person for more than two guests; two night minimum; no breakfast).

Cabins/Houses. Located next to a working pottery shop, the **PEPIN FARM POTTERY AND GUESTHOUSE** (W3706 110th St.; 715.448.3300; WiFi) is a quaint older home that has been through a complete renovation; it has a modern kitchen, screened porch, a large tub, and walking paths on the property where you can enjoy the sounds of nature ($165+tax with two night minimum).

★ **Author's Pick: THE MAIDEN ROCK INN** (N531 County Road S; 715.448.2608; WiFi in the dining room) has four guestrooms in a 1906-era schoolhouse that has been through a skillful and classy 15-year renovation. Each of the four rooms has individual climate control, an elegant bathroom, wainscoting, and tin ceilings ($150–$180+tax incl full breakfast). Common areas include a recreation room with TV and billiards, grotto and courtyard, sauna, and massage room. Follow the circular stairs to a rooftop deck with great views of the village and river.

Resources

- There is a small monthly publication called the *Maiden Rock Press* that circulates around the village.
- Post Office: N517 County Rd S; 715.448.3771.

BAY CITY
(465)

Once the center of a large commercial fishing operation, Bay City today is primarily a residential community, with less tourism than some of its neighbors along Lake Pepin.

Arriving in Town

State Highway 35 skirts the eastern end of town. Go west on Wabash Street to reach Main Street or the river.

History

Mr. A.C. Morton was the first known European to arrive at the future village site; he built a home in 1855. A.J. Dexter believed he had purchased the land before Morton's arrival, so he got a bit peeved when Mr. Morton's surveyor, a man named Markle, showed up to plat the village of Saratoga; Dexter killed the surveyor for trespassing. This didn't create a positive vibe for the new village, so Saratoga was abandoned and the buildings were moved across the ice to neighboring Warrentown. Charles Tyler bought the site in 1856 for $1700 in back taxes and rebranded the site as Bay City, naming it for the natural bay that was the site's most distinctive feature. Early 20th century businesses included the predictable saloon, a confectionary, a billiard hall, a grain dealer, and a meat market.

Bay City was once home to a major commercial fishing operation. Around 1910, a school of Scandinavian fishermen relocated from Sevastopol (Minnesota) to Bay City, because it was cheaper to get a fishing license in Wisconsin. Bay City also had a rail station, so the fishermen had access to transportation that could ship their catch across the US. The fish were typically packed in barrels with ice but local hero Capp Tyler invented a box (the *Tyler Box*) that proved to be a more efficient packing method. He opened a box making factory in Bay City, and supplied fishermen along the eastern shore of Lake Pepin. Early on, most of the commercial fishermen ran small operations, but over time larger companies pushed out or swallowed the smaller ones. Changing tastes in the eating habits of Americans reduced demand for Lake Pepin fish after World War II; the last major fishing operation in Bay City closed in 1952. Bay City today has little industry; most residents commute to jobs in other places.

Tourist Information ⓘ

Get your questions answered at **Coffee by the Bay** (see below).

Attractions

The **1850s Conlin Log Cabin**, filled with period furnishings, is the highlight at the **River Bluffs History Center** (W6321 E. Main St.; 715.273.6611; call for hours or to schedule a visit). The main building (an old church) has a few historic photos, old farm tools, a buggy, and overview of agriculture in the county.

Saratoga Park (Pepin and Main Streets) has a small playground and places to picnic with a good view of Lake Pepin.

Getting on the River

The **Bay City Resort** (N1202 Wabash; 715.594.3147) has a 14-foot fishing boat available for rent ($20/day); you'll need to bring your own motor.

Entertainment and Events ♪

Bay City Fest (715.594.3168) has events to challenge your skills in wiffle ball, bean bag tossing, and bed racing (2nd Saturday in June). At **Pioneer Day** (715.273.6611) immerse yourself in the 19th century and learn how to make butter and cider, listen to old-timey music, and watch an impressive display of corn stripping (no dancing involved).

Sports and Recreation

Pierce County Islands Wildlife Area (715.684.2914) is 860 acres of protected backwaters islands that are nearly adjacent to Bay City and good places to fish or watch wildlife; you'll need a boat to reach most of it.

There is a small **swimming beach** at the Bay City Park/Campground.

Eating

Get your java fix at **COFFEE BY THE BAY** (W6518 State Highway 35; 715.594.3894; M–Sa 7a–6p, Su 9a–6p; WiFi) and nosh on the freshly prepared food of the day.

Sleeping

Camping. BAY CITY CAMPGROUND (106 Park St.; 715.594.3229; open May–Oct) has 25 cramped sites surrounding a parking lot and next to a busy boat ramp ($25/with utilities), but the tent sites are on a small peninsula away in a more desirable location ($15/tent only sites); no showers.

Cabins. BAY CITY RESORT (N1202 Wabash; 715.594.3147; open Apr–Oct) has two basic cabins that are rough around the edges, but they are inexpensive and next to the bay that connects to Lake Pepin.

Each cabin has a bathroom with shower, full kitchen with microwave, air conditioning, and satellite TV ($60 incl tax); no credit cards.

Resources

- Post Office: W6372 Main St.; 715.594.3862.

HAGER CITY
(Uninc)

Hager City may not look like much (it isn't), but it has a place that you must visit—if you like authentic Jamaican food.

Arriving in Town

County Highways VV and K are the main routes in town.

History

Hager City had the distinction of getting the first post office in the township but apparently not much else worth writing down. When the railroad came through in 1886, the village was platted as Hager Chatfield, but the following year the Postmaster General suggested that Hager City would be a better name. That's all I have.

Tourist Information ⓘ

Contact **Pierce County Partners in Tourism** (800.474.3723/715.273.5864) or on the web (www.travelpiercecounty.com).

Attractions

The rock formation called **Bow and Arrow**, on a hillside visible from the River Road, is quite a mystery. This petroform was first noticed in 1902 by archaeologist Jacob Brower who thought the rocks were arranged in a shape that resembled a bow and arrow pointing toward Lake Pepin. Others have suggested that the shape is more likely a bird effigy, but no one really knows what it was meant to be or when it was made, although all agree it has been there a long time.

Eating and Drinking

THE HARBOR BAR (N673 825th St.; 715.792.2417; kitchen open Su–Th 11a–9p, F,Sa 11a–10p, bar open later) is party central, especially on the weekends, with live music (check their schedule at www.harborbar.net), boaters coming and going, and the grill pumping out the best damn jerk chicken this side of Kingston ($13). The standard menu includes Jamaica-inspired entrées like steam roast red snapper ($11–$24) or you can opt for a salad or sandwich ($7–$12). Unless you're a party animal, you may have a better experience going earlier in the evening rather than later.

Sleeping

Camping. Most of the sites at the **ISLAND CAMPGROUND & MARINA** (N650 825th St.; 715.222.1808; open May 1–Nov 1; WiFi) are strung along a single road on—you guessed it—an island just across from Red Wing with a good view of Barn Bluff. The sites are shaded, with many right on the main channel of the river ($12/adult for primitive sites; $32/ water & elec); no credit cards.

Resources

- Post Office: W8123 165th Ave.; 715.792.2919.

For more information and updates, visit my web site at www.MississippiValleyTraveler.com.

TRENTON
(Uninc)

Arriving in Town
County K is the main drag through the village.

History
Wilson Thing (perhaps an ancestor of Thing T. Thing of *Addams Family* fame) was the first person to settle in the area; he showed up in 1848. Most early settlers in the Trenton vicinity were Scandinavians. The area had a bustling commercial fishing operation in the early 20th century, roughly from 1930 to the 1970s. Nearby Trenton Island was a notorious hangout for gangsters like Pretty Boy Floyd and John Dillinger who probably dropped some cash in the brothels and taverns.

Getting on the River
Everts Resort (N1705 860th St.; 715.792.2333) has a couple of fishing boats you can rent: a 15-foot boat without a motor ($25/day), and a 16-foot Lund with motor and depth finder ($105/day).

Sports and Recreation
Trenton Bluff State Natural Area (608.685.6222) has a couple of parcels with overlooks of the river valley. To reach the east tract, go north on County VV for 0.4 miles from Highway 35 and park along the road; walk due west through the woods and up the hill. For the western tract, go 1.5 miles north from the intersection of Highway 35 and County VV and park in the small pulloff; walk north of the road and up the hill.

Sleeping 🛏

Camping. EVERTS RESORT (N1705 860th St.; 715.792.2333) has a few overnight sites with hook-ups for campers but is not really equipped for tent camping.

Cabins. EVERTS RESORT (N1705 860th St.; 715.792.2333; WiFi near office) has five basic cabins on the river that are well-suited for groups; it is a laid back place in summer but very busy in spring and fall with fishermen. Most of the cabins are equipped a kitchen, full bath, and bunk beds plus a full or queen bed and can sleep up to eight people. Bring a sleeping bag, pillow, and towel ($120+tax/4 people, $20/extra).

DIAMOND BLUFF

(Uninc)

Diamond Bluff is a quiet residential community that is about a mile long but only a few blocks wide sandwiched between the railroad tracks and the river.

Arriving in Town

To get to the river, follow 985th Street; 290th Avenue runs along the river.

History

A French guy lived here from 1799 until he died in 1824. His name might have been Monte Diamond, or he might have called the area Monte-Diamond. I haven't been able to reconcile different sources on that one, yet. In 1852, J.W. Hoyt moved up from Tennessee and bought 1200 acres. His brother, C.F. Hoyt platted 50 of those acres as a town site and named it Diamond Bluff. The village enjoyed a few prosperous years as a center for shipping wheat but didn't attract many settlers. Its steamboat landing was busy enough for a while that some townsfolk did well selling cordwood (for fuel) to passing boats. There was also an active boat yard where the *Sea Wing* was built (see page 343).

Close to town is an archaeological gold mine known as the Diamond Bluff (or Mero) Site, a mile long area that has evidence of several villages, plus hundreds of oval mounds framed by a bird effigy to the south and a panther effigy to the north. This site was occupied continuously for 350 years beginning about 1000 years ago; residents had considerable contact with the

Mississippian culture from Cahokia (Illinois). This site is not open to the public, but there is a display at the Goodhue County History Center in Red Wing (see page 47).

Tourist Information ⓘ

Contact **Pierce County Partners in Tourism** (800.474.3723/715.273.5864) or on the web (www.travelpiercecounty.com).

Sports and Recreation 〰

Sea Wing Park (290th Ave.) is a small village park that has a beach and a few places to picnic next to the river named for the ill-fated boat (see the sidebar on page 343).

The Sea Wing Tragedy

The *Sea Wing* (Area Research Center, UW-La Crosse)

The *Sea Wing* disaster resulted in the worst loss of life in a steamboat accident along the Upper Mississippi River. The *Sea Wing* was a 135-foot long, 22-foot tall sternwheeler that displaced 109 tons. On the morning of July 13, 1890, Captain David Wethern guided the boat and the attached barge, *Jim Grant* (set up for dancing), from its home in Diamond Bluff for a day-long excursion to Lake City and back. He stopped to pick up passengers at Trenton and Red Wing and docked at Lake City around 11:30 a.m.

Passengers enjoyed picnic meals and shopping, but turbulent weather throughout the day limited some of the fun. It wasn't entirely clear if the weather would cooperate long enough to get them back home, but, when a break in the rain appeared, passengers boarded and the boat left Lake City.

An hour later, a strong burst of wind roared across Lake Pepin, and Captain Wethern turned the boat to head into the storm, but fierce circulating winds caused the top-heavy boat to capsize. The barge became separated and the 50 people on board floated helplessly away.

The capsized boat trapped many passengers, who drowned quickly, including Nellie and Perley Wethern, the wife and 8-year-old son of Captain Wethern. The captain survived when he was able to break the glass in the pilot house and swim out. The 50 people on the barge survived—some swam to shore—but most were rescued after floating around for a while.

The accident killed 98 of the 215 passengers; 77 of the dead were from Red Wing. Perhaps most shocking, 50 of the 57 women on board drowned. While the cause of the accident has never been clear, Captain Wethern received most of the blame (primarily for overloading the boat) and was shunned by the communities along the lake. Five thousand people attended the memorial service in Red Wing.

PRESCOTT

(3,764)

Perched at the northern tip of the Wisconsin's Great River Road, Prescott is positioned where the clear blue water of the St. Croix River mixes with the ruddy Mississippi. The two great waterways form the core of an area that has an abundance of recreational options.

Arriving in Town

State Highway 35 enters town as Jefferson Street, then becomes Broad Street as it enters the business district; US Highway 10 is Cherry Street.

History

Philander Prescott, a native New Yorker, arrived when the area was known rather descriptively as Mouth of the St. Croix. He had been in the area as early as 1819 when he supplied goods to Fort Snelling. Officers from Fort Snelling offered Prescott part of their claim if he would go settle on it, which he did in 1839. He had a hard time making a living, though, even with licenses to operate ferries across the St. Croix and Mississippi Rivers, and, after a brutal winter in 1843, he moved away to work as an interpreter at Fort Snelling. Joseph Monjeau moved into the Prescott house but Prescott retained rights to the land.

By 1849, the area was known as Elizabeth and had drawn a few settlers, most of whom worked as traders. After Prescott's claims became official in 1851, he sold most of it to developers. Prescott died on August 18, 1862, one of the first causalities in the Dakota uprising (see page 13).

When the village officially became Prescott in 1851, it had all of two houses, so the vote was probably unanimous. New settlers begin to arrive en masse in 1854 and by 1856 the village had 200 buildings. Sawmills were built and thrived from the 1850s until the turn of the century. In 1866 alone, 3000 men worked in the logging industry, and 70 million board feet of lumber passed through town. Prescott was the primary shipping point for grain from the St. Croix Valley from the 1850s to the 1870s. Wheat was not the only local crop, however, as area farmers also grew sugar beets, corn, tobacco, and onions. Ice harvesting prospered from the 1850s to the 1940s. Other early businesses included a cooper, lime and brick manufacturing, a brewery, commercial fishing, and an organ manufacturing factory. By the 20th century, Prescott counted 1000 residents and dairy-related industries became more prominent. Prescott also had a factory that manufactured spinners that were very popular with fishermen. The Cargill Shipbuilding Corporation of Prescott built 18 tankers for the US Navy during World War II, which must have been quite a sight. In the last couple of decades, Prescott has evolved into a bedroom community for the Twin Cities and a popular weekend recreation destination.

Tourist Information ⓘ

Prescott has two places for visitors to stock up on brochures and ask questions. The **Great River Road Visitors Center in Freedom Park** (200 Monroe St.; 715.262.0104; visitor center open M–Sa 10–9, Su Noon–9 from Memorial Day–Labor Day, Tu–Sa 10–5, Su Noon–5 the rest of the year), which houses exhibits about the Mississippi River, eagles, and Prescott. Also check out the **Welcome and Heritage Center** downtown (233 Broad St.; 715.262.3284; Tu–F 10–3).

Lift bridge at Prescott

Attractions

Freedom Park (200 Monroe St.; 715.262.0104; visitor center open M–Sa 10–9, Su Noon–9 from Memorial Day–Labor Day, Tu–Sa 10–5, Su Noon–5 the rest of the year) is situated high above the Mississippi River and has great views over the valley. The visitor center is a Great River Road Visitor and Learning Center and has exhibits about Mississippi River ecology, commerce, and navigation.

Mercord Park (Front St.) is the location where Philander Prescott built his first cabin in 1839; check out the gear house that sat atop the 1923 lift bridge (Sa,Su 10–3ish).

The current **Prescott Clock Tower** (233 Broad St.) houses a timepiece that was made in 1937 to replace one that was lost when the school in which it was housed burned down in 1935; both clocks were built by the Seth Thomas company. The new clock, among the last of its style built by the Thomas Company, was installed in a tower at the rebuilt school but fell into disrepair and had to be removed. It was eventually restored and placed in a new home in a new tower next to the confluence. It strikes every 30 minutes.

The **Prescott Area Historical Society** (235 Broad St.; 715.262.3284; Tu–F 10–3) maintains exhibit space next door to the Welcome Center, with photos and artifacts from the town's past.

Entertainment and Events ♪

The Prescott **Farmers Market** is held in Freedom Park on Thursdays from late May to mid-October (2p–6p).

Festivals. Prescott Daze (second weekend in Sept; 715.262.3284) gets local folks celebrating with a street dance, an eating contest, a fishing contest, water fights with fire hoses, and a parade.

Music. Muddy Waters Restaurant & Bar (231 N. Broad St.; 715.262.5999) hosts live blues and jazz on the deck on Sunday and Monday afternoons during the summer.

Sports and Recreation ≋

Prescott sits at the southern end of the **St. Croix National Scenic Riverway** (715.483.2274), a 255-mile corridor of river pleasures, varied ecosystems, and historic towns along the St. Croix and Namekagon Rivers. Recreation opportunities include fishing, canoeing, hiking, tubing, boating, snowshoeing, and cross-country skiing. The portions of the Riverway downriver of St. Croix Falls (WI) tend to be used by recreational boaters, while the upper reaches are more natural and wild. Rustic camping is free in designated areas.

The city maintains a public **swimming beach** on the St. Croix River (Lake St. at St. Croix Street).

Shopping

NESBITT'S NURSERY & ORCHARD (N4380 State Highway 35; 715.792.2676; hours vary by season, but summer hours are M,Tu,F 7a–4p, W 7a–8p,

Th 7a–7p, Sa,Su 10–4) is the place for seasonal fruit and produce, local honey and syrup, and fine Wisconsin cheese. **VALLEY VINEYARD** (W10415 521st Ave.; 715.262.4235; W–Su 10–6 from Apr–Nov.) is a newcomer to the wine producing scene. They produce a wide selection of red and white wines from their scenic hilltop location just east of Prescott.

Eating and Drinking

Just south of town, the **OASIS EATERY** at Nesbitt's Nursery & Orchard (N4380 State Highway 35; 715.792.2676; daily 7a–10a & 11a–1:30p) has a café that emphasizes fresh, local ingredients for its strata, quiche, crepes, and sandwiches ($6–$10). The menu changes daily; Wednesday is pie night; get it sweet or savory (4p–8p). Thursday is garden night where you can sample seasonal items (4p–7p).

For a pre-dinner snack, stop at the **PRESCOTT BOAT CLUB AT POINT ST. CROIX MARINA** (101 S. Front St.; 715.262.3161; W,Th 4p–close, F 3p–close, Sa,Su 11:30a–close) and nosh on large broiled shrimp ($1.85/each) while enjoying a great view of the St. Croix/Mississippi confluence; cash only.

MUDDY WATERS RESTAURANT & BAR (231 N. Broad St.; 715.262.5999; Su–Tu 11a–9p, W–Sa 11a–10p) specializes in savory smoked meats and Cajun flavors. The lunch menu consists of salads named for blues musicians and sandwiches ($7–$11). For dinner, choose from hearty steak and fish entrées plus pasta (most entrées $13–$17); enjoy your meal on the outdoor deck and stare at the river while you chew.

THE BOXCAR (211 Broad St.; 715.262.2026; daily 11a–11p) serves solid southern-style barbeque, with entrées ranging from crawdad cakes to catfish to baby back ribs to mac and cheese (sandwiches $6–$13;

entrées $9–$20).

For after dinner drinks in a casual atmosphere, head to the **NO NAME SALOON & MONKEY BAR** (114 N. Broad St.; 715.262.9803; Su–Th 7a–2a, F,Sa 7a–2:30a), where locals mingle with bikers, boaters, and other passers-through.

Sleeping

Budget. RIVER HEIGHTS MOTEL (1020 US Highway 10; 800.522.9207/715.262.3266; WiFi) has 23 simple, unadorned budget rooms in good shape ($67–$80 + tax).

Bed and Breakfast. Let outgoing hosts John and Deb spoil you at the **ARBOR INN** (434 North Court St.; 888.262.1090/715.262.4522; WiFi). The four guest rooms each have a private bath with a Jacuzzi tub, fridge, cable TV, and is furnished with an emphasis on comfort; let your cares melt away as you relax on the screened porch ($159–$199 + tax incl full breakfast).

Resources

- The local newspaper is the weekly *Prescott Journal* (715.262.2153).
- Post Office: 1001 Campbell Street North; 715.262.5166.
- Prescott Public Library (WiF): 800 Borner St. North; 715.262.5555; M,W 10–8, Tu,Th Noon–8, F 10–6, Sa 10–2.

POINT DOUGLAS

(Uninc)

The narrow strip of land between the St. Croix and Mississippi Rivers known today as Point Douglas Park was once a bustling community built around the logging business. All that remains of that community today is a single Greek Revival home from the 1840s.

History

The point of land between the two rivers was an early favorite for settlers. Joseph Monjeau built a log home in 1838, and others quickly followed. The village of Point Douglas was platted in 1849 and named after the Illinois senator and rival to Abraham Lincoln, Stephen A. Douglas, for his role creating the Minnesota Territory. A small community developed that became a supply point for steamboats passing through. Its major industry was milling, though. The first sawmill opened in 1851, but it was the Dudley Mill that grew into the major operator. In the peak years (1871-1889), the mills was designed so that whole logs could enter from the St. Croix River via a conveyor and exit the mill on the Mississippi as cut lumber for loading onto steamboats. When the lumber industry declined in the late 19th century, Point Douglas faded into oblivion.

Attractions

Carpenter St. Croix Valley Nature Center (12805 St. Croix Trail; 651.437.4359; daily 8–4:30; free) is a serene preserve about one mile north of the River Road. It has several walking trails through restored ecosystems (grasslands, oak savanna, etc.) and an overlook of the St. Croix River. The interpretive center showcases animals while they are still alive instead of the usual display of stuffed ones (bald eagle, peregrine falcon, redtail hawk).

Sports and Recreation

There are **swimming beaches** at Point Douglas Park (free) and St. Croix Bluffs Regional Park (10191 St. Croix Trail South; $5/day).

Sleeping

Camping. ST. CROIX BLUFFS REGIONAL PARK (10191 St. Croix Trail South; 651.430.8240; open late April–Oct.) has a large campground in an area shaded by tall pine trees. The sites are reasonably far apart. This is a popular campground that fills up on weekends, sometimes weeks in advance; call first to find out what's available ($15/tent only, $20/elec only, $22/water & elec + $5 daily fee).

REGIONAL INFORMATION

When to Go

The climate along the Upper Mississippi can vary widely, sometimes in a single day. I am sure that more than one local can tell you about a day where they left the house in shorts and were scraping ice off their car by the end of the day. (Actually, that happened to me one January day in St. Louis, but it can happen further north, too.) All locations are in the Central Time Zone, the same as Chicago.

Winters along the Upper Miss are cold and long with healthy accumulations of snow. This should not stop you from visiting, however. North of the Quad Cities, the Mississippi River usually freezes over, with a few patches of open water around locks and dams and discharge pipes; the open water at those locations attracts large numbers of bald eagles on their annual trek south. Ice fishing is a popular sport (but ask around about local ice conditions before venturing out), as is cross-country skiing, snowmobiling, snowshoeing, and brandy-drinking.

The return of warmer weather in spring brings snow melts (and mud), high water on the rivers, and strong storms. Warm is relative, however, as some places along the Upper Mississippi can get snow into April. Warm spring days are great for exploring the overlooks as there are no bugs and the views aren't yet obscured by leaves and other vegetation.

Summers are usually quite comfortable, with just a

handful of hot, humid days. Campgrounds and motels fill up quickly on weekends, and it is peak season for mosquitoes and other insects. Summer is the most popular time for pleasure boating—weekends are not the best time to take your boat out in search of peace and solitude, although backwater areas may get you away from the crowds.

Fall is the busiest travel season along much of the Upper Mississippi. The leaves begin to change colors and the limestone bluffs are brushed with a variety of reds, greens, and oranges. This is also a great time for fresh produce like gourds, apples, and the last of the season's tomatoes. Fall weather is usually pleasantly cool, with more cloudy days than summer. Fall is also prime time for hunting (deer season usually begins in late fall), so you may want to avoid hiking in places that are crawling with people carrying big guns; most state parks do not allow hunting, so those are probably the best options.

Mississippi River Ecology in Brief

From its headwaters at Lake Itasca in northern Minnesota to its delta at the Gulf of Mexico in Louisiana, the Mississippi River is about 2300 miles long and passes through ten states; the exact length is tough to calculate, because the river has a habit of carving new channels. The river drains 41% of the lower United States (and part of Canada), about 1,200,000 acres.

The Upper Mississippi River is remarkable for the deep valley framed by limestone bluffs. As the glaciers retreated a few thousand years ago, water from the melting ice rushed through the valley, carving the landscape in a wide swath. As water washed away the lower layers of sandstone, chunks of the dolomite above it cleaved off, leaving dramatic vertical bluff faces. The Upper Mississippi valley is as narrow as 1 ¼ miles at

Prescott and as wide as six miles at Trempealeau. The bluffs are lowest around Prescott, and highest around Great River Bluffs State Park. The lock and dam system is used to maintain a minimum water depth of nine feet in the navigation channel. Before they were built, the Upper Mississippi was often shallow enough in late summer that folks could walk from one side to the other.

Flora

The Upper Mississippi Valley has a wide variety of plant life in a narrow area. At river level, plants that tolerate a lot of moisture flourish in the floodplain forest: trees such as willow, white oak, elm, sycamore, maple, river birch, as well as water lilies, sedges, and pondweeds. White oak and silver maple are declining because of perpetually high water levels brought on by the lock and dam system, as well as invasive species like reed canary grass which are crowding them out.

> ✔ TIP: In the backwaters, varieties of both water lilies and lotuses are native. There's an easy way to tell them apart: lotus blooms stand upright, lily blooms float on the water. You can thank me later.

Further uphill, trees like oak, hickory, and walnut predominate. Prairies covered most of the bluff tops before Europeans settled in the area. For centuries, Native Americans managed these prairies with spring fires so fledgling grasses would attract buffalo and other game animals. Goat prairies (named as such because they are usually too steep for anything to traverse except goats) usually face south or southwest and have thin, dry, rocky soil. They are home to specially adapted plant species like little bluestem and silky asters, many of which are rare or endangered. Some species of lizards and snakes (including timber rattlesnakes) also like the environment of goat prairies. The heat reflecting off the slopes creates waves of hot air that raptors use to lazily rise higher and higher. Without annual fires, the eastern red cedar is taking over many of these prairies; nothing grows around or under them. Conservation officials are working to restore goat prairies by removing the cedars and implementing selective burns. One of the best remaining goat prairies is at Battle Bluff State Natural Area near De Soto (see page 176).

Fauna

If you live in the city like I do, it's easy to forget how wild much of the country still is. There is a much greater range of animal life along the Mississippi River than you might think. Deer are ubiquitous; aside from squirrels, it is the animal that you are most likely to see. If you are paying attention and have some luck, you may also catch sight of beaver, muskrat, otter, raccoons, and fox. If you are really lucky, you might spot mink or a timber rattlesnake. Animals you might hear but probably won't see are coyotes and bobcats. Black bear are increasing in number along the Upper Mississippi River, especially in the northern reaches.

If you are a birder you probably already know about the Mississippi River flyway. For the rest of you, a few facts: 40% of all North American waterfowl migrate along the Mississippi River; 326 species of birds—one-third of all birds on the continent—migrate through in the spring and fall. Among the migrants are bald eagles in winter, song birds and pelicans in spring and tundra swans in late fall. Species that are fairly easy to spot include hawks, turkey, peregrine falcons, great blue heron, egrets, geese, ducks, cormorants, and turkey vultures. The Audubon Society produced a series of maps for birding along the Mississippi River. They do a much better job than I ever could describing the variety of birds in the flyway and when they can be seen. Some of the maps are still available at tourist information centers; all of the content is also available through their website (www.GreatRiverBirding.org).

Bald eagle

Even with the dramatic man-made changes to the ecology of the Mississippi River, fish still abound. Two hundred sixty species live in the river—one-quarter of all fish species in North America. Many are threatened, but fish that are still common include fishermen's favorites like crappie, largemouth bass, walleye, catfish, white bass, and bluegill, as well as carp, suckers, and buffalo fish. Threatened or endangered species include the prehistoric sturgeon, paddlefish, and alligator gar (the latter is native only in the southern sections of the Mississippi). And of course, there are plenty of turtles—including some very large snapping turtles—and mussels. All of these are under pressure from invasive species like zebra mussels and the very odd Asian jumping carp (silver carp).

Getting There

The only commercial airport in this stretch is at La Crosse (see page 231). The next closest commercial airport is in Minneapolis (less than an hour from Hastings), but the airports in Dubuque (IA), Rochester (MN), Madison, Milwaukee, Des Moines, Chicago, and the Quad Cities all put you within a few hours drive of the river.

Getting Around

You really need a car, motorcycle, boat, bicycle, or ultralight to explore this region. Having said that, Amtrak has a route along the river with stops in La Crosse, Winona, and Red Wing; see those chapters for details. Jefferson Bus Lines also has service to La Crosse to Winona. The Wisconsin Department of Transportation in cooperation with the Mississippi River Parkway Commission and the Mississippi River Trail, Inc. produced a series of maps for bicycling along the river. The maps are only available at: http://www.dot.wisconsin.gov/travel/bike-foot/docs/grr-map.pdf.

Food

In many towns, there isn't much variety to the food. Meat and potatoes rule the day, which often means a burger and fries. The salad will probably be little more than a glorified salad dressing delivery system—a few pieces of iceberg lettuce and shredded carrot. La Crosse has the highest concentration of fine dining. Wisconsin is known for its cheese (which is widely available at many grocery stores and gas stations) as well as supper clubs, which almost every small town has and where local people, especially older folks, go for a nice steak, a trip to the salad bar, and some brandy. In many Wisconsin restaurants, you will be asked how you want your baked potato. The correct answer is not rare, medium, or well done; say everything and you'll get chives, bacon, butter, sour cream, and cheddar cheese.

In the Midwest, making pie is a fine art practiced in every small town and nearly every home kitchen. If we spent as much time on the rest of our food as we do on pie, we would have the best cuisine in the world. You should always save room for a slice of pie when eating in small-town restaurants. In fact, you may want to skip the burger and go right to the pie. I didn't realize how many different types of pie can be made until I started this book. I've been to restaurants that had as many as twelve different pies on the menu every day. While working on this book, I ate slices of Amish Oatmeal, raisin sour cream, apple rhubarb, and butterscotch walnut; the possibilities are endless.

✔ TIP: Not all roadside produce stands sell local products. Some buy from wholesale markets for resale. If buying local produce is important to you, ask where they got the produce.

Culture and Arts

If you want to read more about the river, check out Kenny Salwey's books for stories about river rats and river ecology (see page 283). Martha Greene Phillips wrote a charming book about boathouses (*The Floating Boathouses on the Upper Mississippi River*). Author and humorist Michael Perry lives near Alma; he writes about rural life (*Truck: A Love Story; Coop: A Year of Poultry, Pigs and Parenting*). What are your favorites?

Things That Could Ruin Your Vacation

I'm not into scare tactics and I certainly would never dream of telling you how to live your life. But, to help make your vacation experience a pleasant one, I offer a few tips about things that could ruin your vacation:

1) TICKS AND MOSQUITOES: they can spread disease and make you feel miserable.

• **Remedy**: wear a hat and use bug spray. Here are a few tips on repellents courtesy of the Centers for Disease Control and Prevention:

• Picaridin (works against mosquitoes, ticks, chiggers, gnats, fleas): Irritates skin less than DEET but needs to be reapplied more often; no scent. Available in Avon Skin-so-Soft Bug Guard and Cutter Advanced.

• Lemon-eucalyptus oil: The only commercial product in the US is Repel Lemon Eucalyptus; don't use on children under four years of age.

• DEET: The most widely used, it comes in different concentrations: 5% will last about 90 minutes, while 100% will last 10 hours; 20% will also keep the ticks away; it is oily and concentrations of 30% or greater should not be used on children.

Poison ivy

• Citronella: Not as effective as DEET; at 10% concentration, citronella only works for 20 minutes.

2) POISON IVY: most people will develop a very nasty rash when they come in contact with poison ivy.

Remedy: learn to identify the plant. See the picture on this page but also search for images on the Internet. Wear long pants when hiking. If you think you've walked through a patch of poison ivy, wash your skin as soon as possible and wear gloves to remove your shoes and clothes; wash them right away. The oil from the plant, urushiol, is the main irritant, and it can stick around for years. I once got a nasty rash by petting a dog that had run through a patch of poison ivy. Don't burn the plant or exposed clothes; the oil is carried in the air and can give you a very unpleasant rash in your lungs if you inhale it.

3) FALLING OFF A BLUFF: it hurts.

Remedy: Pay attention to the edges. Duh. Good hiking shoes or boots will also help.

4) IGNORING SIGNS THAT SAY "PRIVATE PROPERTY" OR "NO TRESPASSING": they mean it, and they have guns.

Remedy: Don't ignore the signs.

5) HITTING A DEER WITH YOUR CAR: you'd be surprised at how much that deer will mess up your car.

Remedy: pay attention and don't drive too fast, especially at night.

INDEX

A

Aghaming Park 129
Airports 231, 234, 244, 250, 357
Aliveo Military Museum 46
Alma, Wisconsin 291
  Attractions 293
    Alma Area Historical Society 294
    Buena Vista Park 285, 293
    Castlerock Museum 7, 294
    Lock and Dam 4 94, 293, 295
    Riecks Lake Park 295, 302
    St. Lawrence Catholic Church 295
  Culture & Arts 297
  Eating and Drinking 301
  Entertainment and Events 297
  Shopping 300
  Sleeping 302
  Sports and Recreation 297
    Mossy Hollow Trail 297
  Tours 297
Amish, overview 178
Amtrak 46, 57, 137, 138, 230, 231, 358
Anderson, Alexander, Dr. 45, 49
Apple Blossom Scenic Drive 144, 150, 152
Arches Museum of Pioneer History 126
Armistice Day Blizzard 89
Arrowhead Bluffs Museum 7, 8, 91

B

Barn Bluff Park 46
Battle Bluff Prairie 176
Bay City, Wisconsin 333
  Attractions 334
    Conlin Log Cabin 334
    River Bluffs History Center 334
    Saratoga Park 334
  Eating 335
  Entertainment and Events 335
  Sleeping 335
  Sports and Recreation 335
    Pierce County Islands 335

Birding 31, 69, 105, 129, 166, 258, 289, 300, 356
Black Hawk 15, 16, 17, 18, 21, 22, 23, 165, 182
Blackhawk Park 176, 177
Bluff Siding, Wisconsin 271
Boathouses, about 66, 159, 160, 359
Bonnema, Oepke 255
Bow and Arrow petroform 337
Brice Prairie, Wisconsin 251
  Eating and Drinking 253
  Entertainment and Events 252
  Sports and Recreation 252
    Great River Trail 252
Bridges 22
Brothels, history 226
Brownsville, Minnesota 156
  Attractions 158
    Church of the Holy Comforter 158
  Eating 161
  Entertainment and Events 158
  Sleeping 161
Buena Vista Park 285, 293
Buffalo City, Wisconsin 284
  Eating 289
  Sleeping 290
  Sports and Recreation 289
    Whitman Dam Wildlife Area 289
Bunnell House 140
Bus lines
  Jefferson Lines 138, 230, 358

C

Camp Lacupolis, Minnesota 82
Cannon Valley Trail 50, 51
Canoe/kayak rentals 48, 92, 126, 211, 252, 262, 274, 296
Canoe trails 100, 112, 163, 165, 211, 262, 307, 348
Carpenter St. Croix Valley Nature Center 351
Castlerock Museum 7, 294
Centerville, Wisconsin 267
  Attractions 267
    Trempealeau National Wildlife Refuge 7, 267, 288
  Eating 268
  Shopping 268
  Sports and Recreation 268
Climate 353

Cochrane, Wisconsin 280
  Attractions 281
    Cochrane Village Hall 281
    Prairie Moon Sculpture Garden 281
  Eating 282
Colonization Society of Cincinnati 284
Coulees, defined 104

D

Dakota 13, 14, 15, 18, 36, 37, 38, 41, 42, 46, 59, 76, 83, 86, 106, 110, 117, 125, 128, 144, 146, 345
Dakota, Minnesota 144
  Attractions 146
    Steve Morse Park 146
  Shopping 147
  Sleeping 147
  Sports and Recreation 146
    Great River Bluffs State Park 146, 147, 355
Densmore, Frances 45, 47
De Soto, Wisconsin 174
  Eating and Drinking 176
  Shopping 176
  Sleeping 177
  Sports and Recreation 176
    Battle Bluff Prairie State Natural Area 176
    Blackhawk Park 176, 177
Diamond Bluff, Wisconsin 341
  Sports and Recreation 342
    Sea Wing Park 342
Dorer Memorial Forest
  Hay Creek Unit 51, 55
  Kruger Recreation Area 93, 96
  Reno Recreation Area 162, 163
  Snake Creek Unit 101, 102
Douglas, Stephen A. 351
Dresbach, Minnesota 148
  Attractions 149
    Dresbach Park 149
    Lock and Dam 7 148, 149, 200, 237

E

Eggleston, Minnesota 40
Elmer's Auto and Toy Museum 7, 274

F

Ferris wheel 108
Five Mile Bluff Prairie 314
Foerster, Leona 218
Fountain City, Wisconsin 272
  Attractions 273
    Elmer's Auto and Toy Museum 7, 274
    Fountain City Historical Society 273
    Lock and Dam 5A 273
    Rock in the House 274
  Culture & Arts 275
  Eating and Drinking 277
  Entertainment and Events 275
  Shopping 276
  Sleeping 277
  Sports and Recreation 276
    Merrick State Park 119, 275, 276, 278
French Island, Wisconsin 232
  Attractions 233
    Environmental Sciences Center 233
    Fishermans Road 234
    Nelson Park 233
Frontenac (Old), Minnesota 63
  Attractions 69
    Christ Episcopal Church 69
    Frontenac State Park 61, 69, 70
  Sleeping 70
  Sports and Recreation 69
Frontenac State Park 61, 69, 70
Frontenac Station, Minnesota 61
  Attractions 62
    Florence Town Hall 62
  Eating 62

G

Garrard, Israel 61, 64, 70
Garvin Heights Park 121
Genoa National Fish Hatchery 183
Genoa, Wisconsin 185
  Attractions 187
    Lock and Dam 8 163, 186, 187, 191
    Old Settlers Park 187
  Eating 188
  Entertainment and Events 187

Shopping 188
  Sleeping 188
Gesell, Arnold 298, 299
Gesell, Gerhard 293, 294, 298
Gesell, Justice Gerhard 299
God's Country 248
Goodhue County History Center 7, 47, 342
Goodview, Minnesota 114
  Shopping 115
  Sleeping 115
  Sports and Recreation 115
Goose Island County Park 210, 211, 217, 227
Grandad Park 208
Gray, Putnam 108, 109
Great River Bluffs State Park 146, 147, 355
Great River Road 21, 23, 63, 99, 144, 194, 346, 347
Great River State Trail 239, 247, 252, 254, 263

H

Hager City, Wisconsin 337
  Attractions 337
    Bow and Arrow petroform 337
  Eating and Drinking 338
  Sleeping 338
Harris, John 151, 153
Hastings, Minnesota 24
  Attractions 28
    Hastings City Hall 29
    LeDuc Historic Estate 29
    Lock and Dam 2 28
    Old Mill Park 30
    Vermillion Falls Park 30
  Culture & Arts 30
  Eating 34
  Entertainment & Events 31
  Shopping 33
  Sleeping 34
  Sports & Recreation 32
    Mississippi National River and Recreation Area 32
Hixon Forest 208, 216
Hixon House 205
Ho Chunk 13, 16, 17, 18, 167, 174, 251
Holland Sand Prairie 247
Holmen, Wisconsin 245

Attractions 246
　　　Holmen Historical Center 246
　　Eating 247
　　Entertainment and Events 246
　　Shopping 247
　　Sleeping 249
　　Sports and Recreation 247
　　　Holland Sand Prairie 247
Homer, Minnesota 139
　　Attractions 140
　　　Bunnell House 140
　　Sleeping 140

I
Itineraries 8

J
Jule bakking 246

K
Kellogg, Minnesota 99
　　Attractions 100
　　　LARK Toys 100
　　Culture & Arts 100
　　Eating 102
　　Entertainment and Events 101
　　Sleeping 102
　　Sports and Recreation 101
　　　Kellogg-Weaver Dunes 101
　　　McCarthy Lake Wildlife Management Area 101
　　　Snake Creek Unit/Dorer Forest 101
Kellogg-Weaver Dunes 101
Kentucky Land Company 151
Kruger Recreation Area 93, 96

L
La Crescent, Minnesota 150
　　Attractions 152
　　　Apple Blossom Scenic Drive 144, 150, 152
　　　Eagles Bluff Park 152
　　　Heritage House 154
　　Eating and Drinking 155
　　Entertainment and Events 154
　　Shopping 154
　　Sports and Recreation 154

La Crosse River State Trail 217, 239
Lacrosse, the game 195
La Crosse, Wisconsin 194
  Attractions 201
    Children's Museum 205
    Christ Episcopal Church 205
    Copeland Park 207
    Goose Island County Park 210
    Grandad Park 208
    Hixon House 205
    Houska Park 209
    King Gambrinus 207
    Maria Angelorum Chapel 208
    Mississippi Valley Archaeology Center 208
    Mons Anderson House 206
    Myrick Hixon EcoPark 208
    Myrick Park 207
    Norskedalen 209
    Pettibone Park 201
    Riverside Museum 201
    Riverside Park 201
    Swarthout Museum 206
    World's Largest Six Pack 207
  Culture & Arts 212
  Drinking 214
  Eating 221
  Entertainment and Events 213
  Maps 202, 203
  Shopping 219
  Sleeping 227
  Sports and Recreation 215
    Hixon Forest 208, 216
    Human Powered Trails 217
    Mississippi Valley Conservancy 216
    River to Bluff Trail 216
  Tours 213
Lake City, Minnesota 71
  Attractions 72
    Lake City Historical Society 73
    Wiebusch's Windmill Haven 73
  Culture & Arts 74
  Eating and Drinking 77
  Entertainment and Events 74
  Shopping 75

Sleeping 79
  Sports and Recreation 75
Lake Pepin 7, 8, 9, 65, 69, 71, 72, 73, 74, 75, 76, 80, 82, 313, 314, 318, 319, 320, 321, 322, 325, 326, 327, 328, 329, 333, 334, 335, 337, 343
La Moille, Minnesota 142
  Attractions 143
    Pickwick Mill 143
  Entertainment and Events 143
  Shopping 143
Lansing, Iowa 167
  Attractions 169
    Mt. Hosmer Park 169
    Museum of River History 169
    Our Savior's Lutheran Church 169
  Eating and Drinking 171
  Entertainment and Events 170
  Shopping 171
  Sleeping 172
  Sports and Recreation 170
Latsch, John 107, 119, 261, 276
Latsch State Park 107
Laura Ingalls Wilder Museum 312
LeDuc Historic Estate 7, 29
LeDuc, William and Mary 26, 29
Lincoln, Abraham 15, 17, 351
Little Crow 14, 15, 117
Lock and Dam 2 28, 29
Lock and Dam 3 37
Lock and Dam 4 94, 293, 295
Lock and Dam 5 112
Lock and Dam 5A 273
Lock and Dam 6 260, 262, 273
Lock and Dam 7 148, 149, 200, 237
Lock and Dam 8 163, 186, 187, 191
Lock and dam tour 149
Logging camps 241

M

Maiden Rock Bluff 7, 323
Maiden Rock, Wisconsin 328
  Attractions 329
    Maiden Rock Village Park 329
  Eating and Drinking 331

Entertainment and Events 330
  Shopping 330
  Sleeping 331
  Sports and Recreation 330
    Rush River Delta 330
Maria Angelorum Chapel 7, 208, 285
Marshland, Wisconsin 269
  Eating 269
McCarthy Lake Wildlife Management Area 101
Memorial Park (Red Wing) 46
Merrick State Park 119, 275, 276, 278
Mesquakie 15
Midway, Wisconsin 254
  Attractions 254
    Great River Trail 254
Minneiska, Minnesota 106
  Culture & Arts 107
  Eating and Drinking 109
  Sports and Recreation 107
    Latsch State Park 107
Minnesota City, Minnesota 110
  Attractions 112
    Lock and Dam 5 112
    Minnesota City Historical Association 112
  Entertainment and Events 112
  Sleeping 113
Minnesota Marine Art Museum 7, 121
Mississippi National River and Recreation Area 32
Mississippi River
  Ecology 354
  Fauna 356
  Flora 355
Mississippi Valley Archaeology Center 208
Mosquitoes and ticks 186, 314, 359
Mossy Hollow Trail 297
Mounds, Indian 150, 165, 207, 341
Mount Hosmer Park 169
Museum of River History 169
Myrick, Nathan 195, 197, 248

N
National Eagle Center 8, 90, 93
Nelson-Trevino Bottoms 307
Nelson, Wisconsin 306

Index

   Eating 308
   Entertainment and Events 307
   Shopping 307
   Sleeping 309
   Sports and Recreation 307
      Nelson-Trevino Bottoms 307
      Tiffany Wildlife Area 307, 309
New Albin, Iowa 164
   Attractions 165
      Fish Farm Mounds 165
      New Albin Town Hall 165
      Reburn Barn 165
   Entertainment and Events 166
   Shopping 166
   Sports and Recreation 166
      Pool Slough 166
New Amsterdam, Wisconsin 255
   Attractions 257
      Presbyterian Church 257
   Sports and Recreation 257
      Van Loon Wildlife Area 257
Norskedalen 209

O

Onalaska, Wisconsin 235
   Attractions 237
      Lake Onalaska 237
      Onalaska Historical Museum 238
      Sunfish overlook 238
   Eating and Drinking 239
   Entertainment and Events 238
   Sleeping 240
   Sports and Recreation 239
      Great River State Trail 239
      La Crosse River State Trail 239
Overview map 4

P

Pepie 73
Pepin, Wisconsin 310
   Attractions 312
      Laura Ingalls Wilder Museum 312
      Laura Ingalls Wilder Wayside and Cabin 312
      Pepin Depot Museum 312

Culture & Arts 313
  Eating 315
  Entertainment and Events 313
  Shopping 314
  Sleeping 316
  Sports and Recreation 314
    Five Mile Bluff Prairie 314
Perrot State Park 119, 260, 262, 263, 264, 266
Pickwick Mill 142, 143
Pierce County Islands 335
Poage, George Coleman 216
Point Douglas, Minnesota 351
  Attractions 351
    Carpenter St. Croix Valley Nature Center 351
  Sleeping 352
  Sports and Recreation 352
    St. Croix Bluffs Regional Park 352
Poison ivy 360
Polish Cultural Institute 124
Pool Slough WMA 166
Prairie Island Indian Community, Minnesota 34, 36, 40
  Attractions 34, 37
    Lock and Dam 3 34, 37
  Eating 34, 38
  Entertainment and Events 34, 38
  Sleeping 34, 38
Prairie Moon Sculpture Garden 281
Prescott, Wisconsin 345
  Attractions 347
    Freedom Park 347
    Mercord Park 347
    Prescott Clock Tower 347
    Prescott Historical Society 348
  Eating and Drinking 349
  Entertainment and Events 348
  Shopping 348
  Sleeping 350
  Sports and Recreation 348

R

Reads Landing, Minnesota 83
  Attractions 84
    Wabasha County Historical Society Museum 84
  Eating and Drinking 85

Sleeping 85
Red Wing, Chief 41
Red Wing, Minnesota 41
  Attractions 46
    Aliveo Military Museum 46
    Barn Bluff Park 46
    Goodhue County History Center 46, 47
    Memorial Park 46
    Red Wing Pottery Museum 46, 47
    Red Wing Shoe Museum 46
  Culture & Arts 48
  Eating 53
  Entertainment and Events 50
  Map 44
  Shopping 52
  Sleeping 55
  Sports and Recreation 50
    Cannon Valley Trail 50, 51
    Hay Creek Unit/Dorer Forest 51, 55
  Tours 49
Red Wing Pottery Museum 47
Red Wing Shoe Museum 46
Regional Information 353
Reno, Minnesota 162
  Sleeping 163
  Sports and Recreation 162
    Reno Recreation Area 162, 163
River cruises 37, 48, 74, 92, 170, 210, 296, 313
Rock in the House 274
Rush River Delta 330

S

Salwey, Kenny 283, 293, 359
Sauk 15, 18
Sea Wing 47, 72, 341, 342, 343
St. Croix Bluffs Regional Park 352
Stockholm, Wisconsin 319
  Attractions 321
    Stockholm Museum 321
    Stockholm Village Park 321
  Culture & Arts 322
  Eating 325
  Entertainment and Events 322
  Shopping 323

Sleeping 325
Sports and Recreation 323
  Maiden Rock Bluff 323
Stoddard, Wisconsin 190
  Attractions 191
    Riverland Taxidermy Studio 191
    Stoddard River Park 191
  Entertainment and Events 192
  Sleeping 192
St. Stanislaus Kostka 124
Sugar Loaf Bluff 125
Swarthout Museum 206

T

Thoreau, Henry David 43
Tiffany Wildlife Area 307, 309
Trains
  Amtrak 46, 57, 137, 138, 230, 231, 358
Trempealeau National Wildlife Refuge 7, 267, 288
Trempealeau, Wisconsin 259
  Attractions 260
    Lock and Dam 6 260, 262, 273
    Perrot State Park 119, 260, 262, 263, 264, 266
    Trempealeau Community Heritage Museum 261
    Trempealeau Heritage Museum 261
  Eating and Drinking 263
  Entertainment and Events 262
  Sleeping 264
  Sports and Recreation 263
Trenton Bluff 339
Trenton, Wisconsin 339
  Sleeping 340
  Sports and Recreation 339
    Trenton Bluff 339

U

Upper Mississippi River National Wildlife Refuge
  Camping 12

V

Van Loon Wildlife Area 257
Van Slyke, Rev. David 248
Vermillion Falls Park 30
Victory, Wisconsin 182